Silent Cinema

SILENT CINEMA
AN INTRODUCTION

Paolo Cherchi Usai

New preface by David Robinson

Preface to the First English Edition
by Kevin Brownlow

 *bfi* Publishing

First published 02000 by the
British Film Institute
21 Stephen St, London W1P 2LN

The British Film Institute is the UK national agency with responsibility for encouraging
the arts of film and television and conserving them in the national interest.

Originally translated by Emma Sansone Rittle but
largely modified and added to by the author for this edition

Set in 9½pt/13pt Minion by Fakenham Photosetting Limited, Fakenham, Norfolk
Printed in United Kingdom by St Edmundsbury Press, Bury St Edmunds

Front cover: *Sherlock Jr.* (Buster Keaton, 1924) – The Museum of Modern Art, Film
Stills Archive. Opposite title page: *The Vampire* (Kalem, 1913) – George Eastman
House, Film Stills Archive.

British Library Cataloguing-in-Publication Data
A catalogue record for this book is available from the British Library
ISBN 0–85170–745–9 hbk
ISBN 0–85170–746–7 pbk

Contents

This one is all yours, Simonetta

Foreword

My first encounter with the burning passions of silent cinema occurred in 1975, when I was given the chance to meet a Palestinian *émigré*, Angelo R. Humouda, in his apartment filled with 16mm prints of films by D.W. Griffith, Edison, Porter, the pioneers of animation and the avant-garde movements. 'Here are the films', he said, 'and here's the viewing machine. This is how it works. You put the reel here, then through these sprockets. That's how you control the focus. This knob is for the framing. I got to go now – I'm quite busy today – I have some letters to write. Here's the key to the apartment. Come whenever you wish. See you later'.

So there I was, at the Cineteca Griffith in Genoa, with a background in art history (my doctoral dissertation was originally supposed to be about the restoration of a painting by Piero della Francesca), a little knowledge of cinema, and absolutely no idea that Angelo's 30-word introduction to film archiving was going to determine a radical shift in the course of my life. In the spring of 1989, after a decade of acquaintance with the field as co-organiser of the Pordenone Silent Film Festival, Edoardo Pia – then editorial director of the publishing company UTET in Turin – suggested that it might be a good idea to put down on paper the results of my experience in a subject that was still perceived as the arcane territory occupied by a handful of fanatical collectors and specialists.

At first, *Burning Passions* was the title of a lecture given at the Cineteca del Comune di Bologna in December 1988. A book with the same title – *Una passione infiammabile* – was published by UTET in 1991, an act of faith in the potential of silent cinema as an object of interest and research for a wider audience. Ten years later, I found my wish fulfilled, at least in part. Silent films are screened and talked about at festivals, conferences, and schools. Hundreds of books and essays have been written about them. Their preservation and rediscovery is announced on the front pages of newspapers, and public opinion no longer holds it as a mere expression of nostalgia. Six years after the publication of the first English edition of the book, I am grateful to be given the opportunity of expanding its content with the addition of two chapters on early colour technology and the principles of film restoration. All other chapters and bibliographies have been thoroughly revised and updated, with additional illustrations throughout the text and an expanded set of appendices and indexes. For the sake of clarity (Kevin Brownlow told me that passengers were staring at him while he was reading the book in the London subway, as if he was dealing with some sort of pulp fiction erotica – a thought that I quite enjoy), I have reluctantly agreed to have the title changed to a statement of chastity, but I wish to stress that my own burning passions are alive and well, and I'm actually trying to give them a new twist.

After having attempted to foster a dialogue between film studies and the archival world, I would like now to encourage its further growth and outreach towards the cultural community in general. I have always been dissatisfied with any discipline whose aim does not go beyond its own fulfilment, and wished that knowledge in one area could become a catalyst for enthusiasm, curiosity and the impulse of discovery in other aspects of life. As far as I'm concerned, looking at silent films makes sense only as long as it encourages and develops the art of seeing in itself, regardless of its forms and manifestations.

I have greatly benefited from the help of Clyde Jeavons, Anne Fleming and Elaine Burrows (National Film and Television Archive, London); Michael Friend (Academy Film Archive); Jan-Christopher Horak, Edward E. Stratmann, Robin Blair Bolger, Rachel Stuhlman, Becky Simmons and the past and present staff of the Motion Picture Department at George Eastman House, with the students of the L. Jeffrey Selznick School of Film Preservation; Geoffrey Nowell-Smith; Paul C. Spehr; David Francis, Patrick Loughney, Madeline Matz, Mike Mashon and Zoran Sinobad (Motion Picture, Broadcasting and Recorded Sound Division, Library of Congress, Washington, DC); Bo Berglund (Malmö, Sweden); Jonathan Dennis (Wellington, Aotearoa, New Zealand); Ann Baylis and Ray Edmondson (National Film and Sound Archive/ScreenSound Australia); Laurent Mannoni (Cinémathèque française); Ben Brewster (Wisconsin Center for Film and Theater Research, Madison, Wisconsin); Susan Dalton; Yuri Tsivian and Tom Gunning (University of Chicago); Hiroshi Komatsu (Tokyo); John Belton (Rutgers University); Richard Koszarski; Roger Smither (Imperial War Museum, London); Martin Koerber (Stiftung Deutsche Kinemathek); Peter Kubelka (Österreichisches Filmmuseum); Edith Kramer (Pacific Film Archive); Brigitte van der Elst (Fédération Internationale des Archives du Film, Brussels); Kristin Thompson and David Bordwell (University of Wisconsin, Madison); Joanne Bernardi (University of Rochester); Piera Patat, Livio Jacob, Lorenzo Codelli, Piero Colussi, Carlo Montanaro (my partners in the adventure of the Pordenone Silent Film Festival since 1982); Robert A. Gottlieb, for his timely words of editorial support; and Roland Cosandey (Vevey, Switzerland), whose perceptive critical notes to the 1991 manuscript, beginning with the title 'Une passion inflammable (et transmissible)', encouraged my belief in the potential value of this project.

As with previous versions of this work, the people of San Culebra del Porco helped me with their warmth and discreet encouragement in transforming the tedium of rewriting a book into a gratifying and in many ways fascinating experience. My gratitude also goes to David Robinson for his patient revisions to the manuscript and his devilish persistence in editorial advice.

Eileen Bowser, Harold Brown, Kevin Brownlow, David Francis, Angelo R.

Humouda, Naoum Kleiman, Jacques L'Aumône, Enno Patalas, Vincent Pinel, George C. Pratt, Martin Sopocy and Davide Turconi have been my mentors in the quest for silent cinema, and initiated me in its hidden pleasures. Their generosity and dedication are as important to me as the ideas which inspired their own work, although the responsibility for any omissions or inaccuracies in describing them will be mine alone.

Paolo Cherchi Usai
Meridian Cinema, Wairiki
December 01999

Preface to the Revised and Expanded Edition (2000)

To see Paolo Cherchi Usai open a can of nitrate film that is new to him is a spectacle to cherish. He will fondle (within the limits of archival propriety) this fabric that can be softer and suppler than the beloved's skin, and draw it to his face to savour the vaguely narcotic fumes. The gestures are sensuous, even sensual. You feel yourself a voyeur at a very private function. Not for nothing was the original edition of this book called *Burning Passions* (*Una passione infiammabile* in the original Italian) ...

Here, of course, is an image that will bring a ready smirk to the lips of the bureau-crat-archivist and the bureaucrat-academic, confident that their own high scientific method excludes the contagion of romantic mystique about old film. But the smirks may be instantly wiped away. Cherchi Usai's emotional, corporeal relations with its most basic raw materials are only one part of his commitment to cinema. They co-exist with the rigour of a research scientist, the ruthless logic of a private eye, the aesthetic perceptions of an art historian, the expository talents of a fine teacher, the orderliness of an accountant and the unquenchable excitement of a small boy on an eternal Christmas morning. It is a range of talents and responses, covering the complexities of technology as well as the mysteries of aesthetics, that he shares with the great guardian-redeemers of the film heritage – Iris Barry, Henri Langlois, William Everson, David Francis, Kevin Brownlow, Enno Patalas ... there have not been many.

The versatility and mastery that have made possible this exceptional book are reflected in it, and handed on to the lucky reader. It is a step-by-step practical man-ual to every aspect of the use of film coming from the first decades of cinema – finding, handling, understanding, recording, conserving, restoring, enjoying. Like any technical manual it has charts and diagrams and tables and rules. Unlike any other technical manual its guidance ranges all the way from the most practical – good manners when visiting an archive, the psychological handling of the often whimsical and defensive people who are the curators of the film heritage, the list of tools of the trade ('gauze gloves, a magnifying glass, a micrometer gauge ...'), how to take proper notes – to the complex ethical issues of film restoration and the psy-chic adjustments that must be made to recapture the aesthetic and sensory experience that was silent cinema.

The paradox is that there should be a need for such a manual. After all, cinema, for the most part, began as the stuff of commercial popular entertainment, created for a public that is separated from us (at the start of the 21st century) by no more than a long lifetime. Yet as Cherchi Usai puts it, 'Both the greatest discipline and the greatest imagination are needed in order to bring back to life something which is relatively close to us in time. It is closer to us than prehistoric art or the music of ancient Egypt, but it can be no less mysterious and elusive.'

The imaginative effort, first. In an astonishingly short time – little more than thirty years – the silent cinema evolved as a unique, integral and highly sophisticated expressive form, and then, overnight, became extinct. That extinction suited the purposes of the giant talking-picture industry, which preferred audiences to forget that there had once been another kind of cinema. The public was encouraged to remember silent films only vaguely as something primitive, incomplete, grotesque – shadowy images, streaked with scratches, watched, if at all, in a silence broken only by the clatter of the projectors and uncomprehending guffaws at the 'exaggerated' acting.

It was more than half a century from that extinction until the1980 revival of Abel Gance's *Napoleon* triumphantly resurrected the silent film experience in an electrifying fashion. No-one who was present at those shows, or at many other silent revivals since, would now disagree that to see a great silent film, in a lustrous print, with a symphonic live musical accompaniment, projected in a grand theatre with a packed audience is an experience *de sui generis*. It is not like theatre or ballet or film as we know it, but combines something of them all in a form that at its best can exert a unique power over the senses and the imagination. Though the opportunities for that total experience are rare, Cherchi Usai constantly reminds us that 'when it is a matter of watching a film made eighty years ago you need a special commitment: you should try to imagine the effect of the film when it was first distributed'.

Of course, before it is possible to exert this imaginative faculty, which is an essential part of the process of watching a silent film, the film itself must be found. Even the best-informed reader is likely to be stopped in his tracks by Cherchi Usai's chronicle of the hazards that beset the survival of every silent film, and that leads him to the most startling of his fundamental rules: 'Rule 10 – The "original" version of a film is a multiple object fragmented into a number of different entities equal to the number of surviving copies.' Every copy of the same silent film is different, thanks to the intervention of time, storage conditions, projectionists, editors, colourists, thieves, producers, distributors, re-issuers, titlers, re-titlers, censors, over-enthusiastic archivists, incompetent archivists, and practically everyone else who ever came in contact with it.

It is this factor that makes the work of film restoration at once so stimulating and so challenging; and renders more chilling the perhaps not entirely apocryphal story of one of the world's great film archives that found itself, a few years ago, running out of storage space. The archivists' criterion for junking their duplicate prints was to measure the different copies of each film and retain only the longest.

Alongside the strictly practical advice, too, Cherchi Usai advances a code of ethics
for those who handle, preserve, restore or evaluate silent cinema – a discussion
developed further and, particularly in relation to the economic pressures on preservation policies, more aggressively in his subsequent book *The Death of Cinema*.
Here as in every other aspect of his writing, what is most admirable and touching
is the passion, the irrepressibly human responses and the cool good sense that variously enrich Cherchi Usai's scientific rigour and broad academic view.

He takes, for example, a purgative view of the confidence of the fashion-con-
scious world of film studies that (in Rudolf Arnheim's ironic gloss) 'the passage of
time equals progress, and that the pioneers of today stand on the shoulders of yes-
terday's dwarfs' (*Burning Passions*, p. 90). Cherchi Usai on the contrary teaches us
not just dutifully to honour the pioneer historians and journalists, but to recognise
their continuing significance and utility. 'Blaming Mitry for having misremembered
the development of a sequence or the text of an intertitle, at a time when historiography and militant criticism were the only way of legitimising films as an art,
would be like blaming Vasari for not having used infra-red rays to analyse Michae-
langelo's second thoughts and corrections in the Sistine Chapel'.

Cherchi Usai, in short, offers at once a basic manual and a warm, wise, refresh-
ing, discursive essay on the nature and appreciation of silent film – as useful for the
specialist as for the novice, for archivists and scholars as well as for someone only
just discovering the durable enchantment of this singular island survival in the sea
of twentieth-century art. It is, in the oldest and best sense, an improving book. It
also leaves us an equivocal reassurance: 'If the passion we have contracted is not
ephemeral we can relax: a whole lifetime will barely be enough to plough a corner
of this field.'

David Robinson

Preface to the First English Edition (1994)

Poor silent films! Can any art have been treated so shabbily? Even those who respect the films often treat them with such reverence – projecting them too slow, without music – that the life is squeezed out of them. Those who don't respect them have a record of destruction worthy of Attila the Hun: they have burned them, dumped them in the sea, hacked the reels with axes, or let them rot in the vaults.

From the moment sound arrived, it was commercially useful to dispel the magic of silent films; they were derided in print and on the screen as ludicrous, technically inept and badly acted. Something merely to be laughed at. People of my generation will remember Biographs of the 1910–12 period, in appalling prints, much speeded up, with 'humorous' commentaries, shown among the cartoons at news theatres in the 1940s and 50s.

The propaganda worked. Ask anyone in their seventies and eighties about silent films, and the enthusiasm will be clouded by apology. 'They all moved very fast.'

Some of them undoubtedly did. Projectionists liked to get home, and the more unscrupulous would sometimes 'race' the film – increasing the pace far beyond the speed appropriate for it. They could do that because motors had rheostats, unlike today, when projectors are fixed at a standard speed of 24 frames per second. There was no standard speed in the silent days. D. W. Griffith's Biographs were shot at anything from 14 to 18 f.p.s., but 16 was the average. Over at the Edison studio, at the same time, they shot much faster. Projectionists must have become very confused.

By the 1920s when the pit piano had often been replaced by a pit orchestra, it was essential for musicians and projectionists to know the speed, and cue sheets were issued. They make instructive reading. The 'average' speed was around 20–22 f.p.s., and sometimes 24. I doubt whether any cameraman cranked at 24, but that wasn't the point; the films were shown slightly faster than they were shot. When sound arrived, and everything settled down to the speed at which the films were photographed, audiences complained of a 'slow motion' effect. And now, when *Wings* (1927) is shown by a film society at the so-called silent speed of 16 f.p.s., it lasts an hour longer than it did on its original release.

Yet it would be fair to say that in most cinemas in the 1920s you saw original prints, decently presented at a reasonable speed, which is more than one could hope for today.

Worse than the speed problem is the question of prints. Make no mistake the standard of photography in the silent days was remarkably high. The cameramen had the tradition of Victorian still photographers to draw upon and even the least pretentious film could boast superb cinematography. Seen in a nitrate print projected on a big screen, the best work of the silent era can be an overwhelming artistic experience. Copy it, and at once the magic disappears. It is like copying a Rembrandt with an Instamatic camera. The silver content of black-and-white film stock has been removed to such an extent that the glistening sheen of early cinematography often registers as an out-of-focus smear. The information is there. The art has gone.

Once, any laboratory could make serviceable black-and-white prints. Now, apart from the specialists, none of them can. The men who knew how to cope with black and white have long since retired and few of their replacements have any skill beyond their daily concern with colour film. Ask them to print black and white on colour stock, and you will need a remarkably patient and sensitive technician to work with you.

What else has a silent film apart from its visuals? Its subtitles – or intertitles, as they are now called – convey plot and dialogue points. Everything else comes from the image. Degrade that even slightly and you are removing essential information. How often have you seen a print of a silent film in which the actors' faces register as white blobs? Without the benefit of those expressions – which were often very subtle – you have not seen those performances, or, for that matter, that film.

I remember watching a rare film during a Garbo season at a London cinema. It was a beautiful print, but shown out of focus. I asked an usher to contact the projectionist. 'Nothing you call do about that,' said the usher. 'It's an old film, you're lucky to see anything.'

As a film collector, I have had to give up acquiring new prints of silent films, because the results simply depress me. I am old enough to have seen silents in their original nitrate form, shown during the 1950s and 60s, and I have never forgotten the impact of the razor-sharp exteriors, the gauzed closeups, the ravishing use of tints and tones, and the sheer depth of the image. They say depth of focus was invented for *Citizen Kane*; take a look at a few silent pictures! (They say ceilings first appeared in *Kane*, too, and, as much as I revere *Kane*, a forgotten historical epic of 1924 called *Lady of Quality* made a feature of showing astoundingly elaborate Tudor ceilings on all its interior sets.)

Whenever my wife and I find ourselves in the country on a day when the light is immaculate, she invariably says, 'What wonderful nitrate weather!' She is not a specialist, but she refuses to watch silent films on video, and I cannot blame her. Video is a wonderful medium; it releases you from the tyranny of the programme controllers, and it makes films as cheap and as widely available as paperback books. But while the impact of, say, Dickens is as powerful in paperback as in the finest binding, the effect of a silent film is disastrously diminished. The photographic quality undergoes severe degradation, even if the transfer is made from the finest prints. In America, the old-fashioned NTSC softens the definition and flattens the contrast and often produces a double-image. Laserdisc can be an improvement, but all too often transfers to disc are made from videotape rather than film.

With video, you are at the mercy of those who make the transfer for what speed you get. And what grading you get. And how much of the picture you see. One company in America puts out Buster Keaton's *The General* (1927) at the so-called silent speed of 10 f.p.s., even though Buster Keaton wanted it shown at 24. When I wrote to ask why they had committed such an unnecessary sin, they said they had made a close study of the movement within the film – including the smoke (!) – and had come to a corporate decision; it looked better at 16. It also added the equivalent of four reels to the running time. Keaton's comedy can survive almost everything – even terrible prints – but it cannot survive a deadly pace. Anyone watching that particular video could be forgiven for dismissing silent comedy as unbearably slow.

The opposite is equally awful – as when you buy a video of D. W. Griffith's *Intolerance* (1910) to discover that it has been transferred at 24 f.p.s. The cameras on *Intolerance* turned at 16 and 18 f.p.s. and to increase the speed transforms Griffith's epic drama into farce. One of the drawbacks with video – which should be a strength – is that once the speed is set there is no way of altering it.

Why is it that the combined efforts of specialised film and video distributors make the technicians responsible for the old films look like idiots? The sad fact is that the public don't blame the people who made the print – they blame the age of the film, and those who produced it.

Archives are sometimes guilty as well. Some have done magnificent work over the years. Others have merely served as tombs for decomposing nitrate. How many of us mourned when we saw at Pordenone Lois Weber's remarkably realistic drama *Shoes* (1916), surviving in a copy savaged by the marks of bad storage and decomposition? Had it been kept by some eccentric collector in a hen house? No, it was preserved by one of the world's leading archives, by an old regime concerned only with copying films of its own nationality. The new broom has swept away that destructive idea and it rescued *Shoes* – albeit in fragile and fragmentary state – just before it finally gave up the ghost.

Fortunately, there is good news in all this. A new generation of silent film enthusiasts are achieving miracles. Pordenone holds a festival of silent films – Le Giornate del Cinema Muto – once a year, the only place in the world that does so. Pordenone has a long list of achievements to its credit, and the fact that at last there is a place where silent films are regularly shown has encouraged archives to make more rarities available. Pordenone aims at showing the best available prints, but sometimes the heads of the archives are present to witness the cultural crimes committed by their predecessors: murky and incomplete copies. Pordenone always provides live music, either a piano, or, when they can afford it, a full orchestra.

Silent films are high on the agenda of Bologna (Il Cinema Ritrovato) and Paris (CinéMémoire) both of which were inspired by the example of Pordenone. More and more silent films are being restored, and no one who saw them will forget Renée Lichtig's restoration of Volkoff's *Casanova* (1926) for the Cinémathèque Française, or Bob Gitt's of Chester Franklin's *Toll of the Sea* (1922), the first successful Technicolor feature, for UCLA Film Archives.

Paolo Cherchi Usai has been in the vanguard of all this activity as one of the founders of Pordenone. With the indomitable Pordenone team, he has opened our eyes to aspects of the silent era we never dreamed existed. To achieve this he has had to immerse himself in archives all over the world. Recently, he has been working full-time at George Eastman House, in Rochester, NY. I have often wished that a book could be written about the problems of researching silent film, and the problems of dealing with archives. Paolo Cherchi Usai has written that book.

Kevin Brownlow

Introduction:
Burning Passions

Ah! les cow-boys du muet, les vampires du tacite, les maxlinder du
silencieux, les charlots de l'aphone, combien passionné fus-je de leur
geste, épique en son genre, dirais-je.

Raymond Queneau

This book is intended as a researcher's guide to the moving photographic images
produced during the so-called 'silent period'. Normally, this definition covers the
years 1893 to 1927, between the recording of the first photographic images on
35mm perforated film in the Edison Kinetograph, and the first public projection of
Alan Crosland's *The Jazz Singer*, which included some sung and spoken sequences.

A date frequently, if to an extent arbitrarily, invoked as the birth of cinema is 28
December 1895, when the Cinématographe Lumière was first shown to a paying
audience in Paris. Yet the effect of motion achieved by showing photographs in
quick succession had already been known to the public for more than a year before
the Cinématographe was patented in February 1895. The Edison Kinetoscope had
enabled the reproduction of animated images on light-sensitive material, shot by
the Kinetograph camera. The machine allowed a single spectator to see sequences
lasting a handful of seconds: but they were already photographic sequences on film,
not drawings or painted glass slides. From the summer of 1889, Étienne-Jules Marey
was certainly recording life in movement on film. It was not 35mm (actually 60mm
or 90mm) and not perforated, nor could it be projected at the time, but the photographic images are there and somehow they can be projected today.

At the other extreme of the era is the long twilight of the silent film. This began
with experiments to record sound directly onto film (much earlier than 1927: the
first studies on the subject were published in 1901) and ended only around 1935,
almost a decade after the official beginning of sound films. It is true that by 1930
silent cinema was considered an anachronism in Western Europe and the United
States. However, the universal adoption of such a radical technological innovation
was inevitably subject to many hesitations and delays: *La canzone dell'amore* [The
Love Song], the first Italian sound film, was premiered on 7 October 1930; the
Soviet Union continued to produce silent films until 1935; the last surviving Chinese silent film, *Mi tu de gao yang* [A Lamb Astray], dates from 1936.

Moreover, the absence of a soundtrack on a print is not enough to establish the historical identity of a silent film. Experimental cinema has often been, and sometimes still is, devoid of sound, but that does not mean it can be equated with the silent cinema of the early years. The same holds true for some pornographic productions. In contrast, Victor Sjöström's *The Wind* (1928), which was distributed in a version with synchronised sound after the production company had delayed its release, belongs firmly to the aesthetics of silent cinema and is unanimously regarded as one of its most fully realised works.

For well over 30 years, watching a silent film meant hearing the sound of live soloists and orchestras, the voices of singers and actors in front of or beside the screen, the mechanical music of automatic devices, gramophones, noise effects. So, if spectators of the time were hardly ever surrounded by silence, why insist on calling it 'silent'? Perhaps it is too simplistic to see the change from silence to sound as a unique, isolated and definitive revolution. Some scholars have claimed, for example, that cinema underwent a structural transformation – in productive, aesthetic and technological terms – between 1911 and 1917, long before 'sound' appeared on the horizon, with the dawn of feature film and the development of a codified, 'classical' style. Their arguments are often well-founded, and there is no doubt that the distinction between silent and sound cinema has lost the precise demarcation which general usage still tends to attribute to it.

Yet there are still many excellent reasons for continuing to speak and to write of 'silent cinema' in its long-accepted usage, and for interpreting it as such. Some of these reasons provide the *raison d'être* of this book. But first I would like to remind the reader of something about the era when silent films were a daily entertainment for millions of spectators. To begin with, cinema in the early 20th century was conscious of its characteristic of being silent, and defined itself as such in the certainty that this was the essential component of a new art form. This certainty was accompanied by the belief (or fear) that its condition was bound to come to an end sooner or later. Headlines in trade magazines and periodicals of the period used the term 'silent', often in order to proclaim cinema's independence from theatre and literature. filmmakers identified its creative potential with the concepts of vision and pantomime, and regarded the absence of sound (despite the musicians and actors in the cinema hall) as a defining fact rather than a limitation.

The transition from 'silent' to 'sound' cinema (in the sense already defined) was more than a technological revolution. It threw the film industry into a period of turmoil, affecting tens of thousands of people who suddenly, variously, found themselves out of work, or having to adapt to the new reality, or making their fortunes because of it. Spectators changed too, as their way of perceiving moving images was drastically affected by these events. From being an art of abstraction, displaying a problematic coexistence between the image (the shot) and the written word (the intertitle), cinema became the mouthpiece of an ambiguous, subtle mimesis, which could redefine and shape the nature of collective imagination.

The abruptness of such a change alienated silent cinema from the sensibility of viewers of the decade that followed, and prompted its extinction. Since then, silent film has become more the object of archaeological study than an occasion for public entertainment – not because the moving pictures of the first 30 years were necessarily poor in themselves, but because they seemed to belong to an archaic tradition which most people could no longer decipher.

The aim of this book is to provide the tools necessary to understand this tradition, and to dispel some of the prejudices surrounding it (such as its status as a dead language) through the study of visual artifacts whose primary feature is that they are fragile, and bound to be progressively altered through their repeated exposure to the viewer. Although designed as an introduction, it may also offer the reader already familiar with the subject a useful reminder of concepts, technical data and debates in the field. Like all manuals, this contains information and advice which may appear pedantic, but without which the encounter with silent cinema becomes merely a superficial and, at best, a nostalgic exercise. In this respect, the book is certainly not meant to be used as a manual for film criticism or as a source of ideas for public screenings as practised by festivals and film archives. Neither is it, however, a set of instructions for establishing or joining an intellectual sect.

The admittedly more ambitious purpose of this guide is quite the opposite. We can summarise it with a metaphor: apart from being ephemeral, original copies of silent films are highly flammable. This peculiarity symbolises the aesthetic pleasure which examining a film from the silent period can bring to a discriminating but not cynical eye. Learning how to watch silent films means trying to identify with a lost visual culture. It also means going back to the origins of a truly flammable, even explosive relationship between the image and the mind, provided that such a relationship is cultivated with the rigour of the historian and the imagination of a spectator aware of reliving another's past in a beam of light projected onto a screen.

1
The Romance of Celluloid

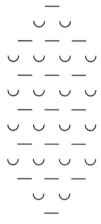

Christian Morgenstern,
'Nocturnal Song of the Fish' (1905)

Physical Structure

Motion picture film stock manufactured in the period of silent cinema consists almost entirely of highly unstable organic materials. Some photographically obtained moving images were printed on carriers other than film: the Kammatograph (United Kingdom, 1898–1900), for instance, used a glass disc with about 550 frames arranged in a spiral (see Plates 26, 27 and 43; a similar technique was adopted for Charles Urban's Spirograph, which used a flexible disc, (Plates 24 and 25); the Mutoscope is a cylinder holding several hundred rectangles of thin card (see Plate 9), each of them bearing a photograph so that, if observed in rapid sequence through equipment for individual viewing, an impression of continuous movement is generated. The same effect is obtained through the Théoscope, produced in France by Théophile Lacroix using a principle similar to that of the Mutoscope.

From the end of the 19th century, cellulose film was established as the preferred material for the reproduction of moving images. Its components remained essentially unchanged for several decades: a base; a very thin gelatin adhesive layer; a light-sensitive emulsion – recognisable as the opaque side of the film – connected to the base by the adhesive layer, and normally consisting of a suspension of silver salts in gelatin. There are sometimes two additional layers: a thin gelatin layer, protecting the emulsion from mechanical damage caused during projection, and a further layer to prevent a haze from forming on the image, or to prevent the film from curling.

The base of most films produced up to February 1951 is cellulose nitrate, a highly flammable substance; from then on, nitrate was replaced by cellulose acetate – which is much less flammable – and, more recently, by polyester. From the first decade of the 20th century, however, some companies were already experimenting with the production of so-called 'safety' – that is, non-flammable – films, in cellulose acetate (this invention by Eichengrun and Becker dates from 1901) or in nitrate covered by non-flammable compounds (the first known examples of this film stock date from 1909). Ozaphane, a French patent for motion picture stock on extremely thin (0.05mm) cellophane film, was presented in 1927 and manufactured in various formats, sometimes without perforations (Plates 34 A–E).

The Birth of 35mm Film

The commercial development of cinema dates from the production of film – with perforations on either side of the frame so that it may be mechanically pulled through the projector – printed on a 35mm wide flexible carrier developed in 1889 by Henry M. Reichenbach for George Eastman from an invention attributed to, among others, the brothers J.W. and I.S. Hyatt (1865), Hannibal Goodwin (1888) and Reichenbach himself. This was the format which Thomas Edison adopted for his Kinetoscope, a device allowing one spectator at a time to see 50-foot strips of film. The Kinetoscope was so successful commercially that subsequent machines for the reproduction of moving images adopted 35mm as a standard format. This tendency was also encouraged by the Eastman company, as their standard film for still picture cameras was 70mm wide. This meant they could simply cut the film in half lengthways to obtain a motion picture film base of the desired size. The success of cinema as a form of mass entertainment is tied to this type of film, officially adopted by all production companies in 1909.

The mechanics of Edison's Kinetoscope also determined the standard format of 35mm film with four vaguely rectangular perforations on either side of each frame. At the end of the 19th century, other inventors tried different types of perforation. The one most commonly used prior to the general adoption of Edison's design was that of the Lumière brothers: the film is drawn along by means of one single, circular perforation on either side of the frame (see Plate 1). Other shorter-lived systems were employed by Max Skladanowsky in Germany (three circular perforations on each side, two of them corresponding to the frame line, as in Plate 21; later, four perforations on both sides of the frame, as in the Edison system, but much smaller and also circular; see also Plate 42) and by the British company Prestwich (three circular perforations on each side of the frame).

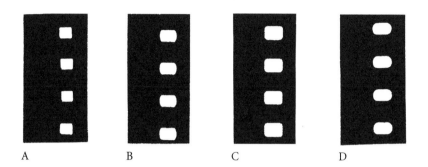

A   B   C   D

35mm film perforations: (A) Small-gauge perforations, pre-1905; (B) Bell & Howell; (C) Kodak Standard ('positive'); (D) Pathé.

Until about 1905 the size and shape of perforations varied from one company to another. They were also smaller than the later standard negative and positive perforations (see A). Around 1905 their profile and size evolved to the point where the Bell & Howell company standardised the features of a larger perforation with straight top and bottom edges, and rounded sides. Perforations of this shape (see B) came into use for all films (both positive and negative) until 1924, when Kodak introduced a rectangular perforation with rounded corners – generally called 'positive perforations' or KS, 'Kodak Standard' – only for positive projection prints (see C). Since then, negative prints continued to have Bell & Howell perforations while all projection positives used the Kodak Standard perforations. The aim was to adapt the prints to different kinds of mechanical stress during shooting and repeated projection. A proposal to unify the two kinds of perforations (the Dubray-Howell system) met with little favour. From 1905 to the late 1920s, Pathé used a perforation of distinctive shape, similar to the Bell & Howell but with rounded corners (see D).

From 1895 to 1916, especially in the United States, a record was often kept of the images printed on 35mm film: the images were reprinted on strips of photographic paper, frequently including the perforations (paper prints: Plate 14). Clearly, these 'films' cannot be screened; each frame, however, can be reproduced on motion picture stock with good results. Many early American films are currently available only on copies obtained from these paper prints, deposited with the Library of Congress by producers in order to obtain legal copyright protection against possible forgeries.

Emulsion

Black and white film stock commonly used until the mid-1920s, called orthochromatic film, was sensitive to ultra-violet, violet and blue light, and partially sensitive to yellow and green radiations, while red had no effect on the silver bromide emulsion. In order to prevent certain objects appearing on the screen as indistinct dark stains, technicians had to monitor the colour balance on the sets, avoiding certain colours for costumes and even painting backgrounds in various shades of grey for interior shots. Orthochromatic film emulsion remained in use until the early 40s, mainly for special effects and for the blue strip in the three-strip Technicolor process after the late 1920s.

Panchromatic film, developed at the end of 1912 by the Eastman Kodak Company on behalf of Gaumont, was sensitive to almost the entire spectrum of visible radiation. At first, it was used only sporadically, partly because it was expensive. However, within a four-year period (from 1922 – the year of Ned Van Buren's *The Headless Horseman*, the first full-length feature shot entirely on a panchromatic negative – to 1926), panchromatic film became the standard stock used by all major production companies; it was less sensitive to light (and therefore forced a change in interior lighting systems), but it allowed for the reproduction of a much wider range of intermediate shades of grey.

Frame

Each frame of a 35mm positive film was about 23mm wide and 18mm high, with slight variations in the early years. Every metre of film held 54 images (16 frames per foot), like present-day film stock of the same format. The aspect ratio of the frame (ca. 1:1.28 to 1:1.31) remained basically unchanged until the soundtrack was introduced (the aspect ratio of silent films reissued with a variable density soundtrack is ca. 1:1.16, very close to a square image: see illustration B on page 61). In 1927 an anamorphic system was devised in France by Henri Chrétien, whose Hypergonar system was used, for instance, in Claude Autant-Lara's short film *Construire un feu* (1925–1929). With the exception of the films in which the widening of the field of vision was a consequence of changing the aspect ratio of the frame, or because the lenses of the projectors magnified the image size on the screen (as with Magnascope, 1926), the two most important attempts to expand the field of vision were Grimoin-Sanson's Cinéorama (1900), with its ten 70mm projectors arranged through 360 degrees to show an image surrounding the spectators, and the equally short-lived Polyvision system (1927) used in the famous triptych sequence of Abel Gance's *Napoléon* (1926): three adjacent 35mm cameras showing three abutting films simultaneously to form a widescreen image. Finally, we must mention Filoteo Alberini's experiment in Italy (1911) with a machine for a 70mm film whose shooting angle reached 110 degrees (Plate 11).

Non-Standard Formats

In spite of its success, 35mm had several rivals in the theatrical and amateur market. The majority of them met with little or no commercial success, but a few became highly popular formats for home distribution, or the ancestors of systems adopted in later years. For instance:

- the first cameras used by the American Mutoscope & Biograph Company, active between the end of the 19th century and the beginning of the 20th century, employed 68mm films without lateral perforations. The ratio between the height and width of the frame (the aspect ratio) is about 3:4; as there are no perforations, the image takes up almost the whole width of the film (Plates 9 and 10). The original intention was to produce the individual images on cards for use in the Mutoscope peepshow device; but when a projector was developed to match the films, the resulting picture projected on the screen was substantially sharper than that of the standard 35mm image, and contributed to the company's success;

- from 1896 onwards, some 60mm films were produced. A 60mm Prestwich film, with four perforations along the edges of the frame and an aspect ratio similar to the 35mm image format, is preserved at the National Film and Television Archive in London. The 58mm film by Georges Demenÿ (France, 1896; see Plate 2) has 15 perforations every four frames. In 1897, the American Veriscope Company made a 63mm film of which only one specimen is known: *The Corbett-Fitzsimmons Fight*, the chronicle of a boxing match (Plate 3). The Veriscope format has five perforations per frame on each side; the aspect ratio of the frame is 1:1.75. The 75mm format (with a frame 45mm high and 60mm wide) was suggested, as an experiment, by Louis Lumière in 1898 (Plate 29). Two years later, in 1900, Gaumont distributed the Chrono de poche, a portable motion-picture camera which used 15mm film with central perforations (Plate 15). In 1902, the Warwick Trading Company introduced a 17.5mm film for amateur use in the Biokam, a machine which could shoot, print and project film. Here, too, there is only one perforation, on the frame line; this idea was taken up by Ernemann, in Germany (with a different-shaped perforation: Plate 6) and by Pathé in the 20s, among others;

- after the 68mm film stock used by the American Mutoscope and Biograph, the next alternative format to 35mm that met with a degree of success (perhaps because its frame is only slightly smaller than that of 35mm film) was the 28mm film introduced by Pathé in 1912 as the Pathé-Kok brand. The Pathé-Kok was a popular and unusual home projector: the hand-cranked mechanism not only operated the film movement, but also the generator to power the electric illuminant. A characteristic of the Pathé-Kok film, printed on a non-flammable (safety) base starting from nitrate negatives, is the asymmetric perforation system:

three perforations per frame on one side, one perforation per frame on the opposite side (Plate 12). In the copies printed in the United States from 1917 (Pathescope) there are three perforations on each side;

- the amateur film *par excellence*, 16mm, was invented by Eastman Kodak in 1920. The first version of this format, known as Kodascope, is a 'reversal' positive film: it could be taken directly from the camera and transformed into a positive copy which could be screened straight away. Almost all film in this format was produced on safety stock (Plate 13). In 1923, Pathé launched another amateur format, 9.5mm (Pathé-Baby), a strong competitor with 16mm for some years. Positive copies in 9.5mm were made on safety film (Plate 17);

- different producers thought up even more unusual formats, and sometimes reached bizarre extremes: for instance, Itala Film of Turin tried a 35mm frame divided into four parts to accommodate four different shots; Edison's 22mm film (Home Kinetoscope) accommodated three strips of frames just over 5mm wide, each of them separated by a line of perforations (Plate 5); the German firm Messter's Kino-Salon had four series of frames and two lines of perforations on a film just under 35mm wide (Plate 7); Oko film by Kazimierz Proszynski (Poland, 1913) was a 120mm film divided into rows of 15 frames. Experiments in 3-D film were also made from the very early years to the end of the silent era, some of them with standard 35mm film to be viewed with anaglyph glasses (Plate 56). None of these systems (with the partial exception of the Home Kinetoscope) went past the experimental stage or achieved wide sales. The often unique images recorded on these 'orphans' of technology (some other examples are given in Plates 4, 8, 16, 20, 30–3 and 35–8) are in danger of disappearing sooner than the others because the machines needed to project them are extremely rare and it is difficult and expensive to transfer them onto more familiar formats.

Sound

From the outset, silent cinema had an aesthetics and a technology of sound. In the beginning, performers had accompanied the projection of moving images with comments and interpretations for the benefit of the public. This had both an educational and a dramatic purpose: the showing of Edwin S. Porter's *Parsifal* (1904) involved the presence of actors in the cinema hall, the projection of magic lantern slides alternating with episodes from the film, and the performance of arias from the Wagner repertoire. Two actors accompanied the Russian short, *Boris Godunov*, produced by the Khanzhonkov company in 1912. For many years, in the long era of silent cinema in Japan, film screenings were integrated by the voice of interpreters known as *benshi*, who emphasised the content of the action with movements and prepared or semi-improvised texts.

A group of technicians performing sound effects behind the screen of a projection hall. Illustration from a Gaumont catalogue of film equipment, US edition, *c.* 1912 (George Eastman House).

With words came music. Initially, music was improvised on a piano; later it was adapted from the current musical repertory, and sometimes composed on commission and performed by orchestras, choirs and opera singers on great occasions, by chamber music ensembles or pianos again in more modest establishments. Camille Saint-Saëns' score for Calmettes and Le Bargy's *L'assassinat du Duc de Guise* (Pathé, 1908) is often said to be the earliest landmark of live music for silent films. The event was particularly significant, since an academic composer had finally agreed to write a score for a product of the new art distrusted by intellectuals. There were also some extreme examples of the alliance between music and the moving image: on 5 September 1916 the first official public showing of D.W. Griffith's *Intolerance* was accompanied by a 46-piece orchestra and a 16-voice choir; the following year, in the Netherlands, Johan Gildermejer made *Gloria Transita*, a film set in the world of opera which required performers to stand beside the screen and sing in time with the characters' lip movements.

Exhibitors who could not afford such luxuries usually had two options. The first was to entrust a pianist, an organist or a small instrumental group with brief scores summarising the tunes thought necessary to accompany each episode in the film; often they were not even true scores, but cue sheets indicating which widely known popular or classical pieces to play (from these cue sheets it is sometimes possible to reconstruct the narrative structure of films preserved in an incomplete form). The other, more drastic solution involved doing without musicians and using mechanical instruments, from pianolas to huge poli-instrumental carillons driven by compressed air, into which rolls of perforated paper were fitted reproducing the music scores. The repertory available from the many companies which produced these rolls was vast; even well-established academic musicians such as Paul Hindemith contributed to it. Sometimes 'noise effects' were produced live in order to enhance the realism of the events depicted in the film. To this end, noise machines or noise performers were deployed to simulate the sounds of natural or artificial occurrences. They relied on ingenious and at times bizarre devices.

The fathers of the moving image had demonstrated from the beginning that they had even greater ambitions. As far back as April 1895, Thomas Alva Edison had presented a system for synchronising a cylinder phonograph with his kinetoscope: while watching the moving images through a peephole viewer, the spectator listened to a sound recording through earphones (Kinetophone: Plate 41). According to some sources, the synchronisation between phonograph discs and film was supposed to have started in 1896 with the use of the Berliner Gramophone by the French company Pathé. From then to 1906 many tried to follow the same direction: among them were Gaumont (Plates 19 and 46), Pineaud and Joly in France, Goldschmidt and Messter in Germany. All, to some extent, had to contend with the problem of amplifying the feeble sound of the phonograph in large halls.

In 1900, the year of the Universal Exhibition in Paris, Ernst Rühmer in Germany, William D. Duddell in United Kingdom and Th. Simon, working independently, perfected a revolutionary idea aiming to reproduce sound photographically on film. This was taken up and developed in 1906 by Eugène-Auguste Lauste, who patented a machine capable of recording images and sounds simultaneously on the same strip of film. However, for some time, production companies went on using synchronised discs. For example, Oskar Messter in Germany (1908), Giovanni Pastrone in Italy (1909) and Léon Gaumont in France (1909–10) distributed short films accompanied by texts and arias from light theatre and opera.

The premonitory signs of the real revolution, and the end of the silent era, emerged around 1918 in Germany, thanks to Vogt, Engel and Massolle. Their equipment for recording sound photographically on a separate film (the Tri-Ergon system) was presented to the public four years later in Berlin. Also working in this field were V.N. Kovalenkov in the Soviet Union (1920), Axel Petersen and Arnold Poulsen in Denmark (1922), Theodore W. Case, and Lee de Forest, whose Phonofilm (United States, 1923) involved reading a soundtrack, placed on the same film stock which held the images, by means of a photo-electric cell. In 1926 Warner Bros. presented *Don Juan*, starring John Barrymore. The film was synchronised to several 33⅓ rpm records with a 40cm diameter, played with a stylus which started in the centre of the record and went out to the edge (the Vitaphone system). Meanwhile another American company, Fox, was buying the rights to the Tri-Ergon and Phonofilm systems, and adding sound to previously made silent films.

The year 1926 thus marks the beginning of the history of sound cinema in the current sense of the term. In the same year, P.G. Tager published in the Soviet Union the results of his research on a variable density soundtrack; a few months later, Fox was proud to show Lindbergh, Mussolini and George Bernard Shaw with their own voices (Movietone News, April 1927). For some time films synchronised with records would run parallel to those with a soundtrack; but in less than two years the latter definitely became dominant. Soundtracks were added to works which had recently been finished as silents or to those which belonged to a past that suddenly seemed remote, almost intolerable without sound and dialogue (Larry Semon's pre-1920 Vitagraph comedies, for example, were provided with a soundtrack for their revived commercial exploitation).

Projection

What differentiates projected film from its ancestors (including the Kinetoscope patented by Edison and Dickson in 1891) is not only the fact that the resulting image could be seen by a community of viewers. In the Kinetoscope, the film strip was run continuously in a peepshow machine. Lumière's *cinématographe* (Plate 40) is based upon a radically different principle: each image would be held still in front of the lens for a small fraction of a second, and then replaced by another one at regular intervals with the aid of a metal claw taking down the film one frame at a time. British pioneer Robert William Paul further developed the idea with a mechanism called the 'Maltese cross', where a tiny pin connected to a cam would engage with the slots which were cut between the arms of a cross-shaped device, thus ensuring that the film moved down one frame. The intermittent movement obtained through this ingenious method is still the operating principle of modern-time film projectors.

Until the end of the silent era the projectors through which most films passed were variable in speed, operated by hand or driven by an electric motor. The operator had to adapt the projection speed to the rate at which the film had been shot, which in turn depended on various factors: the quality of lighting on the scene, the film's sensitivity, the kind of action the camera had to record. In order to ensure that the movements of characters appeared natural, projectionists of the late 19th and early 20th century showed films at speeds between 14 and 18 frames per second. If projected at less than 14 frames per second, the flickering of the image would have been too annoying for the eyes and heat from the projector lamp likely to ignite the film.

The ideal projection speed might vary even within the same film because the shooting conditions had changed, or the director and cameraman had wanted to obtain particular comic or dramatic effects. Projectionists might also drastically increase the projection speed (sometimes causing protests from the public) in order to add to the number of daily shows, or change it at the suggestion of the musicians to enable them better to follow a certain action, or give a scene the desired emotional impact.

The average projection speed increased with the passing years, until it became established – although after many uncertainties and much debate – at 24 frames per second by the second half of the 20s. Higher speeds were used occasionally for experiments with colour films: 32 frames per second for the Kinemacolor system (1909–14), 40 to 70 frames per second for the various equipments patented by William Friese-Greene from 1898 (Plate 58). The opposite tendency was seen, on the other hand, in some amateur film formats whose projection speed was brought down to 14 or sometimes 10 frames per second (9.5mm projectors were even kept on a standstill for the showing of intertitles).

The quality of projection was also affected by the size and the material adopted for the screen (which was often smaller than those used in the second half of the 20th century) and the lighting sources adopted. Before the introduction of electric light, there were at least four other available systems:

- oxyetheric light, produced by a small cylinder of caustic lime made incandescent with a flame produced by a mixture of oxygen and ether;

- oxyhydrogen light, based on a similar principle but using a mixture of oxygen and hydrogen;

- oxycalcic light, where caustic lime became incandescent in a jet of oxygen combined with a flame produced by alcohol;

- acetylene was tried briefly at the end of the 19th and the very beginning of the 20th century, but was eventually abandoned because the light from the gas was very weak, and the vapours released had an unpleasant smell.

Production

How many films were produced during the silent era? There is no certain record, and perhaps we shall never know. The few attempts at setting out a general filmography of the period failed because the number of titles was too large and reliable documents too scarce, especially for the first decade of cinema's life. According to one very approximate estimate, the copies of silent films currently preserved in the world's most important film archives are no less than 30,000 (including both fiction and non-fiction films). More are being found every year, some decompose before having been saved. If we are to believe the film historians' and archivists' estimate that more than 80 per cent of the world production of silent films has been lost, a complete list of titles made in the first thirty years of cinema would easily reach more than 150,000 entries.

Distribution

When dealing with the above hypothetical figures, we must also consider the number of copies made available for each film by the trade through four procedures:

- the direct sale of films, typical of the first ten years of cinema;

- vertically organised, integrated distribution as practised in France by Pathé Omnia between 1907 and 1909. The company controlled the film from beginning to end: manufacturing the raw stock, producing the film, distributing it and finally showing it in theatres owned by the company;

- rental, introduced in 1909 and established as a standard practice in the following years;

- second-hand sales, which derived from the practice of direct sale but survived the period after which this was replaced by the practice of renting films.

There is little information available on this at present, but it is assumed that an average of fifty to one hundred prints were struck for a fiction film produced by a major European company around 1910. The same applies for films produced in Denmark by Nordisk in its heyday, though for an international success like *Den hvide Slavehandel II* (August Blom, 1911) at least 260 copies were struck at the time of its initial release. On the other hand, some early American films which regularly appeared in company lists sold only one or two copies, or were never actually printed at all (and therefore never existed in the form of positive prints) because nobody requested them. On average, a 1914 Keystone comedy was released in a little over thirty prints, although forty copies of Chaplin's *Dough and Dynamite* and 41 of *His Trysting Places* were struck. Chaplin himself stated that 135 copies of the first film he made for Essanay, *His New Job* (1915), were already booked by the end of shooting. When Mutual released Chaplin's *The Floorwalker* in May 1916, seventy-five prints were needed for New York City alone. It is worth pointing out that any inquiry on the dissemination of a film in its country of origin and abroad must take into account the geography of contemporary distribution: in 1919 there were more than 15,000 cinemas in the United States, and it is certain that any ambitious company had to consider the size of the territory to be covered for a nationwide release.

Before the United States established its worldwide hegemony in the market, the film industry was dominated by European productions (France, Denmark and Italy). The distribution of films made by the most important European and American companies became an industry in itself within a few years: well before 1910, the chief firms had branches and agencies in almost every continent. Intertitles in different languages would be supplied in different ways: filmed and already inserted in each copy; as single frames (called flash titles) for reference; provided in the form of title lists, to be printed and newly filmed; or with a separate negative created for the purpose (shooting a film with two cameras side by side became a common practice within a few years of the invention of film): the second negative was sent overseas, where distributors would often make their own intertitles and sometimes add new ones (especially in France and Italy) whenever they felt it necessary.

If an ending seemed inappropriate to public feeling in a certain country, reels of film containing alternative endings were made available. They were called 'Russian endings' when the print was made for eastern European countries, where a tragic conclusion was generally preferred to a happy one. In the first decade of the 20th century, film was sometimes made available in colour or in black and white, at appropriately different prices. Finally, the film underwent a further revision almost everywhere through censorship: two or more copies of the same American film, where they have been preserved, may look different from each other because the censors in each state or nation have taken different decisions according to prevailing mores.

Decay

Several things happen to a film between the time of its first screening and its entry into a moving image archive or a collection. This segment of time shapes the 'internal' history of the copy: the history of the places where it was shown and kept, and of the people who, with varying degrees of awareness, preserved it. It is also the history of the changes that have taken place within the object in the course of time: the history of its progressive self-destruction and, perhaps, of its final disappearance before it could be restored. The study of this process implies a fundamental distinction between a 'film' as a generic entity and the 'prints' through which the film is known. For example, in referring to the 1905 'film' *Rescued by Rover* by Cecil M. Hepworth, we gather within a single definition every 'copy' and 'version' of this title.

The cellulose nitrate stock on which almost every film from the silent period was made is a resilient yet vulnerable entity. It cannot be used beyond a limited number of showings, and it seems that its average expected life outside a climate-controlled environment seldom exceeds about a hundred years (some Lumière films still look in excellent shape, though, and other early titles suffer little more than a slight shrinkage). Film archives are trying to transfer it onto more long-lasting media, but it is an unequal struggle, made even more dramatic by the enormous quantity of material to be duplicated, the limits of the technology and the scarcity of financial resources.

'Nitrate won't wait' is a catchphrase once fashionable in film archives. From the moment it is produced, film stock begins its decomposition process, even in the best storage conditions (that is, at very low temperatures and in ideal humidity). In the course of this process the film emits various gases, especially nitrogen dioxide, which combined with the water in the gelatin and with air forms nitrous acid and nitric acid. These acids corrode the silver salts in the emulsion, destroying the image and the support that bears its traces, until the film is completely ruined.

The stages of this gradual death of a film are sadly familiar, even if the speed of the process is, to a large extent, quite unpredictable. The film shrinks, and the distance between perforations decreases, making projection impossible and copying problematic. There is a strong pungent smell, the image tends to disappear, and the base takes on a brownish colour. The emulsion becomes sticky and it is increasingly difficult to unroll the film. Then eruptions of soft dark matter form on the surface of the reels. This continues until the film becomes an indistinct mass covered by a brown crust. In the final phase of decay, the film is reduced to a whitish mass, or even to powder.

A nitrate film in perfect condition burns at a temperature of 170 degrees Celsius (338 degrees Fahrenheit); a decomposing film can also burn at lower temperatures, down to 41 degrees (105.8 degrees Fahrenheit). If substantial quantities are stored at high temperatures in sealed cans with no air exchange, nitrate film explodes. There is no way to extinguish the flames: the film gives off the oxygen that feeds the fire even under jets of water, sand or carbonic acid. In the initial phases of decay, the film can still be saved by being copied to another carrier, but cellulose nitrate film must be treated with extreme care. In almost every country the projection of nitrate film is illegal or subject to severe restrictions. In our own interest and in the interest of the object's integrity, we must never try to examine nitrate films unless the correct equipment is available. The temptation to look at what may be in the reel we have just found is undoubtedly strong, but giving in to curiosity risks ruining or destroying an already timeworn object.

A nitrate copy can often be recognised by the words 'nitrate film' on the edge of the print. If the writing says 'safety film', we can be almost certain that there is no danger, but that does not mean that we are entitled to treat the print carelessly. When in doubt, it is best to leave the film as it is (and we should not throw away the box it comes in, at least not before taking note of what is written on it).

RULE 1

In the event of finding a nitrate film,
do not try to project it!
Contact a competent film archive immediately.
The archive staff will preserve it safely
and, if necessary, duplicate it.

A film on safety stock is not to be considered stable, either. The base of non-flammable film produced during the silent era (16mm film, for instance) is cellulose diacetate, which is safer than nitrate but, like all polymers, is subject to decay. This phenomenon also affects films from later times printed on cellulose butyrate, cellulose propionate, and, from 1949, on cellulose triacetate base. The principal traits of this sort of decay are described by technicians in graphic yet effective terms:

- vinegar syndrome, so called because of the strong acidic odour given out by the deteriorating film;

- rancid butter syndrome, produced by the butyric acid which develops in the acetate stock;

- pisces syndrome (or rotten fish syndrome), believed to be the effect of the decay in the photographic gelatin.

In many of the above cases the film becomes fragile and tends to curl up. At this stage it should not be unrolled because, if we attempted this, we would find ourselves holding a handful of semitransparent shavings. Decay can be retarded but not stopped (this is why film archivists fight to prolong the life of nitrate film until it becomes possible to duplicate it onto another carrier). Unfortunately, this is also true for cellulose acetate films, whose long-term survival is connected to the rigorous control of temperature and humidity in the premises where they are kept. Archivists are hoping that polyester, whose lifespan as well as physical and chemical compatibility with the photographic emulsion are now undergoing laboratory trials, may offer a viable alternative. Contrary to common belief, digital technology is not necessarily the solution to our problem. We shall return to this point in Chapter 3.

Reproduction

Because they are rare and extremely fragile, original prints should not – with few exceptions – be projected at all. These prints first must survive as long as possible if archives are to be able to restore these films, to duplicate them onto more durable and accessible material, or to preserve them until such time as the techniques of transferring the endangered images to another carrier have improved.

Archives affiliated to the Fédération Internationale des Archives du Film (FIAF) share the opinion that a restored film should be seen in a form as close as possible to the original. An increasing number of institutions provide scholars with reproductions of the most requested films on electronic media, since the wear and tear of a 35mm viewing print may necessitate re-use of the archive negative, at the cost of money that would be better spent on restoring endangered films. (The technological and moral implications of this policy are further discussed in Chapter 7.) Nevertheless, a silent film viewed in an appropriate archival or museum site is still a 35mm or, at least, a 16mm copy. This copy is the result of a preservation process involving print duplication. The main phases of this process will be examined in Chapter 3. In the meantime, it is important to bear in mind that a viewing copy obtained through preservation work may be affected by optical flaws or manipulations that reflect not the 'original' itself but the way it was handled and then duplicated:

- a 'double frame' line: the image is crossed horizontally by an opaque line, most often next to the upper or lower edge of the frame (see photo overleaf);

- stretching: this procedure allows a silent film to be shown at 24 frames per

A 16mm acetate print of *The Navigator* (Donald Crisp and Buster Keaton, 1924) showing printed-in 'double' frame line – next to the upper edge of the frame (George Eastman House).

second (or faster for television). The method, now rejected by most major film archives, consists of reprinting some frames two or more times, at regular intervals. Copies made with this system are recognisable by the dreamlike or irregular pace of moving figures;

- cropped frame: the reproduction of each image obtained by eliminating the peripheral areas of the original frame in order to insert a soundtrack (on the left side of the image on screen) or to adapt the frame ratio to the mask fitted on modern projectors;

- the reproduction in black and white of films originally made in colour;

- alteration in contrast, due to careless reprinting or deliberately done in order to 'improve' the grading of the original print, to compensate for the absence of colour in the duplicate, or to adapt the contrast range to current taste;

- a soundtrack may have been added long after the copy was initially distributed and commercially exploited as a silent film;

- the editing may have been altered by zealous 'preservationists' and archivists (we are not including here the alterations made before the print entered the archive);

- freeze frames may have been added corresponding to shots or intertitles which were damaged or which survived only as fragments, and which are reprinted several times in order to make them visible;

- apocryphal intertitles may have been inserted by the archive because the originals are missing or severely damaged;

- production stills, explanatory titles or other images may have been inserted in the film to plug gaps in the narrative.

The above list is far from being exhaustive. (We shall return to some of its points in Chapters 3 and 6 when dealing, respectively, with film preservation and the viewing practice.) It does, however, serve the purpose of introducing a key concept in silent film studies: there is a huge difference between the moving image we are allowed to see today and what audiences saw at the time of its initial release. What this difference means, in silent cinema and beyond its chronological boundaries, is the question at the core of our inquiry.

Further Reading

Physical structure

See the bibliography at the end of Chapter 3. A short film produced by Metro-Gold-wyn-Mayer, *The Romance of Celluloid* (1937), describes the process of manufacturing nitrate film stock.

Formats

Raife G. Tarkington, 'Early History of Amateur Motion-Picture Film', *Journal of the Society of Motion Picture and Television Engineers*, vol. 64 no. 3, March 1955, pp. 105–16; Brian Coe, *The History of Movie Photography* (Westfield, NJ: Eastview, 1981), pp. 162–9; John Belton, 'The Origins of 35mm Film as a Standard', *SMPTE Journal*, vol. 99 no. 8, August 1990, pp. 652–61; by the same author, *Widescreen Cinema* (Cambridge, MA: Harvard University Press, 1992), pp. 12–33; Paul C. Spehr, 'Unaltered to Date: Developing 35mm Film', in John Fullerton and Astrid Söderbergh-Widding (eds), *Moving Images: From Edison to the Webcam* (Sydney: John Libbey, 2000).

Sound

Historical sources (in chronological order)

E.A. Ahern, *What and How to Play for Pictures* (Twinfalls, ID: Newsprint, 1913); John S. Zamecnik (ed.), *Sam Fox Moving Picture Music* (Cleveland, OH: Sam Fox, 1913 [vols. 1 and 2], 1914 [vol. 3]); Giuseppe Becce, *Kinobibliothek* (Berlin: Schlesingersche Buch- und Musikhandlung Robert Lienau, 1919 ff.); Edith Lang and George West, *Musical Accompaniment of Moving Pictures* (Boston, MA: Boston Music, 1920; reprinted, New York: Arno Press, 1970); George W. Beynon, *Musical*

Presentation of Motion Pictures (New York: G. Schirmer, 1921); P. Kevin Buckley, *The Orchestral and Cinema Organist* (London: Hawkes, 1923); Erno Rapee, *Motion Picture Moods for Pianists and Organists: A Rapid-Reference Collection of Selected Pieces* (New York: G. Schirmer, 1924; reprinted, New York: Arno Press, 1970) and, by the same author, *Encyclopedia of Music for Pictures* (New York: Belwin, 1925; reprinted, New York: Arno Press, 1970); *Cinema Music as a Profession* (Torquay: Educational Section, Screen Music Society, 1925); Hans Erdmann and Giuseppe Becce, *Allgemeines Handbuch der Film-Musik I & II* (Berlin-Leipzig: Schlesingersche Buch- und Musikhandlung Robert Lienau, 1927).

Critical and historical studies

A summary of experiments with sound cinema during the first thirty years of the 20th century can be found in Brian Coe, *The History of Movie Photography*, pp. 90–111. For an introduction to music in silent film see Gillian B. Anderson (ed.), *Music for Silent Films, 1894–1929. A Guide* (Washington, DC: Library of Congress, 1988); by the same author, 'The Presentation of Silent Films, or Music as Anaesthesia', *The Journal of Musicology* 5, 1987. pp. 257–95, and *Film Music Bibliography I* (Hollywood, CA: Society for the Preservation of Film Music, 1995); see also Charles Hofmann, *Sounds for Silents* (New York: Drama Book Specialists, 1970); Charles M. Berg, *An Investigation of the Motives for and Realization of Music to Accompany the American Silent Film, 1896–1927* (New York: Arno Press, 1976); Martin Marks, 'Film Music: The Material, Literature and Present State of Research', *The Quarterly Journal of the Music Library Association*, vol. 36 no. 2, 1979, pp. 282–325; Walther Seidler (ed.), *Stummfilmmusik gestern und heute* (Berlin: Volker Spiess Verlag, 1979); Hans-Jörg Pauli, *Filmmusik: Stummfilm* (Stuttgart: Klett-Cotta, 1981); Sergio Miceli, *La Musica nel film. Arte e artigianato* (Fiesole: Discanto Edizioni, 1982); David Robinson, *Musica delle ombre / Music of the Shadows: The Use of Musical Accompaniment with Silent Films, 1896–1936* (supplement to *Griffithiana*, vol. 13 nos 38–9, October 1990); Martin Marks, 'The First American Film Scores', *Harvard Library Bulletin*, vol. 2 no. 4, 1991, pp. 78–100; Emmanuelle Toulet and Christian Belaygue, *Musique d'écran, 1918–1995. L'accompagnement musical du cinéma muet en France, 1918–1995* (Paris: Editions des Musées Nationaux, 1994); Philip C. Carli, 'Musicology and the Presentation of Silent Film', *Film History*, vol. 7 no. 3, Autumn 1995. pp. 298–321. 'Global Experiments in Early Synchronous Sound', special Domitor issue of *Film History*, vol. 11 no. 4, 1999. A bibliography of over 800 titles, mostly from the silent period, can be found in Steven D. Wescott (ed.), *A Comprehensive Bibliography of Music for Film and Television* (Detroit, MI: Information Coordinators, Inc, 1985, Detroit Studies in Music Bibliography 54, pp. 25–67). Early films with synchronised phonograph recordings: Jan Olsson, *Från filmjud till ljudfilm* (Stockholm: Proprius Förlag, 1986), including an audio cassette containing 17 recordings from phonograph discs for silent films in the period 1903 to 1914. Mechanical instruments for film theatres: *Das Mechanische Musikinstrument enhält Die Drehorgel*, vol.

11 no. 41, April 1987. The transition from silent to sound film: Scott Eyman, *The Speed of Sound: Hollywood and the Talkie Revolution, 1926–1930* (New York: Simon & Schuster, 1997); Martin Barnier, *Le Cinéphone et l'Idéal-Sonore, deux appareils sonores Gaumont des années 1920–1930, 1895*, no. 24, June 1998, pp. 37–53. A dissident, deliberately heretical view on the subject is brought by Rick Altman, who believes that 'silence was in fact a regular practice of silent film exhibition': 'The Silence of the Silents', *Musical Quarterly*, vol. 80 no. 4, 1997, pp. 648–718.

Projection

Given the fundamental role of the screen in the film experience, it is startling to see that so little, if anything, has been published on its history, a fascinating topic still awaiting proper attention. Even the history of film projection has so far been marginalised to specialised technical literature in periodicals such as the *SMTE* (later renamed *SMPTE*) *Journal*. No study on the subject should miss *The American Projectionist*, a journal published in New York between 1923 and 1931 by the American Projection Society. Useful readings on the topic are Raymond Fielding, *A Technological History of Motion Pictures and Television* (Berkeley: University of California Press, 1967); Laurent Mannoni, *Le Mouvement continué* (Milan-Paris: Mazzotta/ Cinémathèque française/Musée du cinéma, 1996); John Hiller, 'Film History for the Public: the First National Movie Machine Collection', *Film History*, vol. 11 no. 3, 1999, pp. 371–86. The debate on projection speed is summarised in Kevin Brownlow, 'Silent Films. What Was the Right Speed?', *Sight and Sound*, Summer 1980, and *Classic Images*, June 1984; a heterodox viewpoint on the subject comes from James Card, 'Silent-Film Speed', *Image*, vol. 4 no. 7, October 1955, reproduced in Marshall Deutelbaum (ed.), *'Image' On the Art and Evolution of Film* (New York and Rochester, NY: Dover Publications Inc. and George Eastman House, 1979), pp. 145–6.

Production

The only production catalogues reprinted after the silent era have been published in the United States and United Kingdom: Stephen Herbert, Colin Harding, Simon Popple (eds), *Victorian Film Catalogues, A Facsimile Collection* (London: The Projection Box, 1996); Reese V. Jenkins (ed.), *The Thomas A. Edison Papers: A Guide to Motion Picture Catalogues by American Producers and Distributors, 1894–1908* (Frederick, MD: University Publications of America, 1985 [6 reels of 35mm microfilm]) is an invaluable source of information on the films produced in the United States during the early period. The microfilms are accompanied by a 50-page guide edited by Charles Musser. Bebe Bergsten (ed.), *Biograph Bulletins, 1896–1908* (Los Angeles: Locare Research Group, 1971); *Biograph Bulletins, 1908–1912* (New York: Octagon Books, s.d. [1973]). A partial exception is Henri Bousquet's chronology of the films produced by Pathé Frères in France (see the Filmographies section at the end of Chapter 5).

Distribution

Kristin Thompson, *Exporting Entertainment: America in the World Film Market, 1907–1934* (London: BFI, 1985); Richard Koszarski (ed.), *Exhibition*, special issue of *Film History*, vol. 6 no. 2, Summer 1994; Richard Abel, *The Red Rooster Scare. Making Cinema American, 1900–1910* (Berkeley: University of California Press, 1999); Robert C. Allen, 'Motion Picture Exhibition in Manhattan, 1906–1912: Beyond the Nickelodeon', *Cinema Journal* 18, Spring 1979, pp. 2–15; Ben Singer, 'Manhattan Nickelodeons: New Data on Audiences and Exhibitors', *Cinema Journal* 34, Spring 1995, pp. 5–35. The lively debate following the publication of Singer's essay, also documented in *Cinema Journal*, is well worth reading.

Architecture

David Atwell, *Cathedrals of the Movies. A History of British Cinemas and their Audiences* (London: The Architectural Press, 1980); Ben M. Hall, *The Best Remaining Seats* (New York: Bramhall House, 1961). A useful bibliography on the subject appears in Joseph M. Valerio and Daniel Friedman, *Movie Palaces: Renaissance and Reuse* (New York: Educational Facilities Laboratories Division, Academy for Educational Development, 1982). The preservation of historical buildings dedicated to film exhibition is discussed by the periodical *Marquee*, published by the Theatre Historical Society of America (ISSN 0025–3928).

Reception

In the absence of a general history of film reception during the silent era, here's the best of the crop: Yuri Tsivian, *Historiceskaja recenija kino kinematograph v Rossii, 1896–1930* (Riga: Zinatne, 1991), translated into English and revised as *Early Cinema in Russia and Its Cultural Reception* (London and New York: Routledge, 1994). See also Gregg Bachmann, 'Still in the Dark: Silent Film Audiences', *Film History*, vol. 9 no. 1, 1997, pp. 23–48; Miriam Hansen, *Babel and Babylon: Spectatorship in American Silent Film* (Cambridge, MA: Harvard University Press, 1991); John Belton (ed.), *Audiences and Fans*, special issue of *Film History*, vol. 6 no. 4, Winter 1994); Janet Staiger, *Interpreting Films: Studies in the Historical Reception of American Cinema* (Princeton, NJ: Princeton University Press, 1992); Donald Crafton (ed.), special issue of *Iris*, no. 11, Summer 1990, on early cinema audiences.

Decay

(Roger Smither (ed.), *This Film is Dangerous: An Anthology in Celebration of Nitrate Film* (Brussels: FIAF, 2000); David Pierce, 'The Legion of the Condemned: Why American Silent Films Perished', *Film History*, vol. 9 no. 1, 1997: 5–22. A bibliography on film preservation is provided at the end of Chapter 3. Those who are curious to see what an actual fire of nitrate film looks like may enjoy watching the eerie short film, *Das Verhalten von brennendem Nitrofilm gegenüber löschmitteln* (Österreichisches Filmarchiv, Austria 1978, 19').

The poem by Christian Morgenstern 'Fisches Nachtgesang' (1905) is reproduced from *Über die galgenlieder* (Berlin: B. Cassirer, 1921).

2
The Way of All Flesh Tones

I know that my colours are not yours. Two colours are never the same, even if they're from the same tube. Context changes the way we perceive them. I've usually used one word to describe a colour, so red remains red with lapses into vermilion or carmine. How could I be certain that the shade I wanted could be reproduced by the printer? I prefer that colours should float and take flight in your minds.

Derek Jarman

The Heritage of Magic Lantern Slides: Hand-Colouring and Stencil

The first attempts to apply colour manually to the film emulsion derive from the methods normally used for magic lantern slides. Experiments in this direction were made in the United States and France almost as soon as the photographic moving image came into existence. Already in 1895 the Edison Kinetoscope Company had marketed *Annabelle's Dance* – the first of a vast repertory of single-shot views dedicated to the genre of the 'serpentine dance', which Loïe Fuller had made an international rage – in colour versions. Annabelle's white veils were tinted by hand by the wife of Edward Kuhn in the Edison Laboratories at Llewellyn Park, New Jersey, using half a dozen hues, in an attempt 'to simulate the effect of the coloured lights that were projected on the ballerina during her performance on stage'. Early attempts in this direction were also made by Lumière in France and by Robert William Paul in the United Kingdom.

The application of colour was later improved with the use of powerful enlarging lenses and extremely fine brushes. Georges Méliès, more than anyone else, took advantage of the limitations inherent in this practice (it was difficult to follow precisely the contours of people and objects) by producing some of the most fascinating colour films of the early period (Plate 45). *Le Palais des mille et une nuits* (1905) has ample strokes of brilliant dyes, sometimes with a dominant golden yellow, pervading the entire frame and creating an effect similar to tinting; more complex is the colour scheme in *Le Royaume des fées* (1903), in which the variety and density of the hues has no equal among surviving nitrate prints of the early period. The colours in this film have been compared to those of medieval miniatures, not only because of the minute detail and the clever articulation of delicately hued patterns within a tiny surface, but also because of their effect in locating the story in a realm of mythic atmosphere, deliberately alien to any historical context (although derived from the visual codes of late nineteenth-century books of fables), and by their capacity to enhance the beauty of the settings and the depth of the *trompe-l'oeil* perspective.

In order to reduce the very high costs involved in hand-colouring a film, standardise the product – for obvious reasons, manual application of colour resulted in noticeable differences from copy to copy, affirming the uniqueness of each – and satisfy a growing market demand, systems were devised for mechanical colouring after 1905. (It is worth noting, though, that hand-colouring never disappeared altogether. From the early 1920s and well into the sound period, for example, Gustav Brock would manually apply color with the same system used by Méliès on prints of several Hollywood productions.) The industrial, rather than aesthetic, nature of the innovation is confirmed by the fact that these coloured films originated with Pathé, then a rapidly expanding company whose drive to control all phases of production culminated in 1908 in its policy of 'vertical integration' of the market. The motive underlying the technological breakthrough was clear: guarantee the standardised quality and regularity of the product, therefore enhancing control over the distribution process. More copies, better quality, at lower cost. The areas of the frame to be coloured were cut (by hand or by needles connected to pantographs) onto matrix copies which were then placed on the positive prints; each colour was applied to the film through the outlines thus obtained, with brushes or pads soaked in the appropriate aniline dye (Plates 49, 51 and 52).

Since its early adoption for trick films and *féeries* (*La Poule aux œufs d'or*, 1905; *Aladin ou la lampe merveilleuse*, 1906) whose chromatic effects were still indebted to manual techniques in use at the time, the patented Pathécolour – also known as '*au pochoir*' in France and 'stencil' in English-speaking countries – justified its owners' claims to supremacy in the colour reproduction of reality. It was then that 'cinematography in natural colours' became a criterion of taste in the evolution of moving images, as important as the 'talking picture' (the coupling of colour and sound came to be considered at a certain point as the ultimate goal of film experiments). The principal arena for the innovation shifted from the domain of fiction to non-fiction: authenticity and realism were the main goals in the reproduction of a landscape as it was actually seen: the warm brown tones of the walls of ancient castles, the uniform blue of the sky, the contrast between the green expanse of a meadow and the vivid rose bushes within it, the emerald texture of the sea spangled with the sails of ships. The principle of authenticity was further extended to the myth of historical accuracy and the legitimisation of cinema as an aesthetically elevated subject; the Pathé series 'Film d'Art' and the adaptations from drama and literature produced by the company's 'Film d'Arte Italiana' between 1909 and 1912 displayed a refinement of colour and precision of outline unequalled in the period. Their palette and their audience alike sprang from the appreciation of academic painting. Stencil colouring became infrequent after 1915, but there are extraordinary examples of it up until the mid-1920s (*Cyrano de Bergerac*, Augusto Genina, 1923).

The Aesthetics of Uniformity: Tinting and Toning

It is not known precisely when uniform colouring of the film stock began to be a component of film production. This uncertainty is somehow surprising, since much has been documented and published regarding other colour techniques in an era when the paternity of a discovery was the frequent object of contention, and competing claims were made by the presumed pioneers of this or that device. A plausible explanation for the absence of reliable evidence on chronological priority might be that tinting and toning were adopted by different producers more or less at the same time. It should be emphasised, however, that the introduction of tinting was gradual, and withouth much fanfare. On the basis of surviving films of the era, it seems that it must have been used only rarely until the end of the 19th century; the first significant example of this kind was to be seen in October 1901, when James Williamson's *Fire!* was released, containing footage tinted red to depict the conflagration in an apartment building.

Although anonymous – perhaps simply because not subject to any form of proprietary ownership – the invention spread to all the producing countries with great speed. No statistical analysis of this diffusion has been attempted, but an estimate based on surviving nitrate prints suggests that the technique went through three phases. The first, from 1900 to about 1907, saw the occasional use of tinting and toning. In the second, from 1908 to 1925, the uniform colouring of the film base became a widespread practice. The great majority of films during this time were coloured using one or the other technique, or both combined. This period may be further subdivided into two trends – initially, the frequent use of both tinting and toning; later, the slow decline of toning in the years 1921 to 1925. In the third phase, corresponding to the twilight of silent film, there was an increase in the number of films distributed in black and white, even though tinted films were still common. The decrease in uniform colouring of the film base is in all likelihood connected to at least three concurring factors: the increasing availability of more sophisticated techniques, such as the first experiments in Technicolor; the gradual introduction of panchromatic film, less suited to the general application of colour than the orthochromatic film for which the techniques of tinting and toning were originally designed; the introduction of soundtrack on film in the late 20s (as tinting and splicing would be likely to interfere with the optical cells in the projector).

Surviving nitrate copies of silent films suggest that some form of tinting or toning was employed in approximately 85 per cent of the total production. This estimate does not take into account a practice quite common even in the earliest cinema, that of colouring the intertitles in films otherwise released in black and white. Intertitles tinted at first in blue and later in red (which was customarily done at least until 1914) was one of the distinguishing elements of the Pathé company's products, a device for discouraging bootleg copies. Similarly, Gaumont intertitles were often tinted blue-green.

Tinting and toning films became such a widespread practice that some companies produced brochures and catalogues on the subject (Plate 44). Eastman Kodak was by far the most prolific, issuing no less than five editions of its manual on the tinting and toning of positive film between 1916 and 1927. These are works of great historical value, as they contain not only the chemical formulas used to create the coloured baths but also actual samples of nitrate film coloured in each tint and by each technique discussed. They deal with processes of remarkable complexity, allowing the creation of a vast range of colours that sometimes differed from one another only by subtle variations in density and luminosity, difficult for the untrained eye of a modern observer to identify.

Tinting was implemented in three different ways:

A initially, by applying a coloured varnish on the film emulsion (Plate 46);

B from the early years of the 20th century, by immersing the film stock in an aqueous solution containing the colouring agent;

C towards the end of the silent era, using a pre-tinted stock (a sophisticated instance of this is given by the Sonochrome film, manufactured by Kodak in the late 1920s and promoted through a vague yet intriguing 'philosophy' of correspondence between colours and emotions; see Plate 62).

Toning was achieved through a process where a coloured compound was substituted for the silver of the emulsion without colouring the gelatin of the film. This could be obtained in three ways:

A by direct toning, in which the silver salts are replaced by another coloured metallic compound;

B by toning in two baths, where the silver image is transformed first into a colourless salt, and then into a coloured salt;

C by mordanting, in which the silver is replaced by an insoluble silver salt capable of fixing organic colouring agents.

The three different systems of toning – devised to increase the variety of available colours – cannot easily be differentiated by a cursory examination of the prints from this era. The possibilities offered by toning alone were in fact limited by the number of metals (such as iron, uranium and copper) which would yield colour compounds. With mordanting, however, because some organic compounds can be altered by colouring solutions, the variety of colours that could be obtained was practically equal to the quantity of basic substances available. The introduction of toning by the use of mordants, towards the end of the 1910s, was a response to aesthetic requirements, and to a market which demanded ever more complex and sophisticated colouring effects.

In the direct examination of a piece of nitrate film, a tinted print shows colour-

This chart will aid in visualizing the chromatic relation-ships of the sixteen Sonochrome tints in the hue cycle.   The tints range from NOCTURNE, *a cold violet-blue, to* INFERNO, *a fiery red tinged with magenta. Between these two on one side lie the purples* PURPLEHAZE, FLEUR DE LIS, AMA-RANTH, *and the purple-pink* CAPRICE, *on the other side the cool blues and greens from* AZURE *to* VERDANTE, *the warm yellows and oranges from* SUNSHINE *to* AFTERGLOW, *and the pinks* PEACHBLOW *and* ROSE DOREE.

Kodak Sonochrome, *c.* 1929. Illustration from *New Color Moods for the Screen*, published by Eastman Kodak Company (George Eastman House).

ing in both the dark and the light areas of the frame, and on the edges of the film (Plate 47). With toning and mordanting, only those areas retaining the silver of the emulsion are coloured. The remaining parts of the frame appear as white, and the edges remain uncoloured (Plate 48). Tinting, toning, and stencil (or, more rarely, hand-painted) colour may be seen together in the same shot, thus multiplying the creative possibilities of these techniques (Plates 44, 51 and 52). Every individual scene with tinting, toning, or a combination of the two had to be immersed in a separate bath, so the film stock to be treated was wound on reels containing all the scenes to be treated with a particular colour. In most tinted prints and all toned prints, segments with different colours had to be rejoined with splices in every positive print. In a nitrate copy of *The Red Lantern* (Albert Capellani, 1919) held by the Cinémathèque Royale in Belgium there is a scene set in a dance hall where changing effects of light are achieved by fragments in various colours, joined with splices. There are no such splices, however, in nitrate prints of *The Four Horsemen of the Apocalypse* (Rex Ingram, Metro Pictures, 1921) in the shot where a woman sings the 'Marseillaise' while the colour changes from blue, to black and white and then red, alluding to the French flag. In this case, the effect was possibly obtained by consecutively immersing portions of the footage corresponding to the entire shot in different colour baths without cutting the positive print (Plate 50).

It has been stated so often as to become a cliché that a colour in a motion picture was chosen most frequently for its specific dramatic, atmospheric, or psychological connotation, such as blue for heavenly scenes (as in Robert William Paul's *The ? Motorist*, 1906), or for night-time settings, the transition from blue to yellow or ochre where a character enters a dark room and switches on a light, or red to indicate fire. The utility of this approach to colour is undeniable, but that alone is not adequate to explain the enormous variety of options that were available to filmmakers and their audiences. If it were simply a matter of associating colours with events or such emotional states as hatred or passion, the palette would have been rather limited, if only because the symbolic meanings of colour were never codified or generally agreed upon by the public. In popular wisdom at the turn of the century, yellow was widely associated with compromise and cowardice, yet only rarely used this way in film. In the often-cited instance of *The Lonedale Operator* (David W. Griffith, Biograph, 1911), blue tinting supports the stratagem of the heroine who, in the dim light of a room, holds a monkey wrench in her hand in order to make it seem to the two bandits that she has a gun. It is true that in this case the association of the colour blue with lack of light has more than a conventional value. But this derives from a theatrical tradition, while the philosophy and use of colour in silent cinema also obeyed other criteria, which were not necessarily more sophisticated but certainly made no effort to simulate reality.

One could say: primary colours for primary sensations. But then, if red equates with fire and violence, blue with the sea, with rain and darkness, and green with the natural world, what was done with purple, orange, mauve, and all the intermediary shades (including silvered dark gray toning, often difficult to distinguish from plain black and white) cited in the manuals and recognisable only after close examination of a nitrate print? And why was such a diversity of shades exploited in non-fiction subjects? Production companies tinted and toned their films using the resources at

their disposal. In some feature films, the first reel would show a relatively wide variety of colours, gradually decreasing in the remaining footage. Here, the spectacular
display of tinting and toning might be compared to black and white films of the
1920s with Technicolor sequences occurring at critical points in the story, or the concentration of grand scenic and sound effects in the first ten minutes of a feature film.

For the major companies of the 1910s (among them Pathé, Ambrosio, Gaumont,
Metro, Cines, Famous Players-Lasky, Nordisk), the use of a gamut of tones was often
a point of prestige; to middling and minor companies, colour was an expensive luxury to be used only when necessary (and at times even contrary to the sense of the
scene, as we see in the many nocturnal settings tinted in amber yellow). An ochre
yellow predominates in the feature films of the poverty row companies, sometimes
alternating with blue. Elsewhere, the same colour would be used just to give a feeling of comfort and warmth to the viewing experience. Apparently, one colour was
better than nothing, and it would allow low-budget firms to claim that their films
were not in black and white after all. By and large, the poorest companies produced
films with no colour at all; others avoided colour altogether in certain genres of film
addressed to lower-class audiences, such as one- or two-reel comedies of the 1910s,
which are largely in black and white.

Tinting and toning in a silent film could also vary according to the time and
place of distribution. A company might re-release copies of its films using colours
different from those initially distributed, more or less elaborate as circumstances
dictated. Once exported abroad, moreover, a film was virtually abandoned to its
fate in matters of colour. If the production company sent a second negative to
another continent (as was the practice from the early 20th century), it might send
recommendations on the tinting and toning, or indicate colour on the blank
frames preceding each scene in the negative, but there was no guarantee that the
recipient would follow those instructions, and little or no supervision of what was
actually done. Local distributors would have the last word in this matter, and determine colour schemes following their own taste or the predilections of their
clientele.

'Natural Colour' and its Utopias

At the extreme opposite of the synthesis of reality by means of symbolism and sim-
plification stands the work of those technicians who sought to endow film with the
presumed qualities of the human eye. The fact that these efforts came principally
from scientists, rather than arising out of the demands of filmmakers – with the
notable exception of Cecil B. DeMille – helps to explain their relative detachment
from most attempts to control colour for stylistic reasons. Following on from the
experiments by James Clerk Maxwell (1831–79) and Arthur-Louis Ducos Du Hau-
ron (1837–1920), at the end of the 19th century, the British photographer, William
Friese-Greene undertook a series of experiments to achieve 'animated natural
colour pictures'. Although unsuccessful on a commercial level, his pioneering work

laid the theoretical foundations of the Technicolor process. The work of Friese-Greene underwent at least six successive stages:

A installing in both the camera and the projector a disc of glass divided into three equal sectors, each with a filter of one of the three primary colours in the additive synthesis (red, green and blue). This disc was then rotated – at speeds varying between 40 and 70 frames per second – so that each sector of the disc corresponded to a frame filmed and then projected (1898);

B abandoning the coloured disc in favor of a prism located in front of the camera lens and the projector;

C arranging three cameras and three projectors, stacked vertically, horizontally or in a triangle, each fitted with a filter of a primary colour. The film would then be projected at the standard speed of 16 frames per second, but required triple the quantity of film, while exact registration of the three images during projection was extremely difficult to achieve;

D directly tinting alternate frames with two primary colours (red and green), after the film was shot through a rotating disc using alternating filters of these same two colours (1909). According to surviving fragments, a three-colour variation on the same system was experimented shortly afterwards (Plate 58);

E shooting simultaneously two parallel reels of black and white film, each moving in synch with an endless band of transparent celluloid whose empty frames were coloured alternately green, red and blue. After processing, the positives were projected in parallel, with the same two loops of transparent film;

F using the same system of two parallel reels of film, successively shot and projected through rotating colour-segmented discs instead of loops of transparent, coloured film.

All these systems had problems when put into use: the need to speed up projection, which consumed an inordinate quantity of film, the rapid deterioration of the print from this high speed projection, the flickering of the image, and the blurring of contours. In 1911 Colin Bennett tried various means to overcome these defects, registering under the trade mark Cinechrome (1911–25) his system of a lens divided into two sectors for a 70mm film, also divided into two zones, each of a different colour. Claude H. Friese-Greene, the son of the inventor, experimented further with the idea of a rotating filter, pursuing research along the lines initiated in 1897 by the German researcher, Isensee. All of them met with negative results. The solution – developed by Frederick Marshall Lee and Edward Raymond Turner in the London laboratory of Frederic Eugene Ives, copyrighted in 1899, bought in 1902 by Charles Urban, and refined further by George Albert Smith – was essentially a compromise. Smith discovered that the use of just two colours, with a rotating filter of green and red sectors, could give adequate results without radically modifying the projection apparatus while running the film speed at 32 frames per second.

The development and success of the system copyrighted by the Natural Colour Kinematograph Company, founded by Urban after a successful demonstration in 1909 and his acquisition of Smith's shares (Smith being more interested in the scientific aspects of the invention than in its commercial exploitation) were part of a series of business moves. In the form in which it was exploited in the United States and Europe, the Kinemacolor film needed only a single chemical treatment, the panchromatisation of the motion picture stock (achieved by immersing the base in a sensitised solution) in order to make it sensitive to the red end of the spectrum. The Kinemacolor image provided a modest but serviceable chromatic range. Charles Urban exaggerated its capabilities to the point of maintaining that the new process could capture accurately all the colours of the spectrum. Nothing was further from the truth, but the fact that neither journalists nor the general public objected to this claim shows the extent to which audiences were captivated by the images created with this system.

The colour palette in Kinemacolor was in fact rather limited. The reproduction of blue and purple in particular left much to be desired, and required corrections which could be effected by projecting the film onto a light blue screen. Eyestrain was often reported when long films were shown. All the numerous subjects of Kinemacolor were shot in bright sunlight, as artificial light gave disappointing results. Other limitations are clearly visible in surviving prints: green and red predominate, while objects in other colours appear with a brownish cast that gives the whole a pastel tonality, recalling the look of Lumière Autochromes. There is a tendency towards homogenisation of diverse hues and a reduction in the depth of field.

Besides these drawbacks, other basic technological flaws precluded Kinemacolor from becoming the dominant system for natural colour. Exhibitors objected to adjusting their projection equipment every time a Kinemacolor film was threaded into the machine, while producers resented making 1,000 foot reels whose running time only equalled no more than a reel of 500 feet. All in all, Kinemacolor never reached a full integration into the normal exhibition circuit. However widespread, its success was confined to the status of a special attraction for a select audience. In the early 1910s, however, the relative lack of commercial success of Kinemacolor was attributed more to its inherent qualitative shortcomings than to its technical challenges. The competition between Kinemacolor and other rival systems was partially stimulated by a utopian faith in the potential of film technology to achieve 'natural colour', reality 'as it is' being the goal of the cinematic spectacle. An elaborate system launched at this time by Gaumont had this same goal: bringing the spectator to this 'new world' of the image.

Following research undertaken in France by the Établissements Gaumont, the Société Française de Photographie presented on 15 November 1912 a demonstration of a new two-colour additive system, 'Biochrome', the latest entry into the field of cinematography with 'natural colours'. The response encouraged Léon Gaumont to continue his efforts, and less than a month later to organise another screening, this time before an invited audience at the Gaumont-Théâtre, 7 Boulevard Poissonnière in Paris. The first commercial presentation was in April of the following year at Gaumontcolor in rue du Faubourg-Montmartre.

Within two months, the invention – now christened 'Chronochrome' – crossed the Atlantic, in an attempt to conquer the American market for 'natural colour' cinema, which until then had been ruled by Kinemacolor. The subjects presented in New York in June 1913 were largely those already shown in Europe. An agent of the Eastman Kodak company was present at the screening, since Kodak had produced especially for Gaumont an experimental panchromatic safety-base film, sensitive to the full range of the spectrum, which was destined to overtake orthochromatic emulsion by the end of the 20s. Alone among all the systems hitherto developed, Chronochrome had the advantage of displaying a very rich range of colour while using a film of standard 35mm format.

The system employed a triple lens fitted with three filters (green, red, and blue) for both the camera and the projector, by means of which each black and white image was split into three frames. The three images were projected simultaneously, each through its respective filter, to form a single image (Plate 61). Instead of the usual two- or three-blade shutter, a one-blade shutter was used. The width of each frame was identical to that in conventional films, but its height was reduced from the standard 18mm, thus giving the projected image a panoramic format, with an aspect ratio of approximately 1:1.71. The reduced height of the frame achieved a considerable saving of material, requiring 2.25 times the quantity of film stock used for normal film projection, rather than three times as much, as would have been required for frames of standard dimensions.

The filter corresponding to the central lens was fixed. The green and blue filters were adjustable both horizontally and vertically, in order to keep the three colour images in register on the screen. It was a delicate operation, requiring constant adjustments by the projectionist, and complicated by the distance of the projector from the screen. At first, correct registration demanded the help of an assistant projectionist in the hall, relaying instructions to the projection booth by telephone; later, a technician in the hall would modify the positions of the three lenses by means of an electrical remote device.

Another drawback proved to be more serious and ultimately decisive: Chronochrome could not be shown with a conventional projector, whereas Kinemacolor required only a single adjustment to the projection mechanism, the insertion of a two-blade shutter fitted with filters (green and red). Other disadvantages were shared by both systems. Kinemacolor filters absorbed up to 33 per cent of the light, and required 250 per cent more electric power to achieve a luminosity equivalent to that of a conventional projector. It was even worse with Chronochrome, whose blue filter alone absorbed almost one third of the available light. Furthermore, both Kinemacolor and Chronochrome had problems with image sharpness. George Albert Smith's positives suffered from blurred contours, particularly noticeable with people and objects in rapid motion. Chronochrome projection tended to suffer from a stereo-parallax effect, as the three lenses projected the image from slightly divergent angles. This was another reason for reducing the height of the frame, so the three complementary images could be positioned closer together. Finally, both systems required twice the amount of footage needed for a conventional film. In this respect, however, Chronochrome had the important advantage of being shot and projected at the standard speed of 16 frames per second, slow enough to make panchromatic film compatible with artificial lighting.

The Chronochrome image was of a noticeably higher quality than that of other systems using filters. Two extant short films, known by their English titles *Reproduction of a Bouquet with Ordinary Cinematography* (to be projected without colour filters) and *The Same Bouquet by Chrono-Chrome Gaumont* (both 1913), provide eloquent evidence of the impression this system must have created on the spectator of the period. The definition and the variety of colour is striking, with predominant red, blue, and especially a gaudy green, particularly noticeable in the detail of a lady's hat in *Paris-Fashion: Visiting* (1913). Seen as a whole, the sheer variety of tones is nothing less than astonishing. In the filming of inanimate objects at close range, Chronochrome endows the image with a startling sense of three-dimensionality. In long shots and outdoor scenes this effect is less marked; sunlight tends to give a brownish cast to primary colours, and small objects tend to go out of focus because of the trouble in keeping the three superimposed images in registration.

Handschiegl, the Lithography of Nitrate

The impracticality of systems based on additive synthesis, all of which required special projection arrangements, led the industry to search for alternatives which would present fewer problems for commercial deployment. One symptomatic example of this approach is a solution prompted by Cecil B. DeMille in 1916, which was a fundamental step in the transition from the technology and aesthetics of tinting and toning to the dawn of Technicolor.

The principle of the Handschiegl Process, later also known as the Wyckoff-DeMille Process (probably because the cameraman Alvin Wyckoff actively participated in its development) is an ingenious adaptation to motion picture film of the process of lithography in multiple colours. This technique (devised by Max Handschiegl, a craftsman from St Louis who specialised in lithography and photo-engraving) is by far the most complex system of direct colouring ever devised during the silent era. Starting with a normal black and white print, sequences were chosen for treatment, using a maximum of three colours. This required a separate matrix for each colour chosen. The portion of the film to be coloured was covered by a masking liquid. Once dried, an internegative was made: the area to be coloured appeared in it as a transparent outline, while the rest of the frame retained the silver salts of the emulsion. Following the principle that the exposed portions of the emulsion are less soluble than the unexposed ones, Handschiegl then immersed the internegative in a tanning bleach in order to fix the exposed portions, solidifying them in such a way that they would not absorb the colouring agent, while the unexposed parts remained viscous and transparent.

After fixing, washing, and drying, the internegative was immersed in a bath with an aqueous colouring solution to tint the transparent areas. After the bath, the internegative was cleaned to eliminate excess colour, so that only the permeable area remained tinted, and was then dried. The matrix thus obtained was run in direct contact with a positive copy of the same segment, under sufficient pressure to transfer the colour from the internegative to the positive. To ensure the transfer of colour, the positive was treated with an emollient solution which moistened the emulsion, allowing it to absorb the colour from the internegative matrix. The internegative was therefore used as a sort of stamp that left its imprint on the positive copy. Because of this – in the same way that a stamp cannot leave a clear impression unless it is reinked frequently – the internegative had to be reimmersed in the dye bath after every two transfers.

The fixing solution for the internegative could not be used indefinitely; after a certain number of copies the internegative began to dissolve, and the colouring solution permeated the entire emulsion, making the internegative of no further use as a matrix. About forty copies could be made successfully with one internegative matrix. Because the area to be coloured had initially been outlined manually – as the covering substance was applied to the master positive by brushstrokes – the entire procedure had to be repeated when preparing a new internegative.

But the Handschiegl process was too cumbersome to be adopted on an industrial scale, in cases where a large number of copies were required for distribution. For the same reason, the system could be used only for relatively brief portions of a film. In fact, the Handschiegl process was employed in about twenty feature films (alone or combined with the Technicolor No. 2 system) from 1916 to 1927, shortly before the death of its inventor. Its swift descent into obsolescence points to another element of incompatibility with mass production: Handschiegl personally supervised the creation of every matrix, and closely monitored all phases of the process.

Thus a craftsman's method, similar to the procedures of a studio for applied graphics, proved unable to meet the industry's demands. The amount of work required by the Handschiegl process was comparable to the labour involved in hand colouring or stencilling film, since the area of the internegative matrix to be coloured had to be traced by hand, frame by frame. The Handschiegl image has the look of early films, but its pastel colours have a much greater transparency and a subtler texture, which gives an atmospheric quality to the scene. While direct colouring appears as imposed upon the objects represented, like a lacquer overlay

altering contrast values and drastically weakening detail, this system seems to coex-
ist well with the photographic image, and to endow it with a liquid softness that
is almost tactile. Because of this quality, DeMille and Handschiegl preferred above
all to use it for scenes with mutable elements like water and fire: *Joan the Woman*
(1916) has a Handschiegl final scene where Geraldine Farrar's body is enveloped
in flame and smoke; in *The Ten Commandments* (1923), the Egyptian army, pursuing the Hebrews in the desert, is first obstructed by a barrier of fire, then
drowned in the Red Sea where the Pharaoh and his horse are immersed in brilliant emerald foam. No less remarkable is the glowing yellow of a golden tooth in
a surviving frame (Plate 55) of Erich von Stroheim's *Greed* (1925). Projected on a
large screen, original Handschiegl colour has the power to dazzle the eye in a way
that no reproduction can possibly imitate. While it is true that all modern copies
of any original colour process reduce its impact, Handschiegl is virtually impossible to duplicate without a fatal loss of its outstanding pictorial attributes. Existing
viewing copies make it look like a faded Technicolor, or a hand-coloured film worn
out by time; sadly enough, there is no way to fully appreciate it without viewing
the original. This makes its rarity and extreme physical vulnerability all the more
lamentable, reinforcing as it does the notion of the photographic moving image
as a simulacrum of a 'present' lost to our time, witnessed by no one other than the
audience of the past.

Before and after Technicolor: Additive and Subtractive Processes, 1911 to 1928

The various efforts to create films in colour which could be exploited commercially
on a large scale gave rise to a period of aggressive competition (mostly among the
United States, United Kingdom, and France) between processes which each in turn
emerged, enjoyed an ephemeral public life, and then sank into oblivion. This pattern, whose chronology covers the period from 1911 to 1928, is among the most
exciting and at the same time frustrating in the history of cinema, as most of the
physical evidence on the subject appears to be lost. We have the theoretical rudiments of these techniques, but not the actual experience of what the films and their
colours were like. This handicap should not lead us to ignore or denigrate these processes. They played a formative and decisive role in the evolution of colour, and we
must at least try to formulate a set of reasonable conjectures about them. From this
standpoint, a substantial part of the history of colour in silent film has not been
written yet. Much research is needed on the processes described below and their
operating principles.

   A brief digression on colour terminology is necessary before describing these systems. In the additive synthesis process, a colour image is produced by black and
white images made and then projected through colour filters (green, blue and red)
and superimposed one upon the other. In the moving image, the same effect is produced by projecting the images through different colour filters in rapid succession.

In the subtractive synthesis, objects absorb certain wavelengths of light in the visible spectrum, and reflect others, which the eye perceives as colours. In the resulting coloured film, the colours that appear on the screen are those which have been filtered – that is, subtracted – from the entire spectrum of white light. A complete picture obtained through this process is a combination of partial images in yellow, magenta, and cyan.

Colorgraph (1911–seqq.), a subtractive synthesis process – the first of its kind known to date – created by Arturo Hernandez-Mejia for coloured film stock. The key elements of the system were the creation of two negatives, one exposed through a red filter, the other through a green filter; the reversal of two successive frames one on top of the other (a device that would prove decisive in the development of Technicolor); and the idea of printing the film with the emulsion on both sides. The images from the two negatives were reproduced one on each side of the positive, and then tinted or toned a blue-green on one side and a red-orange on the other.

Panchromotion (1913), the first system (additive, in four colours) among many created by William van Doren Kelley at the beginning of a 22-year career that influenced the development of colour cinema as much as did the inventors of Technicolor. The principle behind Panchromotion was similar to that of Kinemacolor, but the rotating disc used for shooting and projection was divided into sections of red-orange, blue-green, blue-violet, and yellow, each separated by a small transparent segment.

Warner-Powrie Color (1914–seqq.), a three colour additive system developed by J.H. Powrie from a photographic colour process and later perfected with financing from the Warner Brothers Research Laboratory. A 47mm panchromatic negative, divided into 900 longitudinal lines per inch and tinted with the three primary colours, was run horizontally in the camera and the printer (the oversize frame covered about four times the area of a standard 35mm frame). A positive print, also striped with very fine lines running lengthwise, was run vertically in the developer. In order to achieve a correlation between the 47mm negative and the 35mm positive, the printer would be fitted with reduction lenses for the negative. The horizontal lines of the negative and the vertical lines of the positive intersected at 90 degrees; the image was projected through a filter that reproduced the grid thus obtained.

Berthon/Keller-Dorian/Kodacolor (1914–28), additive systems derived from an invention copyrighted in France in 1909 by R. Berthon, a specialist in astronomical optics. The film base was transformed into a lenticular surface, which functioned like a net of microscopic lenses in front of a lens fitted with a filter having three vertical sections of red, blue, and green. In 1914, A. Keller-Dorian registered a system that gave a lenticular structure to cinematographic film, a patent which the Eastman Kodak Company acquired in 1915, in order to to introduce it on the amateur 16mm market under the name of Kodacolor .

Brewster Color (1915). Following the premises of one of William Friese-Greene's systems, this two-colour subtractive process required that two reels of film be printed in parallel through a lens fitted with a prism that split light in two directions, through red and green filters respectively. The two negatives were then printed on a positive coated with emulsion on both sides, tinted green on one side and red on the other. In 1935, after the success of Technicolor, Brewster Color introduced a three-colour system with the addition of yellow tinting, with no success.

Douglass Color No. 1 (1916), a two-colour additive synthesis system developed by Leon Forrest Douglass. The camera held two reels of film, with a mechanism that intermittently moved two frames at a time. On one reel, every other frame was filmed through a red filter; on the other, through a green filter. In both reels every second frame was unfiltered. The two negatives thus created were printed onto a single positive with alternate images from each of the camera negatives, and projected at 32 frames per second with a shutter equipped with red and green filters, similar to that used in Kinemacolor.

Kodachrome (1916), a two-colour subtractive synthesis process conceived by J.G. Capstaff on behalf of Eastman Kodak. *Concerning One Thousand Dollars* (1916) was the first experimental short produced to verify the quality of the image created by a camera fitted with two lenses (one above the other) with green and red filters. The latent colours of every pair of frames were matched when printed on reversal film stock (negative, transformed into positive) with two emulsions, tinted blue-green on one side and red-orange on the other (Plate 54).

Prizma No. 1, No. 2, No. 3 (Kelley, 1917–18). The first Prizma system, based on additive synthesis, used a rotating disc similar to the one designed for Panchromotion, but instead of having small uncoloured segments between the four filters, each had colours whose intensity grew and then diminished. In the second system the colours were reduced to three, as in Kinemacolor, but calibrated to produce softer tones, and the disc was made for easy installation on Simplex and Powers projectors, the most widely used machines of the period. With the third system, derived from the principle of subtractive synthesis, the rotating disc was eliminated altogether, and the frames of the positive copy were treated with alternating primary colours; the film could then be projected on any standard apparatus.

Gilmore Color (1918) of Frederic Eugene Ives, a two-colour additive system. The frames of a standard 35mm film were divided longitudinally into two equal sectors, and the two corresponding images were recorded vertically through a green and a red filter. The two images were then projected through their respective filters and superimposed so as to form a single image.

Polychromide (1918), a two-colour subtractive synthesis process, patented in England by Aron Hamburger. The positive film bore emulsion on both sides (bipack), and was printed with two different negatives, one orthochromatic, the other panchromatic (a subsequent patent substituted a single bipack negative for these), then toned red-orange on one side and blue-green on the other.

Kesdacolor (Kelley, 1918), a two-colour system based on subtractive synthesis. The positive had emulsion on both sides, with vertical stripes of green and red complementary to the stripes of the opposite side. The film could be projected at the standard speed of 16 frames per second, without any modification of the projector.

Douglass Color No. 2 (1919). The two negatives of the Douglass Color system No. 1 were printed on a positive. In this updated version of the process, rather than projecting the frames through red and green filters, both latent images were printed and then dye-toned on the same frame, one in contact with the emulsion side, the other with the base. This meant that the positive film had a layered emulsion.

Prizma (Kelley, 1919–23), a two-colour subtractive synthesis patent. The positive, printed from a negative created by a camera equipped with a rotating filter, had two emulsions, uniformly coloured blue-green on one side and red-orange on the other. *The Glorious Adventure* (Vitagraph, 1921, still extant) by J. Stuart Blackton was the first feature-length film 'in natural colour' to enjoy some commercial success in the United States and United Kingdom.

Zoechrome (1920), additive process invented in the United Kingdom by T.A. Mills, based on the printing of a positive film with one full-aperture frame and three smaller images arranged in a triangle on the next frame, each filmed and subsequently projected through a different colour filter.

Kelley-Color (1924), a two-colour subtractive synthesis process. Little information is available on this system. Apparently, its main advantage over Kelley's earlier systems was that the film bore an emulsion on one side only, reducing the risk of scratching during projection.

Spicer-Dufay (1925) resulted from the collaboration of Spicers Limited, a paper manufacturer, and the French photographer Louis Dufay. Its essential feature – an image divided into a large number of semi-microscopic primary elements, each provided with a minuscule colour filter – is similar to the operating principle of the

Lumière Autochrome plates. After languishing during the twilight of silent films, Dufaycolor had noticeable commercial success from the mid-1930s.

Kelley Color Films No. 1, No. 2, No. 3 (1926–28), hybrids of the Handschiegl process, whose films were printed at the Kelley laboratory. In broad terms, the positive was made of consecutive frames in black and white, blue-green, and red-orange. After Max Handschiegl's death on 1 May 1928, Kelley briefly tried out two other systems. In the first, the film alternated a black and white frame and a frame with red, green, and blue superimposed; in the second, three separation negatives were printed on a single emulsion which was then subjected to toning.

Color Film Process (1927) of A.G. Waddingham (Color Cinema Productions), a two-colour subtractive system similar to Polychromide. A bipack negative, with orthochromatic emulsion for the green and panchromatic emulsion for the red, was printed onto a positive, also a bipack, the two sides toned blue-green and red-orange respectively.

Towards an 'Invisible' Technology: The Origins of Technicolor

Names, dates, patents, film coated with one or two emulsions, filters, tinting and toning. Despite the scarcity of original footage pertaining to these experiments, film historians should be discouraged from considering the few well-documented systems (such as Chronochrome or Kinemacolor) as representative of the whole spectrum of possibilities explored at the time. A truly exhaustive inventory of colour processes in silent cinema still waits to be made; meanwhile, the refinement of research methodologies brings to light previously unexplored sources, testifying to the existence of obscure pioneers endowed with fertile imaginations but little or no sense of business (Plates 59 and 60). The same caution should be applied to the assessment of the early years of the most influential colour process of the classical Hollywood era: Technicolor, the arbiter of taste for the film entertainment industry in the years following the advent of sound. Three of the four Technicolor systems created by Herbert T. Kalmus and his associates from 1915 – the founding date of the Technicolor Motion Picture Corporation – to the advent of sound are extensively documented, yet barely known in terms of accessible motion picture footage.

It is difficult to judge, for example, the merits of the Technicolor Process No. 1 (1916), the only one based on the principle of additive synthesis, achieved here by running two reels in parallel before two lenses and two filters (red and green), using a single light source split by a prism. A projector with two lenses equipped with filters superimposed the two complementary images using a complex (and difficult to regulate) registration device. Critics who saw *The Gulf Between* (Wray Physioc, 1917) were torn between admiration and puzzlement, very much as they had been with Kinemacolor. It is impossible to verify their views by direct examination, since no nitrate print of *Way Down East* (D.W. Griffith, 1920), apparently the second and last fiction feature film with sequences made with the system, is known to survive with its Technicolor sequences (for the record, it could even be that no print of the film was ever made with this process, as Griffith had the habit of announcing projects that would never see the light.)

The merits of Technicolor Process No. 2, the first subtractive system designed by the company, are hardly easier to appraise. A single negative was exposed to light separated by a prism as the negative was drawn intermittently through the mechanism, exposing two frames at a time. Following the principle of Arturo Hernandez-Mejia's Colorgraph (patented in 1916 but conceived five years earlier), every other image was reversed with the bottom edges of the two frames in contact (Plate 28). The latent red frames were then printed on one roll of film, the latent green ones on another. The two positives were glued together and tinted, respectively, red and green.

The Toll of the Sea, directed by Chester M. Franklin for Metro Pictures, was officially premiered in New York on 26 November 1922. The judgment of contemporary critics and the wisdom of hindsight agree: the copy restored by the UCLA Film and Television Archive shows a tidy and stable image, with brilliant red and orange tones, but with a certain tendency towards brown in the greenery of outdoor scenes, and a blurring of the finest details and distant objects. Despite this, Technicolor No. 2 was superior to all two-colour subtractive systems of the time, and the advantage of not requiring special projection apparatus ensured it such immediate success that the company was at first unable to keep up with the demand for release prints. Twenty-eight feature films and at least six shorts were made with this system. At least one third of them survive, often visible only in black and white prints. In the others, printed by more recent methods that barely approximate the originals, the colour has so deteriorated that (at least until a more adequate restoration methodology is found) it is impossible to pass judgement, other than to state that the colour sequences have more of a decorative than a dramatic effect, and are to be found in those spectacular scenes that could most benefit from the 'luxury' of colour, like the episode of the masked ball in *The Phantom of the Opera* (Rupert Julian, 1925) and the fashion parade in *Irene* (Alfred E. Green, 1926).

The trouble with the second Technicolor process became apparent soon after the release of *The Black Pirate* (Albert Parker, 1926). The adhesiveness and shrinkage of the two lengths of film glued to each other would cause the base to curve, making it difficult to keep the film in focus. The problem was eliminated only in 1928 with Technicolor Process No. 3, first seen in the release copies of *The Viking* (R. William Neill, 1929). Kalmus went back to the first additive synthesis Technicolor system by creating two separate negatives, each in a primary colour, exposed simultaneously by means of a prism splitting the light from the camera's single lens. Instead of using the two negatives to print a positive directly, however, the improved process involved the production of two positive matrices with a thicker emulsion. After receiving their respective primary colours, these positives were then pressed in succession upon unprocessed film stock with an especially absorbent emulsion (very much like lithographic matrices, as with the operating principle of the Handschiegl process) with the utmost attention to achieving perfect registration of the two monochromatic images. Further progress would be attained soon afterwards with the three-colour Technicolor Process No. 4 (1930), but the concept introduced by its immediate predecessor was revolutionary in itself: there were no more positives with two emulsions, nor lengths of film to be glued together. The Western race drama *Redskin* (Victor Schertzinger, 1929; see Plate 57) was already a Technicolor film in the 'modern' sense of the term. Its warmth of tone and subtle control of colour saturation were critical to the notion of a smoother, more versatile palette whose overall effect seemed finally to transcend the technological rationale of the process. Viewers of *The Viking* and *Redskin* would complain of blue skies sometimes tending towards green, uneven flesh tones, details that were 'not quite true'. But these were matters of taste, not function. For cinematic colour had already achieved its first goal: to make 'invisible' the technology that produced it.

A Note on Imaginary Colour

Understanding colour in aesthetic terms means confronting the ontological problem of its permanence and transformation. In this respect, film analysis does not much differ from the interpretation of canvases, frescoes, miniatures and handcrafted objects. What makes the difference is the chronological pattern of colour decay (Plate 53), its scale, and our perception of it. Indeed, fewer moving images of the silent period will be experienced in their original colours in the years to come, but that is not the only problem. At stake is our awareness of colours, our memory of their previous state, and the sense we are able to make of the ongoing shifts affecting the appearance of a film. We know very little about the colours of Erich von Stroheim's *Greed*, as no restoration project can use original positive prints from the full-length 1924 version. Stanley Kubrick's *The Shining* was released more than fifty years later, yet those who viewed it in 1980 no longer find the same brilliancy in the golden tones and the contrasts of yellow and red in prints which are only twenty years old. Colour in the moving image is the most unstable component of an inherently ephemeral medium; anything we can say about it comes from a contradictory mediation between memory and present visual experience.

The dilemma is all the more striking when applied to the first years of cinema. Our knowledge of colour in silent films is largely derived from a treasured misconception that we are accustomed to accept without question: tinting, toning, colouring by hand or stencil, first and second Technicolor are loosely translated in the duplicates struck by preservation laboratories into systems radically different from the original techniques. Projection equipment has changed, too. Light sources bear no resemblance to those employed in the early 20th century. Faced with the reality of colour decay in modern film stock, film archives have duplicated in black and white reference prints the vast majority of surviving films made with colour before 1930, thus still further altering the viewer's perception of silent cinema. Improved restoration methods and the introduction of low-fade motion picture stock has revived the ambition to preserve colour film, but the underlying premise of this renewed interest is as deceptive as not preserving colour at all. From a cultural standpoint, colour film preservation (as much as film preservation in itself) is a necessary, interesting mistake.

Such awareness does not exempt us from an even more challenging paradox. Much as we may know that a certain colour once existed in a silent film, we must also acknowledge that it is now virtually impossible to experience its actual rendering on the screen. As time goes by, the entity slowly mutates into an imaginary object, a creation of the mind. We collect the few surviving fragments, the apparatus, the chemical formulas, the memoirs of the technicians who designed the systems, the opinions of those who saw them at work. Whatever remains of the moving images made with these systems is drifting out of reach, and we are left with the option of explaining their oblivion, or reinventing them according to our own predilections and constraints. Have we the right to create a system of aesthetic judgment from all this? If the object of this judgment is not the evidence itself but its reincarnation (be it arbitrary, or the product of a dominant technology), how can we give it a meaning, and to what end?

Further Reading

Colour in Pre-cinema

For an overview of the literature on colour and optical devices prior to the photographic moving image, see the bibliography on pre-cinema at the end of Chapter 5.

Surveys

Frederick A. Talbot, *Moving Pictures. How they are made and worked* (London: Heinemann, 1912), pp. 287–300; David S. Hulfish, *Cyclopedia of Motion-Picture Work* (Chicago, IL: American Technical Society, 1918), Vol. I, pp. 262–77; Vol. II, pp. 149–54 (the reprint of an earlier 1915 edition, in a single volume, was published in New York by Arno Press/The *New York Times* under the title *Motion Picture Work*); Brian Coe, 'The Development of colour Cinematography', in Roger Manvell (ed.), *The International Encyclopedia of Film* (New York: Crown, [1972]), pp. 29–32; by the same author, *The History of Movie Photography*, pp. 112-39; Robert A. Nowotny, *The Way of All Flesh Tones: A History of Color Motion Picture Processes, 1895–1929*, Master of Arts thesis for the University of Texas at Austin, 1979, published in 1983 (New York-London: Garland); *Il colore nel cinema*, special issue of *Fotogenia*, vol. 1 no. 1. (Bologna: Editrice Club, 1994); Paolo Cherchi Usai, 'Le Nitrate mécanique. L'imagination de la couleur comme science exacte (1830–1928)', in Jacques Aumont (ed.), *La Couleur en cinéma* (Milan-Paris: Mazzotta/La Cinémathèque française, 1995): pp. 95–109; Monica Dall'Asta, Guglielmo Pescatore and Leonardo Quaresima,

Il colore nel cinema muto. Proceedings of the 2nd International Conference on Film Studies, March 23–25, 1995. (Udine-Bologna: Dipartimento di Storia e Tutela dei Beni Culturali, Università degli Studi di Udine/Mano Edizioni, 1996); Daan Hertogs and Nico De Klerk (eds), *'Disorderly Order': Colours in Silent Film. The 1995 Amsterdam Workshop* (Amsterdam: Stichting Nederlands Filmmuseum, 1996 [distributed by BFI]).

Tinting, Toning and Mordanting

Léopold Löbel, 'Les Virages et les teintures', *La Technique cinématographique* (Paris: Dunod et Pinat, 1912), pp. 268–303; by the same author, 'Les Nouveaux procédés de virage par mordançage', *Bulletin de la Société Française de Photographie*, 3, 1921 (second edition, revised and expanded. Paris: Dunod, 1922, pp. 293–333); J. Crabtree and C. Ives, 'Dye Toning With Single Solution', *Abridged Scientific Publications from the Kodak Research Laboratories*, Vol. 12, 1928; 'Tinting and Toning Motion Picture Film', in Hal Hall (ed.), *Cinematographic Annual*, Vol. 2, 1931 (Hollywood, CA: The American Society of Cinematographers, 1931), pp. 576–90; 'Virages et teinture des images positives. Coloris', in *Le Cinématographe muet, sonore, parlant. Le cinématographe scientiphique et industriel* (Paris: Albin Michel, 1933); J.M. Nickolaus, 'Toning Positive Film by Machine Methods', *Journal of the Society of Motion Picture Engineers*, vol. 38, July 1936, p. 67. Sample frames of tinted and toned nitrate film are included in *Tinting and Toning of Eastman Motion Picture Film* (Rochester, NY: Eastman Kodak Company. Five editions: 1916, 1918, 1922, 1924, 1927) and L. Didiée, *Le Film vierge Pathé. Manuel de développement et de tirage* (Paris: Établissements Pathé-Cinéma, 1926), which also contains frames of non-standard formats and 35mm negative film exposed and developed with different methods.

Handcolouring and Stencil

Jacques Marette, 'Les Procédés de colouriage mécanique des films', *Bulletin de l'Association Française des Ingénieurs et Techniciens du Cinéma*, 7, 1950, pp. 3–8; reproduced in *Journal of Film Preservation*, vol. 22 no. 47, October 1993, pp. 54–9; M. Ruot and L. Didiée, 'The Pathé Kinematograph Colour Process', *The Photographic Journal*, new series, vol. 65 no. 3, March 1925, pp. 121–6; Harold G. Brown, *An Account of the Hand and Stencil Colouring Processes* (London, document mimeographed by the author and distributed at the FIAF Berlin Congress, 1967), published in Italian as 'Tecniche di colourazione a mano e a pochoir', *Griffithiana*, vol. 10 nos 26–27, September 1986, pp. 72–3.

Chronochrome

Filmparlants (Talking Pictures) and Chronochrome Gaumont (Flushing, Long Island, NY: Gaumont Company, 1913); Paolo Cherchi Usai, 'Le Miracle du Chronochrome', *Cinémathèque* [Paris], no. 3, Spring/Summer 1993, pp. 83–91.

Kinemacolor

Charles Urban, *Kinemacolor Press Appreciations: British, Continental and American* [collection of articles, n.d., at the Science Museum Library, London]; Henry W. Joy, *Book of Instructions for Operators of Kinemacolor Appliances* (London: The Natural Color Kinemacolor Company, 1910); Anon., *Kinemacolor and Some American Criticisms* (London: The Natural Color Kinematograph Co., 1910); Anon., *Handbook* (London: The Natural Color Kinematograph Co., Ltd, 1910); Colin N. Bennett, *On Operating Kinemacolor* (London: The Kinemacolor Company, 1910); by the same author, 'Filter Absorptions for Two-Colour', *British Journal of Photography* [Supplement on colour Photography], 7 July 1911, p. 45, and *The Handbook of Kinematography* (London: The Kinematograph Weekly, 1911); George Albert Smith, 'The Kinemacolor Process', *The Moving Picture News*, vol. 5, 9 March 1912, pp. 12–17; St John Hamund, *Explanatory Lecture on the Pageants, Processions and Ceremonies Connected With the Imperial Durbar at Delhi as reproduced by Kinemacolor for Use at the Scala Theatre* (London: The Natural Color Kinemacolor Company, 1912); *Catalogue of Kinemacolor Film Subjects. Animated Scenes in Their Actual Colors* (London: The Natural Color Kinematograph Co., Ltd, 1913); Gorham Kindem, 'The Demise of Kinemacolor: Technological, Legal, Economic and Aesthetic Problems in Early Color History', *Cinema Journal*, vol. 20 no. 2, Spring 1981, pp. 3–14.

Technicolor

Surprisingly enough, the most fertile of all innovations in colour technology has so far received scant attention (most of the published studies are limited to the sound era). Richard W. Haines, *Technicolor Movies: The History of Dye Transfer Printing* (Jefferson, NC: McFarland, 1993); Herbert T. Kalmus (with Eleanore King Kalmus), *Mr. Technicolor* (Absecon, NJ: MagicImage Filmbooks, 1993). The journals of the inventors of Technicolor are held by the Motion Picture Department at George Eastman House. This extraordinary (and unpublished) document on the development of colour technology consists of several handwritten and typed volumes, compiled between 1916 and 1944 and containing narratives, diagrams, formulas and film samples, including the fragment of a positive print made with Technicolor system No. 2.

Brewster Color

'The Brewster Colour Process', *The Photographic Journal*, Royal Photographic Society of Great Britain, August 1935, in Roderick T. Ryan, *A Study of the Technology of Color Motion Picture Processes Developed in the United States*. Doctoral thesis presented September 1966 at the University of Southern California (published Ann Arbor, MI: University Microfilms International, 1979), p. 150.

Handschiegl Process
William V.D. Kelley: 'Imbibition Coloring of Motion Picture Films', *Transactions of the Society of Motion Picture Engineers*, vol. 10 no. 28, 1926, pp. 238–41; 'The Handschiegl and Pathécrome Color Processes', *Journal of the Society of Motion Picture Engineers*, vol. 17 no. 2, August 1931, pp. 229–34.

Kodacolor
'Kodacolor Finishing Stations', in Hal Hall (ed.), *Cinematographic Annual*, vol. 2, 1931 (Hollywood, CA: The American Society of Cinematographers, 1931), p. 591.

Sonochrome
New Color Moods for the Screen (Rochester, NY: Eastman Kodak Company, s.d. [ca. 1930]).

A bibliography on the restoration of films in colour is provided at the end of Chapter 3.

The quote from Derek Jarman on p. 21 is taken from first American edition of *Chroma* (Woodstock, NY: The Overlook Press, 1995, pp. 42–3).

3
The Ethics of Film Preservation

A motion picture lives three months at most. There is no use pretending we are making pictures for the ages.

Darryl F. Zanuck

Genealogy: Print Generation, Provenance, Format

The silent film we are about to watch is not an abstract entity brought to us through a logical pattern designed by history on behalf of posterity. It is the survivor of a complex, often random process of selection, not much different from a Darwinian evolutionary scheme. When we consider the limited number of prints struck for a film of the early years, and take into account the variety of factors contributing to their loss or decay, the very existence of a nitrate copy one hundred years after the making of the film may be seen as something close to a miracle.

A large group of silent feature films was found several years ago in a barn somewhere in the American Midwest. Most of the reels were in good condition, but for no apparent reason each individual film was lacking the first or the last reel. It was later determined that the missing reels had been used by some local kids for a rather daring form of fireworks display, in which the film was removed from the cans, unspooled, and then ignited at one end of the leader. The game was dangerous – gases produced by burning nitrate are extremely toxic; inhalation can cause death within a few hours. Still, the witnesses to this playful destruction of film heritage were not aware of that, and the sight of flaming celluloid must have been quite spectacular.

No less astounding was the discovery in 1978 of a swimming pool in Dawson City, the most unlikely repository for 510 reels of nitrate film forgotten by distributors after their exploitation in that remote region of Canada. The severe cold temperatures in northern Yukon, and the unusual protection given to the prints in the underground shelter, uncovered by an excavator half a century after their burial, ensured the physical survival of about 435 of these long forgotten treasures. Several factors, including the temperature shock caused by the sudden retrieval of the films from the frozen ground and their contact with sunlight and humidity, might have contributed to the melting of the emulsion around the edges of the reels. Several prints in the Dawson City Collection at the Library of Congress are easily

The Half-Breed (Allan Dwan, 1916), 35mm acetate print (Library of Congress/ Dawson City Collection).

recognisable by this characteristic, which blurred the contours of the frame. These episodes are among the most bizarre in the history of film preservation, but they are not isolated. Nitrate prints can turn up anywhere, and we often know about it only when it is almost too late to do anything to protect them. What has safely reached the vaults of the archives is only the carefully monitored tip of a thawing and highly volatile iceberg. The sheer dimensions of this iceberg may be better appreciated by turning it upside down and viewing it as a genealogical tree, at the apex of which is the camera negative originally used to make distribution prints at the time of a film's initial release.

Let us imagine, for argument's sake, that two parallel black and white camera negatives of an American feature film were made in 1914, according to the practice mentioned on page 11. The first negative was to be used for the domestic market, while the second was recut for the European market and sent to London. In our example, let us suppose that nineteen positive prints (tinted and toned) were made from the first negative in the United States, while sixteen copies of the edited version were struck abroad, with intertitles translated in different languages, and with different tinting and toning schemes, for each country where the film was shown. Let us also assume that by the end of World War I, both camera negatives had disappeared, and that in 1925 one of the 'domestic' positive prints was used to create a black and white duplicate negative from which to make prints for the re-release of the film. Pursuing our imaginary case study, twelve positive prints (not tinted) were then struck from the duplicate negative. In 1936, a private collector found one of these prints, loved the film despite the absence of colour, and made another duplicate negative and three prints, for personal use and trade. In 1948, an entrepreneur got hold of another copy of the 1925 re-release version, trimmed all the shots to make the editing snappier, and from this created a duplicate negative and ten prints for distribution in the non-theatrical market. One of these 1948 prints was borrowed in 1952 by a film society, and on this occasion someone kept it long enough to send

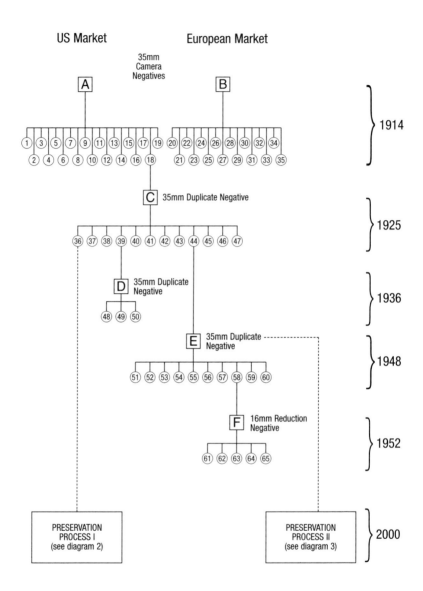

Figure 1: Print generation in history.

it to a laboratory and make a 16mm reduction negative. From this she printed five copies of the film, eliminated from each of them some scenes which seemed to her controversial, and then sold the abridged versions to schools and public libraries.

Our story could go on like this indefinitely; but if we decide to interrupt it at this point, the plot could be summarised by Figure 1.

All in all, our film came to exist in six negatives and sixty-five positive prints, five of which were made on 16mm stock. The scenario described above may look excessively complex; in fact, it is a wildly oversimplified mirror of reality. Many silent films were subject to a much larger number of duplications, and in most cases we have no idea of how many prints were made at any given step of the process, nor can we reconstruct its actual chronology. More often than not, we can't even tell whether the process has come to a conclusion, or is being continued in forms and circumstances that are – and will probably remain – forever unknown to us. Take any early Chaplin short, and you will soon realise that the 'big bang' of the original camera negative has created a constellation of copies we will never be able to quantify.

What really matters in our fictional account, however, is that we have come to terms with two crucial issues. First, the fact that the archive print we are looking at may belong to any one of the phases identified in our imaginary duplication process. Exactly where the print stands in the genealogical tree may make a world of difference, both in terms of its completeness and its visual quality. For example, watching a 1948 print corresponding to item number 52 in the diagram would probably tell us very little of how print number 4 looked in 1914. Furthermore, what we have so far called a 'step' in the duplication process (the making of a negative and the subsequent creation of one or more prints) corresponds to a print generation. Broadly speaking, each photographic generation involves a loss of approximately 15 per cent from the image information of the previous print. Think of a copy derived from a tenth generation negative, and you will get a rough idea of the gap between its appearance and the look of a print struck from the original camera negative. The frame enlargement of Fritz Lang's *Metropolis* reproduced overleaf (A) comes from a 35mm nitrate positive print made from the original camera negative. Frame B is taken from an 35mm acetate print of unknown generation, possibly the third, made in 1987. Frame C shows the same frame as it appears in a 16mm print made in 1954. See the difference between this one and the first of the series? Don't ask what generation it belongs to. It takes many of them – or just a very bad printing job – to make the image so foggy, but don't ever think this is how *Metropolis* was intended to be seen. Now, look again at Frame B, and note how little difference there is between its image quality and the appearance of the same frame in the enlargement of the 16mm copy. In both prints, the title is barely readable, but the 35mm has a coarseness and a contrast surprising for a print that should definitely look better than a 16mm duplicate. There are at least two possible reasons for this. First, the processing of the 35mm copy may have been less than appropriate; second, the 16mm print may have been struck from a source belonging to an

A

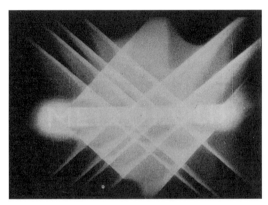

B

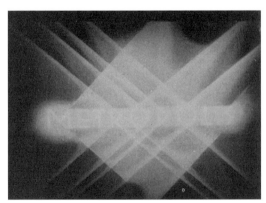

C

Metropolis (Fritz Lang, 1926), main title. From top to bottom: (A) first-generation 35mm nitrate positive print from the National Film and Sound Archive/ScreenSound Australia; (B) 35mm acetate print from the 1987 restoration, Münchner Filmmuseum; (C) 16mm triacetate print made in 1954, George Eastman House.

earlier generation than that used for the 35mm positive. The lesson to be drawn from this instance has been hard to learn for film archives, which have traditionally considered substandard formats as objects of little or no archival significance. Never underestimate the potential value of a 16mm print – nor, for that matter, of any format under 35mm, such as 28mm, 22mm or 9.5mm. Print elements made in forms other than the original one might represent the best quality copies you will ever see for certain films, and might prove to be in much better shape than a battered, incomplete 35mm duplicate print from a very remote generation.

Obviously, the goal of every film archive is to locate and acquire a print as close as possible to the original camera negative. When it comes to silent film, finding the camera negative itself is a fortunate yet rare occurrence. (Two remarkable exceptions are the Metro-Goldwyn-Mayer negatives preserved at the George Eastman House and the D.W. Griffith shorts of the Biograph period, held by the Museum of Modern Art in their original form, although without intertitles). Most curators would be more than happy to settle for a first generation print, often recognisable by the absence at the edge of the frame of any photographic evidence of sprocket holes other than those belonging to the negative (see below). This goal, however, is thwarted by a near-universal law of film preservation: while a film of little or no commercial fortune is unlikely to have been duplicated much, and so will probably be found in prints of very early generations, pictures that were great popular successes in their time and have remained in demand by subsequent audiences are often to be seen in copies several generations away from their origins. The examples of *Metropolis* and the Chaplin shorts are two obvious cases, but the list of masterworks available only in prints far from ideal is quite extensive. There is for instance no copy of *Sunrise* (Friedrich Wilhelm Murnau, 1927) that approaches the beauty of a first generation print, and whatever is left of *The Blue Bird* (Maurice Tourneur, 1918) is a far cry from the beautiful nitrate prints originally struck from the camera negative. To make a long story short, archives have only two options: to be content with the best they can find, or to keep on searching for better copies, believing in miracles and hoping for the best.

Print generation as seen through the profile of sprocket holes. *The Voice of the Violin* (D.W. Griffith, 1909), 35mm acetate print. The white profiles of the four sprocket holes visible in the right margin of the image are from the 35mm nitrate positive used for the creation of the 35mm viewing print reproduced here. The dark profile of the single sprocket hole on the center left edge of the image is from the 35mm camera negative of the film (George Eastman House).

Miracles do sometimes happen, as in the case of a gorgeous 35mm nitrate print of
La Passion de Jeanne d'Arc (Carl Theodor Dreyer, 1928) which lay quite forgotten for
several decades in a mental hospital in Norway until it was retrieved intact in 1981.

Given the situation, there should be no surprise that the assessment of print generation and the retrieval of relevant clues about the provenance of a copy play such
an important role in the preservation process. Film historians who care about this
aspect of archival work are often frustrated by the scarcity of information surrounding the circumstances under which a particular film was acquired by an
institution at the end of the nitrate era. At that time, finding a lost film was all that
really mattered: who would care, after all, whether a print was found in a dumpster,
or bought from dealers who had no interest whatsoever in letting people know where
the print came from and how it got into their hands? The irony of all this is that they
were secretive mainly out of fear of being stalked or legally threatened by copyright
owners, whereas production companies couldn't care less about what happened to
a used print. Periodically, it is true, they might get worried – as they did for a brief
period in the 1970s, when FBI officers would question collectors such as William K.
Everson – only because they were suddenly afraid of an unlikely resurgence of illegal, non-theatrical distribution. Today, the cost of putting corporate companies'
lawyers on the trail of a private collector who is showing the film in a basement to a
group of friends is not generally considered worth the effort. The money obtained
through the distribution of bootleg videos for personal use is less than peanuts for
the majors. Corporate firms know all too well that there are duplicate prints all over
the place, but they would not make much profit in taking control of the collectors'
world. On the contrary, they would no doubt lose face from being perceived as the
enemies of non-profit film culture, and moreover lose the invaluable advantage of
potential cooperation from an underground army of enthusiastic cinephiles. It's
much better to get their help instead. As we will see further on, film preservation has
become a useful public relations tool for the film industry, but never be astonished
if a production or distribution company's legal office is unaware of a title owned by
its firm. Once in a while, archivists who have found a film and would like to know
if the producer has other elements of it may even receive startling answers: 'What are
you talking about? We don't have copyright on this film. In fact, it looks like we did-
n't make it. It doesn't appear in our inventory.' As a rule, film entrepreneurs were not
good filmographers, and their successors may not even know what they own.

Archivists have traditionally been very fearful of letting researchers browse
through the historical papers related to the acquisition of a silent film. Today they
are generally less paranoid about this, and are actually becoming quite active in
keeping records of whatever written material they come across, and scrutinising
their departmental records for correspondence, memos, shipping orders and laboratory bills – all useful stuff for nowadays' determined researcher, leading to
revealing hints of how and when a certain film first ended up in the vaults. Archive
managers will have a hard time figuring out how their first prints entered the

premises of the institution, but it is as much their problem as ours, and we now all have to live with it.

Let us now return to the diagram on page 46, and suppose that the genealogical tree represents the printing history of a hitherto missing film, now found as a single print (say, the 35mm nitrate positive number 36), the only one known to exist. The archivist is happy. Film scholars are happy, too, but that's only the beginning of a completely different and no less intricate story.

The Preservation Process

What now happens to that surviving print is the object of the art and technique of preserving moving images. In a museum context, our positive copy number 36 is considered as a unique object, and is therefore withdrawn from public access. There is already an important principle to be stressed here. If she knows that the print is far from being unique, and the existence of another two hundred copies of that film is documented, the archivist would probably decide to retain it anyway, because its presence in the vaults is consistent with the educational mission of the institution; and she would leave it at the viewer's disposal, subject only to limitations pertaining to the basic need to minimise the physical consumption of the artifact. This is a tricky argument, though. When a print is worn out, it may not be that easy to replace it. Since it was generally thought that the films of Charlie Chaplin could be found all over the place (there are indeed hundreds of copies around the world), everybody kept showing them freely until it was discovered that in fact acceptable preservation elements were no longer to be found. Now we are desperately searching for nitrate prints of Chaplin's early titles, and it is clear that there aren't that many left in an acceptable condition.

Another example may further clarify the issue. A film archivist in Indonesia finds the print of a film that is already preserved in China. Should the Indonesian archivist consider his print a reference copy, and let it be projected indefinitely? What if the preservation elements held by the Chinese archives are less than perfect? What if they are incomplete? What if they didn't preserve the other print at all? What if a fire destroys their vaults? In that case, the Indonesian print would become truly unique and therefore an 'archival master' in the fullest sense of the term. Predictably enough, there is no easy solution to this dilemma, and some archives have no other choice than to take the hard line and consider as an 'archival master' every print that is not otherwise adequately protected within the premises of the institution, regardless of its status in other fellow archives.

What 'protected' means is roughly summarised in Figure 2.

Our print number 36 is cleaned, repaired, and put in cold storage, as it is known that constant low temperatures and humidity levels normally guarantee a longer life to the film. It is at this point that preservationists must decide how to make the film accessible to present and future generations. As much as it is useful as a tool for altering or recreating portions of a damaged moving image, digital technology

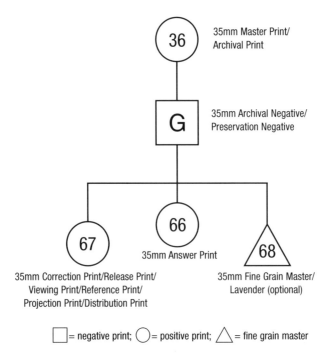

Figure 2: The preservation process. Duplication pattern from a positive print.

has not found a way to protect it for an extended period of time; in fact, a restoration pursued exclusively with digital means is bound to have a much shorter
lifespan than a reproduction achieved with photomechanical means. Scientific
research has focused on a number of possible long term solutions. One of these
involves the etching of the visual information by digital means on a metal plate
(steel, or nickel, as in the case of optical disk stampers) – a technology which is relatively well known, but has limitations in terms of data density and also in terms of
the survivability of the metallic surface upon which data is encoded. Another entails
the creation of data resources in the form of ion-etched quartz (where accelerated
ions are used to create a pattern at the atomic level within an artificially grown crys-
tal of quartz). This latter method offers the possibility of high-density data storage
and the ability to store both digital and analog information in a substance which
appears to be stable over extremely long periods of time and is largely unaffected
by storage environment. Yet another proposal is holographic bubble memory that
could inhere in a relatively permanent medium such as quartz or glass.

    Unfortunately, none of these technical options is developed enough to offer a sol-
ution today. Furthermore, none of these systems presents a simple image (as does
a film master); all of them require the migration of data into a non-iconic, coded

data form for storage, and then a device for rendering the decoded image data back to film. Regardless of the permanence of the data substrate of such exotic media, the long-term viability of these technical systems (the hardware and software necessary to make them work) is seriously in doubt. Thus, the most durable preservation carrier for the moving image is still an object resulting from the use of photographic methods. The rest of this chapter will therefore address the issue of film preservation on the basis of this assumption.

As soon as financial resources allow it, the print is taken to a laboratory, and a negative element (of the same format, if possible or required) is produced. Optical printing with photographic means can be achieved through normal contact printing (a positive and a negative film are continuously run through the printer), or through step printing (each frame of the film is exposed individually in front of the duplicating element). The latter is a much slower but accurate process, used for severely damaged or shrunken copies. The laboratory strikes one print ('answer print') in order to verify the quality of the negative, makes corrections if necessary, then produces one or more prints for access. Terminology varies from archive to archive: 'viewing print', 'projection print', 'reference copy', 'distribution print', 'access copy', 'release print', 'show print' may mean slightly different things, but what they have in common is the fact that they can be viewed because their gradual loss of quality or accidental damage will not endanger the survival of the archival master and the negative. It is clear, however, that the negative is in itself a fragile object which should not be used indefinitely, whenever a viewing print gets in bad shape; in fact, archivists would very much prefer not to use it at all, in order not to jeopardise its status of 'preservation negative' (as this element is frequently called). That is the reason why it is always a good habit to make at least two prints from a newly preserved film, and leave one as a reserve in case of irreversible damage to the other. If a certain film has to be used several times and in different venues, it would even be advisable to take an additional step: create a 'fine grain master' (such as print number 68 in Figure 2; we will explain in a minute why it is called that) and an 'intermediate negative' (not reproduced in Figure 2) from the fine grain master, and only allow additional copies to be made from this printing element; but very few archives have enough resources to do this. While producing a fine grain master is always a good idea if the institution can afford it, going any further would almost defeat the purpose for the existence of an archive, making the institution an awkward equivalent of a distribution company.

Now that we have dealt with the average scenario, it may be worth mentioning the second most likely one (Figure 3). The archive has found item E in our genealogical chart, a nitrate negative. Its preservation involves a different treatment, starting with the creation of a 'fine grain master'. This looks like a positive print (theoretically, it can even be projected), except for the fact that it is printed on a film whose emulsion – made of much tinier molecules – is particularly suitable for making an intermediate negative to be used for the positive prints destined for access.

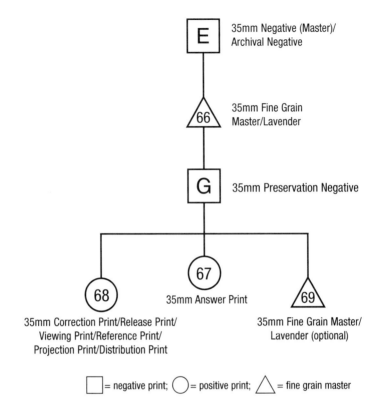

Figure 3: The preservation process. Duplication pattern from a negative print.

The Colour It Might Have Been

A film surviving only in the form of an 'archival negative' and a 'fine grain master' is materially preserved, in the sense that we don't have to worry too much about the decomposition of the first element; but this does not mean that the film it represents can be viewed. Whether we like it or not, the archive may have decided that this is where the preservation process is going to stop for the time being, and no viewing print is going to be made. It is now time to look again at Figure 2, and imagine that the element number 36 has some colour on it. As we have seen at the end of Chapter 2, archives have dealt with the ontological problem of the inevitability of colour decay without being able to give a final solution to the issue. For years, preservation of colour film on black and white prints (their emulsion is much more stable than the multi-layered colour emulsion) seemed the only viable alternative to colour degradation, but its contradictions have become increasingly apparent. Plates 45A and B, respectively taken from a nitrate original and a duplicate in black and white, provide ample evidence of this point. Museums have now grown a little more daring, and in the meanwhile image technology has improved enough to justify other approaches to the question. At least four possibilities ought to be mentioned:

1 *The positive print is tinted and/or toned*. Until the 1980s, this kind of colour was generally reproduced through a standard colour negative and positive prints, vulnerable to the degradation process mentioned above. Since then, three different options have been taken into consideration.

   A The first is the creation of a black and white negative, whose processing is timed in such a way that the resulting positive could be struck on colour stock through the use of coloured filters or computer-generated tints. This system has the advantage of involving the production of a black and white conservation element, comparatively easy to preserve for a longer time without major image alteration. A relative disadvantage is, of course, the fact that the viewing print is on standard colour stock. Another more important drawback is that the system is good for the reproduction of tinted films, where the image has only one colour at a time, but cannot be applied to films where two colours are combined (tinting and toning).

   B A technique that been applied for some years, but became known in the 1990s in a variation called the Desmet System or Desmetcolor (from the name of technician Noël Desmet, head of the preservation laboratory at the Royal Film Archive of Belgium) entails two consecutive exposures of the positive print, thus allowing the reproduction of a tinted base and a toned emulsion.

   C For many years, specialists have also tried to pursue their goal the hard way, attempting to recreate tinting and toning by following the original formulas for dye baths, still available in various manuals published during the silent era. Interestingly enough, these systems have often proved extremely impractical (as each print must be treated separately) or unsuccessful: some of the original dyes are no longer available commercially, or their application on modern stock rarely results in colours of comparable stability or resemblance to the original.

2 *The positive print has been coloured by hand, mechanically (i.e., stencil or Handschiegl), or was printed with a subtractive process such as Technicolor nos 2 or 3*. There is not much of an option in this case. French film historian, Jacques Malthête, has tried to apply colour manually to modern prints of films by Georges Méliès, but the process was excruciatingly slow and the results have raised severe methodological objections. No better solution has so far been found than the standard duplication on colour negative stock and colour positive prints. Hand-painted, stencil-coloured and Handschiegl prints are traditionally the most difficult to reproduce, and the most disappointing when modern results are compared with the original nitrate sources. Contrary to common belief, 'remaking' a stencil copy is a hopeless task, even with the aid of

modern techniques. It is also an absurd goal, as we will never know exactly what the shape of the stencil really was, and no trace is left of the corresponding matrix.

3   *The positive was made with an additive colour process such as Chronochrome (see p. 30) or Kinemacolor (p. 29).* The original prints in black and white were intended to be shown on projectors equipped with coloured lenses or special blade shutters with coloured filters. Here we have another reminder of how important it is to preserve film equipment with as much care and attention as we give to the film itself. Some of these machines are still extant, but few of them are in working condition, and their use for actual projection is normally out of question. Technology has now been developed to reproduce the effect of these images when projected onto a screen, often with outstanding results (notably in the case of Gaumont's Chronochrome system). Unfortunately, modern prints (normally generated by standard colour negatives and therefore resulting in standard colour films) derived from originals made with these systems can do no more than interpret the impression of a viewing experience achieved through completely different means. With few notable exceptions (with Kinemacolor) they simulate what the audience may have seen, but they necessarily bypass the optical principles of the devices built to display those images, thus falsifying the nature of the process itself.

From a preservationist's standpoint, it may be added that something could be done in theory to make these colour reproductions less ephemeral than we have suggested so far. The principle of the Technicolor process comes to the archivist's rescue: three black and white intermediate elements are created – each of them timed for one of the three primary colours – and then merged into a single-strip positive colour print. This processing technique, generally known as colour separation, produces archival elements whose stability is comparable to black and white material, and results in colour positive prints of excellent quality. It is an extremely expensive system, though, because three masters must be created instead of one. Moreover, colour separation from positive masters has serious drawbacks in relation to the processing stock required for making intermediate elements. The financial resources of film archives allow them to adopt this technique only on rare occasions for the preservation of colour negatives of sound films, almost exclusively in a commerical context.

4   *The surviving element is the nitrate negative print of a film that was originally tinted, toned, hand-coloured or stencilled.* In this case, tough luck. We are in a position of advantage in terms of image quality, especially if we are in presence of an original camera negative, as we are going to obtain prints of much sharper appearance than those we would get from average release prints. But we don't know what kind of tinting or toning was individually applied to the original prints made from the negative. Even when some written sources (such as scripts)

indicate the colours to be added, it is very difficult for us reliably to follow the instructions contained therein, as we have no exact idea of what kind of blue had to be used for a scene indicated as such in the script. We are of course tempted to guess, and if the document in our hands seems accurate, archivists may do so; but they do it at the risk of superimposing their own imagination upon an entity whose actual original appearance is not known. Things get even worse if the camera negative refers to a film that was originally coloured by stencil. It is possible that positive copies made from the negative reproduced in Plate 39 were originally coloured with mechanical means, yet the only evidence left to us is a black and white image which can only remain so unless a positive release print is found (in which case the negative is no longer needed).

So here we are, with a whole array of possibilities, a variety of techniques available to address them, and some aesthetic options, all more or less adequate but always questionable in theory. For each answer, several doubts arise. Are we doing the right thing with colour? Is it worth trying to reproduce it as faithfully as we can? Frustrating as it is, this challenge is one of the most exciting aspects of film preservation, as long as we keep in mind that all strategies are bound to clash with an inescapable truth. We are trying to imitate ancient colour on a modern object, and this object is not nitrate film. We also know that a colour dye looks different every time we apply it on a different film stock, and there is one thing we can't possibly do – create another nitrate print from the nitrate source. Nitrate stock has not been produced since 1951, and will never be manufactured again. Right now we are even at the threshold of a third era: manufacture of acetate film is being discontinued, and replaced by polyester. Once this film stock becomes the only one produced, those who try to restore films made in the acetate era will encounter the same kind of problems. While we're at it, let us make another leap of imagination, to the future time when the manufacture of film stock will be discontinued altogether. It will happen later than experts thought in the 1980s, but it will certainly happen. That will be an interesting time for film archives. We will return to this point at the end of the chapter.

The Concept of Lacuna (I): What's Missing from the Image; or, Careful with that Axe, Eugenios

In all the situations we have considered so far, we have dealt with the print as it was when we found it. True, we have cleaned it, repaired the torn perforations, put the archival material in cold storage. Other than that, however, we have done nothing to the visual content of the film itself. In other words, we have not taken into consideration what will be further discussed in Chapter 6 – the fact that a silent film is never 'complete' in the abstract sense of the term. It is now time to deal with the concept of lacuna, and the ways to deal with it. Broadly speaking, there are two ways of looking at this issue. From a diachronic point of view – that is, from the point of view of the sequential experience of several frames projected in rapid succession – print number 36 is 'incomplete' in the sense that we know that some footage that existed in the camera negative A is no longer there, and we assume that we would like to reintegrate the missing parts in the preserved object if we were given the opportunity to do so. From a synchronic point of view – that is, from the point of view of each frame taken as such – the image may be suffering from the ravages of time: the emulsion and the base are dirty, scratched because of wear and tear or careless handling and projection; colours have faded; parts of the emulsion have peeled off from the base; the image itself has been cropped during the various phases of duplication, including the stage where a soundtrack was added. Predictably enough, scratches have always been a primary focus of film preservation. They are, in fact, nothing but minuscule grooves on the film stock. If we cut a section of such film and look at it through a powerful magnifier, what we would see wouldn't be much different from this:

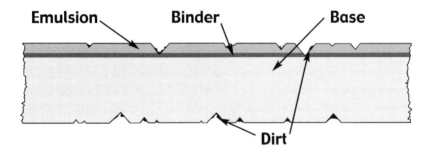

Figure 4: Section of a print with scratches on the base and emulsion sides.

Before going any further, it should be stressed that no matter where the scratches are, or what provoked them, there is nothing you can do about those which were made on prints of previous generations. If you find a pristine 16mm negative struck in 1935 from an appalling 35mm positive, nobody should blame you if your 16mm duplicate positive is less than perfect. (Viewers at festivals and symposia should be reminded of that every now and then.)

Scratches made on all non multi-layered positive prints (that means before Technicolor, where scratches may be visible in different colours because of the multiple emulsion layers) may appear as clear or dark lines on the screen.

Scratches on the emulsion. A portion of the visual information carried by the film has disappeared altogether and cannot be recovered with photomechanic means, unless the scratch is extremely light. If the emulsion scratch is on the positive, it will appear as a clear line. If the scratch was made on the negative emulsion, the positive copy struck from it will make it appear as a dark line.

Scratches on the base. Instead of hitting the film perpendicularly, light from the projector encounters the base from different angles; its refraction provokes the impression of a dark line on the projected image. This impression is further aggravated by dirt increasingly deposited in the groove. After the dirt has been eliminated through various means of cleaning (ranging from basic manual intervention to chemical and ultrasonic cleaning, the latter being preferable because it is environmentally friendly, and does not involve any mechanical contact between the object and a cleaning agent), there are at least two ways of reducing or eliminating this effect. In the first method, generally known as 'light diffusion', the light source used in the printing process is directed from a variety of angles, so that the parts of the base affected by scratches are hit perpendicularly by as much light as the flat surface of the film stock. It is a very safe stratagem, as no chemicals are involved, but the image resulting from the duplication process tends to have less contrast than an average source print, and sometimes looks a little foggier than the original.

The second method requires a printing device where the optical gate is enclosed in a box filled with an extremely transparent liquid, so clear that it fills the scratches and makes the base surface appear as smooth as if there were no scratches at all, long enough for the light of the printer to go through it perpendicularly. The results produced by this system can be amazing, as the 'wet gate printing' is often able to make a badly scratched print look almost new. Unfortunately, most of the chemicals used for it are extremely harmful to the environment, and have become illegal in several countries. Laboratories are now trying hard to find safer substitutes. Despite this serious drawback, wet gate printing has dramatically improved the quality of the printing process and is widely considered a requisite for any serious restoration process.

Scratches can be eliminated in the duplication stage through a digital reconstruction of the missing part of the image: a computer scanner goes to the frame before or after the damaged one, identifies the part of the image affected by the scratch, retrieves the visual information on the 'clean' frame and copies it to the scratched frame. For the time being, digital reconstruction is a slow and expensive process. It can be applied to relatively modest portions of film, and has some disadvantages. Because of the cost involved, it cannot be applied on a large scale. Moreover, computers sometimes tend to take instructions too literally, thus altering parts of the frame that needed no alteration at all, such as the fleeting images of tiny birds in the sky mistaken by the electronic eye for grains of dirt and therefore eliminated from the frame. No doubt, this is no more than a technical limitation that is bound to be overcome with further developments of computer technology. The fact that a machine is being asked to replace a missing portion of visual information with a virtual one is a wholly different matter, an ethical issue which involves broader philosophical questions. Is image enhancement a form of restoration? Do we have the right to make an image look better than it was originally? One example should stand for all. Many filmmakers working before 1908 had trouble in ensuring that the projected image would remain stable. Cameras and projectors were often producing and showing jittering images, and the matter was serious enough to become a discriminating factor in the film industry. (An Italian company born in 1908, Itala Film, used a trademark logo consisting of a veiled woman holding a light, the rays of which form an inscription – the French word '*fixité*', signifying that the work presented by that company had a rock-steady image.) In restoring an early film with this kind of defect we are faced with another unanswerable question: should we reproduce image instability just as it was (because that's how people saw the film), or should we make it look stable, as if the problem never existed? One may argue that of course producers of the time would have loved to get rid of this flaw in the apparatus, and of course it would be better to see an early Lubin film that doesn't make us dizzy by its unpleasant shuddering. So we take care of the problem, as we now know how to do it, but in doing so we open ourselves to a whole range of objections. Early film producers would not only have preferred to see their images stable, but they would probably also, had they been able, have made them sharper, better contrasted, with even, hand-painted contours instead of those floating clouds on clothes and objects. How far are we willing to go in this exercise of wishful thinking? A limit must be set to our right to imagine their intentions, yet the boundaries of that limit are far from being well defined.

This is, again, a matter of choice and responsibility. On the other hand, there is not much of a choice to be made about a quite different kind of fault, caused not by cameras and printing machines but determined by human carelessness or deliberate action: the cropping of the image. If printing is not done with the necessary care, the edges of the frame can be mutilated on all sides. This occurs most visibly when a silent film is given a soundtrack whose area affects the left part of the frame, obliterating between 10 and 12 per cent of the visual content. The viewer is thus forced to look at an unbalanced shot, with people's right arms cut off, intertitles off centre, and some heads closely shaved. There is obviously no way to reverse the loss: the only possible solution is to find a better print. We can now duplicate films without losing any portion of the image, and yet our culture seems so concerned with the power of the centre that the potential sacrifice of peripheral information doesn't seem such a big deal. Consider this in pictorial terms. If we don't care much about the framing of a Murnau film, what about a Rubens painting with the heads and feet of the figures partially cut off in order to repair the edges in a canvas? All available viewing copies of *Ben Hur* (Fred Niblo, 1925) are taken from printing elements with added soundtrack. Since the latest reissue of the film, a full aperture fine grain master has been retrieved, but for the

Ben-Hur (Fred Niblo, 1925), 35mm positive prints of (A) the original release version and (B) the 1931 re-release with variable density soundtrack (George Eastman House).

A

B

time being this does not appear to anyone to be a sufficient reason for embarking on another restoration project on the film. The newly-found fine grain master is also of better quality, because it comes from a negative of an earlier generation, but so what? Untrained projectionists tend to crop the image anyway by using the wrong aperture gate, and as long as nobody protests or argues to the contrary, we will continue seeing this and other silent films a bit more incomplete than they already are. Viewing these films in electronic form is unlikely to make this a hot topic, so be prepared to be called a purist if you indulge in this kind of nit-picking argument.

Imagine, though, what would happen if all archives were to follow the example of director Hans Jürgen Syberberg. At the beginning of his *Parsifal* (1981) there is a caption with specific instructions to the projectionist, and a title surrounded by a thin white line whose meaning is more or less the following: if you don't see the lines at the edges of the frame, the film is not being projected properly (see overleaf). A projectionist in Athens got so humiliated and upset (the upper and bottom lines were not visible on the screen) that he took an axe and butchered the print after the show, but an average audience would just giggle if the lines didn't appear, and then accept the cropped image as it is; a more alert viewer would have every right to make a little fuss about it, although perhaps not as vehemently as the mad Greek technician.

Dieser Film ist im klassischen Normalformat
gedreht (Vorführmaske 1:1,33) und darf
nicht auf Breitwand vorgeführt werden.

This film was shot on
Academy format (aperture gate 1:1,33)
and may not be shown on wide-screen.

Les prises du vue pour ce film ont été
faites dans le format standard classique
(cache d'aperture 1:1,33).
Il n'est pas autorisé de le projeter
sur écran large.

The opening credits of *Parsifal*
(Hans-Jürgen Syberberg, 1981),
35mm acetate print (courtesy of
Hans-Jürgen Syberberg).

Wenn obere und untere Linie sichtbar,
sehen Sie das vollständige Bild.

Full picture visible when upper and
lower edges can be seen.

Si la ligne du haut et celle
du bas sont visibles,
vous voyez l'image complète.

The Concept of Lacuna (II): What's Missing from the Story; or, What Price Completeness?

It is now time to go back again to Print 36 of our first diagram, and consider its 'incompleteness' from what we have called the diachronic point of view. Some sequential parts of the film are missing; that is, a portion of footage of what we assume must have been the complete print is absent altogether. It doesn't matter here whether the 'lost' portions of film are single frames, shots, sequences or entire reels. The fact is that a whole piece of the object is not there, and no laboratory technique is going to do us any good if we don't retrieve another print in a more complete shape. Contrary to what happens in the other arts, the viewer of a moving image doesn't like fragments. Looking at the Venus of Milo without arms is all right, but it doesn't seem all right to imagine *Casablanca* without the farewell scene. Whenever an important film that needs to be preserved is found in such an incomplete form, film archives inquire around fellow institutions in the hope that another print will help complete the puzzle. It is a frustrating search, and disappointment is far more frequent than success. Even in the latter case, the discovery of missing footage gives rise to more questions than answers. Let's now say that another print of our imaginary film is found, and we are swift in comparing it with Print 36. What

The Lost World (Harry O. Hoyt, 1925), 35mm acetate print (Národní Filmový Archiv, Prague).

if it's a print taken from a second negative, with shots taken at a slightly different angle? Do we have the right to incorporate it in the main footage? What if the print is of a much later generation than Print 36, and image quality is considerably worse than what is already in our hands? Are we going to insert the found part in our print anyway? That might help in figuring out what happened in the story of a fiction film, but it is also likely to bring a whole different set of disrupting effects. It all boils down to the question of what price we are ready to pay for the small victory we have gained on the narrative front. Image quality is only slightly inferior to Print 36, so we go ahead in the hope that the eventual viewer won't notice too much (in other words, we will play a little trick on our audience by using laboratory techniques in order to minimise the difference between the two sources). Alternatively, print quality is awful but the portion is too important to be left out, such as the last shot of *The Lost World* (Harry O. Hoyt, 1925), believed missing for many years and then found, but in desperate shape. Film preservationists have acquired a taste for adding footage at any cost to satisfy their concept of completeness, thus neglecting the significance of several dilemmas: if the recovery of the missing image matters so much, are we going to measure every single shot in the search for the print with one or two more frames? If these frames are found, are we going to add them to the main print even if the difference in quality will be obtrusive? Is it worth forcing the viewer to become the coroner in charge of a morgue of the moving image? And does the act of collating different prints in order to create a new one deliberately disregard the very history which has brought the print to the state in which it has come down to us?

There is no single answer to any of these questions. Their solution lies in the mind of the preservationist, and is dependent upon individual judgement, a choice between a wide array of options. The paradox of a mutilated integrity is at the core of the principle of conservative restoration: we leave the film as it is, in the hope that its incomplete evidence will be appreciated as such by the educated viewer. Here's an interesting item in the agenda of film preservation for the years to come. In the 18th century ruins were given an aesthetic value not only because of the implicit memory of what had once been, but also because of the inherent beauty of the ruins themselves. Nothing of this kind is to be found in film culture today. An incomplete film is a museum object of lesser value, something that archives strive to preserve when they can, but only a few hard-core specialists are keen to watch. Some institutions have even declared that their primary goal is the preservation of complete films, thus giving up the crucial challenge of educating the viewer to the intrinsic value of a fragment as an entity with its own right to exist as such. Most of the early films made D.W. Griffith during the Biograph period (1908–13) survive in the form of paper prints (see p. 3) or as camera negatives without intertitles and with disassembled shots. There is of course a reason for their incomplete condition, and the state in which they were found and have come down to us is in itself historically relevant. The need to keep and preserve these sources in that state – which, in museum terms, is always the only sound choice – should not discourage the attempt to make them available in a form that enables us to understand their value (if this is at all possible; admittedly, that's not always the case with the Biograph shorts). In other words, we should be able to see each film as a coherent whole in order to appreciate, even by approximation, the role of these films in the culture of their time.

We are now getting used to the idea that when it comes to film preservation, no principle is absolutely right or completely wrong. Each has its virtues and flaws, depending on the perspective from which we consider it. This becomes all the more evident when we look at the counterpart of the conservative restoration principle discussed above. The opposite paradox – of a fictional completeness made out of a patchwork of ruins – is no less problematic, as it is the sign of a surrender to the authoritarian demands of the viewing pleasure and the market imperatives which exploit it. Other more drastic solutions are likely to exacerbate the problem. Have a look the illustration overleaf, taken from the Library of Congress's restoration of John Ford's *The Blue Eagle*, 1926), and consider its role in the viewing process. Those who preserved this film are telling us that some portions of it are missing, and provide as much information as possible about their content. Film historian Hervé Dumont attempted to explain what happened in the lost reels of Frank

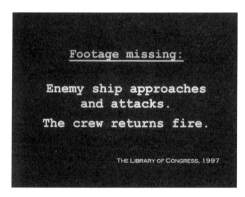

The Blue Eagle (John Ford, 1926), 35mm acetate print. Archival title from the 1997 reconstructed version (Library of Congress, Washington DC).

Borzage's *The River* (1929) by inserting production stills in the surviving footage, a method more effectively implemented by Rick Schmidlin and Richard Koszarski in their 1999 recreation of the four-hour version of *Greed* (Erich von Stroheim, 1925). We now have a better understanding of its plots and themes (that's good news indeed, certainly enough to justify the efforts), but how much is this going to improve the aesthetic experience of the moving images which were left for us to see? How much are we willing to sacrifice to an unrestrained obsession for completeness? However perfectly logical in its rationale, the principle of integrative restoration (as applied to the moving image) may be pushed to unacceptable aberrations, such as beginning over again on the preservation of a film that probably is not in need of urgent care – an attempt, figuratively speaking, at reinventing the wheel. Projects of this kind can tell us more about the people who contrived them than about the films they are supposed to resurrect. True, restoration techniques improve with time. True, restoring a film cannot be considered as something that is done once and once only, and needs no further attention after the printing work is done. Unfortunately, these very good and often forceful reasons have been manipulated and twisted for the sake of far less compelling and sometimes highly questionable goals.

A Very Concise Dictionary of Film Preservation

We may now have a better idea of how complicated and controversial the preservation of a silent film can be, but look how far we have progressed. We started with a single tree of possibilities (one print found among the many that could have survived), and we ended up being entangled in a network of alternative or conflicting options, a variety of possible print generation trees, and a whole set of cultural, financial, and political issues. The treatment of the copies retrieved or created during this intricate process has been described using terms too often used interchangeably, and it may now be the time to try defining them. Since you should not expect to find an overwhelming consensus on the matter, each definition ought to be considered more as a flexible conceptual framework than as a fixed, dogmatically imposed statement on how archival work should be implemented.

PRESERVATION is described in a film archive as the overall complex of procedures, principles, techniques and practices necessary for maintaining the integrity, restoring the content, and organising the intellectual experience of a moving image on a permanent basis. This seemingly vague definition is in fact the implicit acknowledgement of the three-fold purpose of the preservation work: making sure that the surviving artifact is not further damaged; bringing it back to a condition as close as possible to its original state; providing access to it, in a manner consistent with the way the artifact was meant to be exhibited. Outstanding laboratory work does not fulfil the above requirements if the film is then shown without regard to the projection speed or aspect ratio, or if the source copy is destroyed or abandoned after printing. Duplication, restoration, conservation, reconstruction (when necessary), access and exhibition in proper conditions are all constituent parts of the preservation activity.

DUPLICATION is the set of practices related to the creation of a replica of the moving image, either as a backup of existing original or preservation components, or as a means to give access to the moving image. While the duplication process is performed with the goal of obtaining a copy as close as possible to the source, such a process is a necessary but not sufficient requirement of a restoration project. The most accurate duplication (for example, a wet gate printing) may result in a satisfactory imitation of the source copy through the elimination of scratches and the removal of exterior agents such as dust, oil spots and dirt, yet – for better or worse – no further action is taken in order to bring the film back to its presumed original condition.

CONSERVATION involves all the activities necessary to prevent or minimise the process of physical degradation of the archival artifact, whether such an artifact is newly produced by the archive (a preservation negative) or is an already existing object acquired by the institution, with possible signs of damage or instability. An underlying principle of this process is that the above activities should be carried out with the minimum intervention or interference with the object. Storing a nitrate print in a vault equipped with temperature and humidity control systems is part of the conservation process.

RESTORATION is the set of technical, editorial and intellectual procedures aimed at compensating for the loss or degradation of the moving image artifact, thus bringing it back to a state as close as possible to its original condition. Removing alterations or manipulations detected on the artifact (in the reproduction process), retrieving elements missing from it (with reconstruction practices), and reversing the effects of time, wear and tear on the optical, chromatic, and (in the case of sound film) aural content of the motion picture carrier, are all components of the restoration work. Taken individually, none of them is sufficient to fulfil the requirements of a film restoration. The term 'restoration' in motion picture preservation is also different from its equivalent in most other disciplines, in the sense that it necessarily involves the reproduction of a source copy. We clean a painting, treat the canvas, adjust the frame and fix unstable pigments, then we exhibit the painting itself. A nitrate film (and, for that matter, any known moving image carrier) may be cleaned, repaired, edited or treated otherwise. However, as long as it is the object of a preservation process (that is, if a decision has been made concerning its archival status), the artifact as such cannot be exhibited. Another distinctive feature of photographic moving images – comparable only to analog phonographic recordings on disc or tape – is that they cannot be experienced without progressively damaging them. Therefore, they must be duplicated onto another carrier whose eventual decay through wear and tear will not affect the possibility of providing access to their content through a new copy.

RECONSTRUCTION is the editorial process through which a print whose appearance is as close as possible to a desired version, considered as authoritative, is created by interpolating, replacing or reassembling segments within the copy and with footage retrieved from other copies. Some segments (such as intertitles) may be newly created by the archive. Because of its superficial resemblance to the critical edition of a manuscript or printed text, the practice underlying this method has sometimes been pretentiously mislabelled as 'philology', thus endorsing the reductionist implications of the term as applied to the moving image. In this respect, we should follow David Bordwell's advice, and reserve the term 'philology' for the interpretation of a literary work.

RECREATION is a strategy aimed at presenting an imaginary account of what the film would have been if some or all of its missing parts had survived. This course of action is taken when material directly or indirectly related to the film is used in order to give an idea of its original concept. While it is by no means a restoration, the 1999 version of *Greed* made for television (with a mixture of extant footage and production stills following Stroheim's script for the four-hour version) can be adequately described as a recreation. We will never know what the cinematic qualities of the film actually were, but at least we have a glimpse of its overall content.

It cannot be stressed enough that learning how a reconstruction project was accomplished, and sharing its criteria with future researchers and preservationists, is a duty that has only recently been properly recognised, but deserves the archivist's utmost attention.

RULE 2

Any decision taken in the preservation process must
a) be reversible,
b) prevent further deterioration or alteration of the original artifact, and
c) be carefully documented.

Neither the above glossary nor the rule derived from its definitions includes terms such as 'digitised' and 'remastered', already mentioned in this chapter. These words may say something about what has been done to an electronic image obtained from a photographic film (and they may indeed be useful tools in a restoration project), but they are not operational criteria for film preservation. Don't be fooled by their indiscriminate use. The same applies to more traditional concepts. A poster for the 1989 re-release of *Lawrence of Arabia* says, 'restoration produced and reconstructed by Robert A. Harris and Jim Painten'. That doesn't mean much, either. Harris and Painten did a good job for the sake of a new commercial version of the film, but it looks as if the publicity department at Columbia was a bit confused by what they were trying to accomplish. How do you reconstruct a restoration? Or, did they mean that it was a restoration *and* a reconstruction?

The importance of using and not abusing the appropriate terms brings us to an important corollary. As much as film preservationists must make sure that their work is reversible (meaning that the source elements used in the restoration process are kept intact, or are treated in such a way that it is easy to return them to their editorial state preceding the reconstruction process), they also share the responsibility of explaining to others what they have done. Someone may ask why a certain decision was taken; other preservationists may want to do further work, and it will be very useful for them to be given all the information which their predecessors had at their disposal. Caring about what others are going to say or think about us and our philosophy of film preservation is a responsible way of thinking about the future. In all likelihood, our successors are going to question our action as much as we now question the decisions made by those who came before us. Why did we restore certain films and not others? Why did we use our funds for this print, and neglect that one? Why did we restore the films in a certain way and not otherwise?

One of the most difficult things we will have to explain to them is why we never had enough money to preserve everything we wanted. Working in a film archive is an exciting endeavour, but it is also a time-consuming, frustrating task where patience, method and perseverance are as important as creativity. Consider the following scenario, imaginary but totally plausible. One hundred prints in a film archive are in the process of severe decomposition, and we know all too well that they will soon disappear altogether if appropriate action is not taken promptly. We have enough money to save only ten of them, and the choice of which will survive and which will not is entirely in our hands. It is a cruel, thankless duty, similar to the situation of a doctor with a hospital full of dying patients and enough medicine to cure only a handful. Think of it. You are that doctor. How are you going to determine who will be cured and who won't? What will you tell them? How will you justify your actions to their descendants? That's exactly how a responsible film curator feels when reading the inspection reports. Film scholars who are unfamiliar with the museum world are often startled at the supposed indifference shown by the staff when they admit that a film has completely vanished. Their apparent cold blood is not much different from a surgeon's unemotional stance in talking about a moribund human being. Once the film's cancer (be it nitrate decomposition, or the vinegar syndrome) has begun to spread, the preservationist is well aware of the moral challenge involved in deciding whether to salvage at least part of a film, or to let it die because others have to live. Such circumstances demand a remarkable sense of commitment towards posterity. Films will die anyway, but at least we must be fully conscious of why this daily tragedy occurs before our eyes.

The curator's choice will also shape the concept of history in years to come. We will tell future audiences that one film instead of another is worthy of their attention, and only we will know what other film was sacrificed in the name of our opinion. In the curator's defence, it should be added that the choice will also depend on what audiences ask film archives to do. A harsh truth of film culture is that audiences are often – perhaps generally – the most conservative players in the game. We want to see the masterpieces, the films that film history books have taught us to consider as cornerstones in the development of film style. We look for 'the best films ever made', we play with the lists of the 100 titles everybody should see. This immoral and nefarious exercise has become the staple of organisations whose mission should be the preservation of motion picture heritage. Its destructive consequences are obvious. Film culture becomes the equivalent of a tourist itinerary where a certain country is supposedly covered once all the main monuments have been seen. Been there, done that. Fundraising and marketing officers have taken over most of the institutional power in the archive, and now claim the decision-making authority once given to curators and programmers (unless they agree to become fundraisers themselves out of necessity, which is perhaps a lesser evil).

Less than 5 per cent of all the titles preserved in the average film archive is seen by scholars, and even less is requested by film festivals. Much of the remaining 95 per cent never leaves the shelves of the film vaults after preservation has been completed. Despite all the big talk about constantly rewriting the history of cinema and discussing its canons, we keep showing the same classics over and over again. One may say that younger generations have a right to see the great works we already take for granted, and that there's still a difference between a Buster Keaton of the golden years and an Eclair comedy, but that's not a valid reason to refuse them a chance to broaden their horizons. Is this what a film archive is for? A shelter for a privileged minority of cultural icons? A sanatorium for all the rest? An observatory of decomposing nitrate prints, or worse, a cemetery where archivists are paid for the sad duty of witnessing the progressive self-destruction of film history? Saving mummies of what's left, amongst the indifference of our time? Why bother spending fortunes for such an absurd task?

What makes things even more absurd is the fact that the archivist's idea of conservation as applied to the moving image is short-sighted from *force majeure*. Preservationists seem to be happy when a film is declared as saved for the next 100 years, but a century of cultural life is virtually nothing by comparison with the life of architecture and paintings. Let's put it another way: whenever we tackle a long-

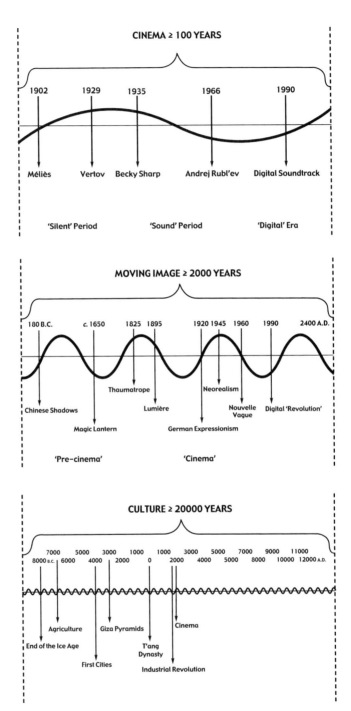

Figure 5: The moving image in history.

term preservation project, what do we mean by 'long-term'? Let's look at Figure 5, adapted from the 1996 manifesto of the Long Now Foundation. Seen from this perspective, a true long-term preservation strategy for cinema has yet to be found, and despite all the archival precautions implemented with great effort and debate we have made no real progress in this direction. We preserve film on film (as long as the industry will allow us to do so: it is still by far the most stable medium available at this time), and then see what happens. The future will be determined by the dictatorship of the moving image and entertainment industry. Let's not forget that manufacturers will eventually stop producing motion picture stock. At that point, film archives will be in big trouble. More visual history will be lost, more than ever (even things you thought were safe), despite the misleading promise of eternity delivered by the digital gospel. It is of course impossible to say now what carrier will bring our silent film heritage to the eyes of a spectator of the distant future, but we may fairly assume that such a carrier will be required to fulfil some basic requirements in order to make moving images visible 10,000 years from now. It ought to be a carrier whose actual use requires a hardware based on low technology. It also must be a carrier requiring a minimal amount of human maintenance in order to survive: a far cry from the costly refrigerated, low humidity vaults we are building now. Finally, it should be something that won't require much knowledge of twentieth-century technology in order to operate and experience. If we really want to make sense out of a lifetime spent in film preservation, we'd better come to grips with imagining the object (because it will also have to be an object: there's no getting over it) containing moving images that will be available to the viewer of the year 12000. In short: film preservationists of the world, let's add one digit to our calendar year. That's right, 10,000 more years. I see no good reason to settle for less than that.

Further Reading

Research on moving image preservation has grown exponentially since the early 1980s in an exciting yet quite chaotic way, and has now reached the arena of daily newspapers, sometimes with questionable side effects. Writings on the struggle for film restoration, the search for hitherto lost treasures, and the efforts made to retrieve them and present them to modern audiences have grown to the status of a literary sub-genre and should soon become the object of a socio-cultural analysis. Such a spectacular surge, however, has not yet brought a systematic corpus of knowledge, and the following selected list of specialised studies on the subject should be seen as nothing but the provisional outcome of a collective work in progress often influenced by political and economic factors. The technology of moving image preservation is in itself undergoing a rapid progress, so swift that a text written only five or ten years ago may quickly be superseded by further progress in the field. A comprehensive bibliography of texts in English is available at the website of the American Film Institute: www.afionline.org/preservation/about/bib.html.

Introductory Texts

If I had to choose a text to be used as a very first reading on the subject, I would have no hesitation in selecting Eileen Bowser, 'Some Principles of Film Restoration', *Griffithiana*, vol. 11 nos 38–9, October 1990, pp. 170–3. *A Manual for Film Archives*, edited by Eileen Bowser and John Kuiper (Brussels: FIAF, 1980; New York and London: Garland, 1991) is still a basic reference tool for those who wish to enter the arena of film preservation, and a useful *aide-mémoire* for more experienced professionals. *Audiovisual Archives: A Practical Reader*, edited by Helen P. Harrison (Paris: UNESCO, 1997) is also highly recommended. A guide to archival terminology is Günter Schulz and Hans Karnstädt (eds), *Terms and Methods for Technical Archiving of Audiovisual Materials* (Munich-New York-Paris: K.G. Saur, 1992). Tom McGreevey and Joanne L. Yeck, *Our Film Heritage* (New Brunswick, NJ, and London: Rutgers University Press, 1997) is a general overview of film preservation in the United States. See also Eva Orbanz (ed.), *Archiving the Audio-Visual Heritage: A Joint Technical Symposium* (Berlin: Stiftung Deutsche Kinemathek, 1987); *Guide de la conservation des films* (Paris: Commission Supérieure Technique de l'Image et du Son, 1995); Ralph N. Sargent, *Preserving the Moving Image* (Washington, DC: Corporation for Public Broadcasting/National Endowment for the Arts, 1974); Ramon Espelt (ed.), *Protection and Preservation of Films* (Barcelona: Oficina Catalana de Cinema, 1988); Chen Jingliang (gen. ed.), *A Collection of Papers Presented at the Symposium on Film Collections in Asia* (Beijing: China Film Archive, 1997); *Film Mutilation and How to Prevent It* (Rochester, NY: Eastman Kodak Company, 1924), reproduced at the end of this volume in Appendix 6. *The Book of Film Care* (Rochester, NY: Eastman Kodak Company, 1983), written from the viewpoint of a major film stock manufacturer, is a practical guide for the non-specialist, filled with odd comparisons ('a film roll may seem like a stubborn horse that resorts to distending its flanks to avoid the solid seating of the saddle by whatever tugging of the cinch strap', p. 68) and empirical evidence which has been refined by further laboratory research. The recommendation that 'when nitrate base negatives have been duplicated, they should be destroyed' (p. 45) is aberrant by today's standards, yet reflects an opinion that was quite common at the time.

Theory

The only comprehensive study on the subject has been written by Ray Edmondson, *A Philosophy of Film Archiving* (Paris: UNESCO, 1998), a landmark in the discipline of moving image archiving. See also *Film Preservation and Film Scholarship*, special issue of *Film History*, vol. 7 no. 3, Autumn 1995; the *FIAF Code of Ethics* (Brussels: FIAF, 1998); Paolo Cherchi Usai, 'Decay Cinema: History and Aesthetics of Moving Image Destruction', *Stanford Humanities Journal*, Fall 1999; revised and expanded versions have been published in Italian, *L'ultimo spettatore. Sulla distruzione del cinema* (Milan: Editrice Il Castoro, 1999) and in English, *The Death of Cinema* (London; BFI Publishing, 2001). While not dealing at all with film, Nicholas Stanley Price, M.

Kirby Talley, Jr., and Alessandra Melucco Vaccaro (eds), *Historical and Philosophical Issues in the Conservation of Cultural Heritage* (Los Angeles: The Getty Conservation Institute, 1996) is a treasure trove of ideas which are quite pertinent to the preservation of the moving image. The institutional gap between preservation in film and the other arts is a lamentable reality which no individual or collective effort has yet managed to overcome; the responsibility of addressing this critical question is now in the hands of a new generation of specialists, but no solution seems to be in sight. A meticulous reading of art historian Cesare Brandi *Teoria del restauro* (Rome: Edizioni di Storia e Letteratura, 1963; reprint Turin: Einaudi, 1977; partial translation in Price, Talley and Melucco Vaccaro, *Historical and Philosophical Issues*) will provide a wealth of insights into most of the controversies related to the topic. Other required readings for the moving image preservationist of the future should be Steward Brand, *The Clock of the Long Now. Time and Responsibility* (New York: Basic Books, 1999), and Peter Schwartz, *The Art of the Long View. Planning for the Future in an Uncertain World* (New York: Doubleday, 1991). Figure 5 is a modified version of the diagram by Stewart Brand and Brian Eno which appeared on the website of the Long Now Foundation (www.longnow.org).

Documentation

An outstanding example of how a preservation project may result in a catalogue of holdings is provided by Roland Cosandey in *Film um 1910*, an analysis of the Joseph Joye Collection held by the National Film and Television Archive in London (Stroemfeld/Roter Stern/Stadtkino Basel, 1993); see also his *Cinéma 1900. Trente films dans une boîte à chaussures* (Lausanne: Payot, 1996). Another corpus of early films, the Jean Desmet collection, is discussed in Ivo Blom, *Pionerswerk. Jean Desmet en de vroege Nederlandse filmhandel en bioscoopexploitatie, 1907–1916* (Amsterdam: Amsterdam University Press, 2001). A promotional approach to the subject is offered by *The Lumiere Project: The European Film Archives at the Crossroads*, edited by Catherine A. Surowiec (Lisbon: Associação Projecto Lumiere, 1996). A much broader range of questions on the rationale of film preservation is presented in the massive report presented by the Librarian of Congress under the title *Film Preservation 1993: A Study of the Current State of American Film Preservation* (Washington, DC: US Government Printing Office, 1993, four vols in three tomes), integrated by *Redefining Film Preservation: A National Plan*, coordinated by Annette Melville and Scott Simmon (Washington, DC: Library of Congress, 1994). The discovery and preservation of the Dawson City Collection referred to on page 44 is described by Sam Kula, 'There's Film in Them Thar Hills!', *American Film*, vol. 4 no. 8, July–August 1979, pp. 14–18.

Films, Video and Electronic Media on Film Preservation

A charming short film on motion picture preservation and history (set in 1999!) was produced by MGM when nitrate film was still in production: *Forgotten Treasure*

(Sammy Lee, 1943, 10′). Over the years, film archives have produced video works as introductions to moving image preservation. Among them are Orly Yadin, *The Work of a Film Archive* (Flashback Television Ltd, 1992, 27′13′′, VHS PAL); Scott Benson, *The Race to Save 100 Years* (Warner Bros./Turner Entertainment, 1997, VHS NTSC, 55′57′′); Jacques Mény, *Sauver les films. Une mémoire pour demain* (Sodaperaga/Centre National de la Cinématographie/Ministère de la Culture et de la Communication, France 1991, VHS Secam, 33′); from the same director, *À la recherche des films perdus* and *La Mémoire retrouvée* (Oneline Productions/La Sept/ARTE, 1996, VHS PAL, 75′ and 63′); Mark McLaughlin, *Keepers of the Frame* (WinStar Cinema/Mount Pilot Productions, 1999, 16mm, 70′).

Technical Literature

The International Federation of Film Archives (FIAF) has published over the years a large corpus of studies in this area. Among them are the *Technical Manual of the FIAF Preservation Commission* (Brussels: FIAF, 1993); *Handling, Storage and Transport of Cellulose Nitrate Film* and *Preservation and Restoration of Moving Images and Sound*, published respectively in 1992 and 1986. Spanish archivist Alfonso del Amo García is the author of a remarkable manual, *Inspección técnica de materiales en el archivo de una filmoteca* (Madrid: Filmoteca Española, 1996). The volume has been translated into English and Italian (*Technical Inspection of Motion Picture Film in the Archive*) by the L. Jeffrey Selznick School of Film Preservation (Gemona and Rochester, NY: Cineteca del Friuli/George Eastman House, 2001). The same series includes two very detailed accounts of the structure, chemistry and identification of motion picture film stock: Luis Fernández Colourado, Rosa Cardona Arau, Jennifer Gallego Christensen and Encarnación Rus Aguilar, *Los soportes de la cinematografía 1*; Fernando Catalina and Alfonso del Amo García, *Los soportes de la cinematografía 2* (Madrid: Filmoteca Española, both published in 1999. Volume 2 is in Spanish and English). See also Mark-Paul Meyer and Paul Read, *Restoration of Motion Picture Film* (Newton, MA: Butterworth-Heinemann, 2000); James M. Reilly, Peter Z. Adelstein and Douglas W. Nishimura, *Preservation of Safety Film* (Rochester, NY: Image Permanence Institute/Rochester Institute of Technology, 1991); James M. Reilly, Peter Z. Adelstein, Douglas W. Nishimura, and Catherine Erbland, *New Approaches to Safety Film Preservation* (1994); Jean-Louis Bigourdan and James M. Reilly, *Environment and Enclosures in Film Preservation* (1997); *Il cinema ritrovato. Teoria e metodologia del restauro cinematografico*, edited by Gian Luca Farinelli and Nicola Mazzanti (Bologna: Grafis, 1994). Despite the convoluted style and jargon-filled language, their article 'Black on White. Notes on Film Restoration: The Reconstruction', co-authored with Michele Canosa in *Cinegrafie* 10 (Ancona: Transeuropa, 1997, pp. 191–202) is a worthwhile addition to the book. On the same topic, see Roland Cosandey, 'Fac-similé non dissimulé: l'édition ordinaire du cinéma (Boolsky, Guillaume Tell, Eisenstein' in *CinémAction* (Paris), no. 97, October 2000. Colour preservation is discussed in *The Preservation and Restoration of*

Colour and Sound in Films (Brussels: FIAF, 1981); *All the Colours of the World. Colours in Early Mass Media, 1900–1930* (Reggio Emilia: Edizioni Diabasis, 1998). For a history of film preservation techniques until 1985, see the bibliography in *Film da salvare. Guida al restauro e alla conservazione*, special issue of *Comunicazione di massa*, vol. 5 no. 3, September–December 1985. Issues of digital restoration are discussed in *The Use of New Technologies Applied to Film Restoration: Technical and Ethical Problems* (Gamma Group [no place of publication, no date, ca. 1994]).

Journals
Reports and discussions on film preservation projects appear in the *Journal of Film Preservation* (produced under the title *FIAF Bulletin* from issue 1 to 46), published twice a year by the International Federation of Film Archives, and in *Moving Images*, distributed for AMIA by the University of Minnesota Press. Essays and notes also appear regularly in the *AMIA Newsletter* (Los Angeles: Association of Moving Image Archivists, 1988–seqq.), *Cinegrafie*, the 'Archival Notes' section of *Cinema Journal* and, occasionally, in *Griffithiana*, *Kintop*, *Film History* and *1895*.

Associations
In addition to the International Federation of Film Archives (1 rue Defacqz, 1000 Brussels, Belgium), representing non-profit moving image archives worldwide (their names and addresses are listed in Appendix 2), a number of regional groups are active in specific areas: in Europe, the Association des Cinémathèques Européennes; in Central and South America, the Coordinadora Latinoamericana de Archivos de Imagenes en Movimiento (CLAIM); in Australasia, the South East Asia-Pacific Audio Visual Archive Association (SEAPAVAA, c/o Ms. Belina Capul, Philippine Information Agency, Visayas Avenue, Quezon City, Metro Manila, Philippines. Fax +63 2 920 4395); in North America, the Council of North American Film Archives (CNAFA). While operating in the United States, the Association of Moving Image Archivists (AMIA) has no inherent geographic boundaries. So far, AMIA is also the only association based on individual membership. Anyone interested in moving image preservation can join the group.

Archival Training
At the time of writing, several institutions provide archival training on a more or less systematic basis. The L. Jeffrey Selznick School of Film Preservation at George Eastman House is the first permanent programme (one academic year for each course) covering all aspects of museum work, with a strong accent on hands-on experience with nitrate print inspection, film programming, and management (website: www.eastman.org). The seminars held by Archimedia in the European Union take place in several institutions on a rotation basis, and are mainly aimed at an audience from the academic and professional world (website: http://europa.eu.int/comm/dg10/avpolicy/media/en/archim). The University of East Anglia has a Film

Studies/Film Archiving program in conjunction with the East Anglia Film Archive (website: www.uea.ac.uk/eafa/). The University of California in Los Angeles has classes, seminars and workshops in archival training held in the context of the Cinema Studies graduate program (website: www.ucla.edu). The University of New South Wales in Australia has organised an internet course in audiovisual management in cooperation with National Film and Sound Archive/ScreenSound Australia (website: www.silas.unsw.edu.au/silas/distedu.htm). A similar project, Film Archives On Line – limited to the laboratory aspect of film restoration – is now being prepared in the European Union (website: www2.iperbole.bologna.it/faol/). By and large, the advantages and disadvantages of training courses held through electronic media are obvious: they offer extensive and often invaluable information on the subject, yet are lacking the direct contact with film, which is at the core of the archival experience. Those who don't have the time or the financial resources necessary to attend any of these courses have some alternatives. The International Federation of Film Archives runs a three- or four-week Summer School every three to four years (website: www.cinema.ucla .edu /FIAF/fiaf.html), mainly for the benefit of staff members of FIAF and FIAT (International Federation of Television Archives). One-day seminars are held at the annual conference of the Association of Moving Image Archivists organised in different locations of North America (website: www.amianet.org). In Australasia, SEAPAVAA periodically offers workshops to its members (website: www.seapavaa.virtualave.net).

PLATE 1
Cinématographe Lumière.
*Inauguration par Guillaume II
du monument de Guillaume Ier*
(September 4, 1896), Lumière
Catalogue no. 221. 35mm
nitrate print with one round
perforation on each side of the
frame (Author's collection).

PLATE 2
Georges Demenÿ. Unidentified film (1896),
58mm nitrate print. The inscription '*Avant
l'assaut – Le mur*', handwritten on the
negative, is visible on the leader of the
positive copy (George Eastman House).

PLATE 3
Veriscope. *The Corbett-
Fitzsimmons Fight* (1897), 63mm
nitrate print (George Eastman
House).

PLATE 4
Duplex, 1915–27.
Unidentified film,
11mm positive print
(George Eastman
House).

PLATE 5
Edison Home
Kinetoscope.
Unidentified film,
22mm diacetate print
(George Eastman
House).

PLATE 6
Ernemann Kino, 1903.
Unidentified film, 17.5mm
negative print (George
Eastman House).

PLATE 7
Messter Kino-Salon,
1908–09. Unidentified
film, 35mm diacetate print
(George Eastman House).

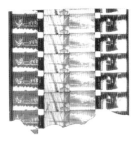

PLATE 8
Duoscope, 1912.
Unidentified film, 17.5mm
positive print (George
Eastman House).

PLATE 9
American Mutoscope & Biograph.
French Acrobatic Dance (1903), 70mm
paper print for Mutoscope equipment
(George Eastman House).

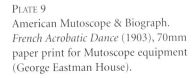

PLATE 10
American Mutoscope &
Biograph. Unidentified film
[*Procession in Italy*] to (*c.*
1895–1905), 70mm nitrate
print (George Eastman House).

PLATE 11
Filoteo Alberini. Unidentified
film [*Street Scene, Rome*] (1911),
70mm nitrate negative (George
Eastman House).

PLATE 12
Pathé-Kok, 1912. *Fifty-Fifty* (Allan Dwan, 1916), reel 2,
28mm diacetate print, three perforations per frame on the
left, one on the right. The US standard (Pathescope, 1917)
has three perforations per frame on each side (George
Eastman House).

PLATE 13
Cine Kodak. Shooting test
by W. Vaeth on reversal
film (May 1920), 16mm
diacetate print (George
Eastman House).

PLATE 14
Paper print. Unidentified
film (*c.* 1912?), 35mm print
(George Eastman House).

PLATE 15
Gaumont, Chrono de
poche (1900). 15mm
unprocessed film stock
(George Eastman House).

PLATE 16
Movette, 1917.
Unidentified film
(*c*. 1918), 17.5mm
positive print
(George Eastman
House).

PLATE 17
Pathé-Baby or Pathex,
1922–23. *Faust* (Friedrich
Wilhelm Murnau, 1926),
9.5mm diacetate print
(George Eastman House).

PLATE 18
Le Maestro Do-mi-sol-do (Georges Méliès,
winter 1905–06), 35mm nitrate print. The
'Star Film' trademark, embossed on the film
base, is made visible by low-angle light
(Davide Turconi Collection).

PLATE 19
Das Schmiedelied aus Siegfried (Messter-Gaumont, 1905?), 35mm nitrate print for
synchronized projection with phonograph recording. Note the shape of the smaller
perforations with rounded corners, common until 1905 (Davide Turconi Collection).

PLATE 20
*Bains de la Jetée de Pâquis,
Genève* (Casimir Sivan,
Switzerland, 1896), 35mm
nitrate print with non-
standard perforations
(George Eastman House).

PLATE 21
Das boxende Känguruh (Max
Skladanovsky, Germany, 1895),
55mm nitrate film. Perforations and
splices are reinforced with metal
studs (George Eastman House).

PLATE 22
A Daughter of Two Worlds (James L. Young, 1920),
35mm nitrate print. Note the Eastman Kodak 1920 edge
code on the right side of the film. The fragment
reproduced here, photographed in 1994, is now
decomposed (George Eastman House).

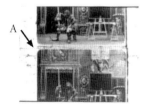

PLATE 23
Le Chevalier mystère (Georges Méliès, 1899), 35mm nitrate print. The cement splice
on the positive copy is visible (A) as a dark line at the edge of the frame. A splice
made on the negative source is visible (B) on the same positive copy as a light area on
the upper part of the frame (George Eastman House).

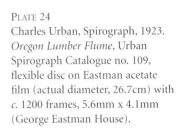

PLATE 24
Charles Urban, Spirograph, 1923. *Oregon Lumber Flume*, Urban Spirograph Catalogue no. 109, flexible disc on Eastman acetate film (actual diameter, 26.7cm) with *c.* 1200 frames, 5.6mm x 4.1mm (George Eastman House).

PLATE 25
Charles Urban, Spirograph, 1923. *Oregon Lumber Flume*, detail (George Eastman House).

PLATE 26
Leonard Ulrich Kamm, Kammatograph (1898–1900). Unidentified film [*Street scene*], glass plate (actual diameter, 30.5cm) with *c.* 550 frames, 8.4 x 6mm (George Eastman House).

PLATE 27
Leonard Ulrich Kamm, Kammatograph, 1898–1900. Unidentified film [*Street scene*], detail (George Eastman House).

PLATE 28
Technicolor Process no. 2. *The Black Pirate* (Albert Parker, 1926), 35mm nitrate negative. Every other image is reversed, with the bottom edges of the two frames in contact (courtesy of Kevin Patton, National Film and Television Archive, London).

PLATE 29
Lumière, 75mm film for the Paris 1900 Universal Exhibition, 75mm nitrate print (courtesy of Vincent Pinel).

PLATE 30
Unidentified film for synchronized phonograph recording, probably *Madame Baron présentant le Graphophonoscope* (Auguste Baron, France 1899), 50mm nitrate print (George Eastman House, courtesy of Vincent Pinel).

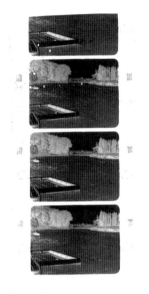

PLATE 31
Unidentified film (Pathé?, *c.* 1910?), 35mm nitrate negative with one Bell & Howell perforation on each side of the frame (George Eastman House, courtesy of Vincent Pinel).

PLATE 32
Pathé-Rural (France, 1927–seqq.), 17.5mm film with one square perforation on each side of the frame. This format was also used for early sound film – Pathé-Rural/Pathé-Nathan (George Eastman House, courtesy of Vincent Pinel).

PLATE 33

Phono-Cinéma-Théâtre. *Air de Roméo et Juliette* (Ambroise-François Parnaland, France 1900), 35mm nitrate positive for synchronized phonograph recording, with three non-standard perforations on the frame line (George Eastman House, courtesy of Vincent Pinel).

PLATE 34

Ozaphane (France, 1927–seqq.), cellophane film in various formats: (A) 16mm, (B) 17.5mm, (C, D) 22mm, (E) 24mm without perforations, to be used on Oehmichen projectors. Original samples (B) and (C) are tinted, respectively, pink and amber; the others are black and white. Ozaphane film stock is extremely thin (0.05mm). Other non-standard formats for sound projectors are also extant (courtesy of Laurent Mannoni).

A

B

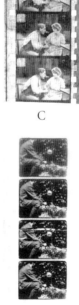

C

D

E

PLATE 35
Unidentified format, 44mm
(courtesy of Vincent Pinel).

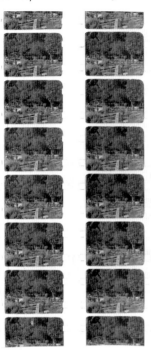

PLATE 36
Unidentified format for
early sound projection,
22mm, France?, *c.* 1930
(courtesy of Vincent
Pinel).

PLATE 37
Unidentified stereoscopic
film (country and date
unknown), 35mm negative
print (courtesy of Laurent
Mannoni).

PLATE 38
Henry-Joseph Joly, Eugène Normandin, *Place de la
Madeleine* (1896–97), 35mm nitrate postive film with
five perforations on each side. Frame size, 21–23mm
(h), 23–24.8mm (w); aspect ratio 1:1.02 to 1:1.08
(Filmoteca Española. Illustration courtesy of Irela
Núñez del Pozo, Lima, Peru)

PLATE 39
Markings for editing or title insertion, *La Grotte des supplices* (Alfred Machin, Pathé,
1912), 35mm nitrate negative print (Author's collection).

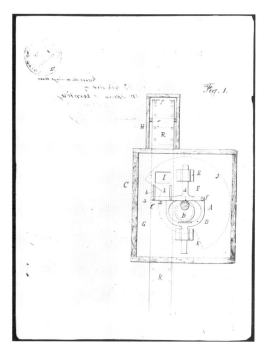

PLATE 40
Drawing for the patent
description of the
Cinématographe Lumière
camera and projector, 1895
(George Eastman House).

PLATE 41
Edison Kinetophone,
1895–1900 (George
Eastman House).

PLATE 42
Max Skladanowsky, film projector with two 55mm film strips (see PLATE 21). The first public screening of Skladanowsky films was held in Berlin on 1 November 1895 (George Eastman House).

PLATE 43
The inside mechanism of Leonard Ulrich Kamm's Kammatograph camera and projector, 1898 (George Eastman House)

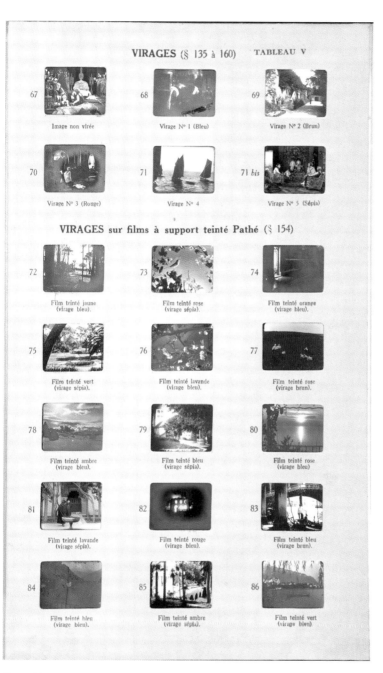

PLATE 44

Toning (frame samples no. 67–71 *bis*) and toning on tinted film stock (no. 72–86). Frame samples from L. Didiée, *Le Film vierge Pathé: Manuel de développement et de tirage* (Paris: Établissements Pathé-Cinéma, 1926), Table 5 (Author's collection).

A   B

PLATE 45
Hand-colouring. *La Danse du feu* (Georges Méliès, 1899), 35mm nitrate print and black and white duplicate (George Eastman House).

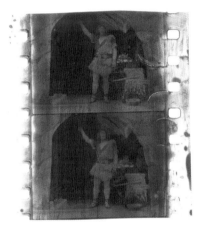

PLATE 46
Tinting by hand brushing. *Das Schmiedelied aus Siegfried* (Messter-Gaumont, 1905?), 35mm nitrate print for synchronized projection with phonograph recording. Note the irregularities of the red tint on the edges of the print (Davide Turconi Collection).

PLATE 47
Tinting by dye immersion. *Firenze* (Milano Films, Italy 1913), 35mm nitrate print. Note the Eastman Kodak edge code stenciled on the right, between the perforations (Nederlands Filmmuseum, Amsterdam).

PLATE 48
Toning. Unidentified film, possibly Gaumont, 1907 (German titles: *Braut des Freiwilligen*, or *1870*), 35mm nitrate print (Davide Turconi Collection).

PLATE 49
Stencil colour process. *Fée aux pigeons* (Gaston Velle, Pathé, April–May 1906), 35mm nitrate print (Author's collection).

PLATE 50
Multiple tinting. The colours of the French flag in the *Marseillaise* sequence of *The Four Horsemen of the Apocalypse* (Rex Ingram, 1921), 35mm acetate print (courtesy of Kevin Brownlow).

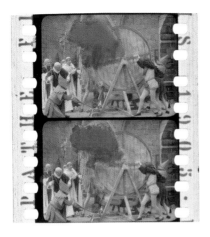

PLATE 51
Toning and stencil. *Les Martyrs de l'Inquisition* (Lucien Nonguet, Pathé, November 1905), 35mm nitrate print. The red cloud in the scene is coloured with the stencil process (Davide Turconi Collection).

PLATE 52
Stencil and hand colouring. *L'Écrin du Radjah* (Pathé, April–May 1906), 35mm nitrate print. Note the irregular shape of the hand-coloured scarves on the dancers' shoulders (Davide Turconi Collection).

PLATE 53
Mein name ist Spiesecke (Emil Albes, Germany 1914), 35mm nitrate print. In all likelihood, colour alteration of the tinted and toned segments was accelerated by inadequate processing of the nitrate copy at the time of release (Nederlands Filmmuseum, Amsterdam).

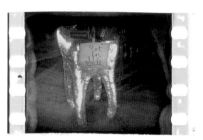

PLATE 55
Handschiegl process (also known as Wyckoff-DeMille process). *Greed* (Erich von Stroheim, 1925), 35mm nitrate print (Seaver Center for Western History Research/Los Angeles County Museum of Natural History).

PLATE 54
Kodachrome process. Unidentified film, probably a colour test (*c.* 1922), 35mm nitrate print. The edge code is visible on the right (George Eastman House).

PLATE 56
William T. Crespinel, [*Stereoscopic Film Test*] (United States, Winter 1919), 35mm nitrate print, the earliest 3-D film known to survive. The full projected image can be seen through anaglyph glasses (George Eastman House).

PLATE 57
Technicolor Process no. 3. *Redskin* (Victor Schertzinger, 1929), 35mm nitrate print (George Eastman House).

PLATE 58
William Friese-Greene, three-colour system, *c.* 1909, 35mm nitrate print (George Eastman House).

PLATE 59
Two-colour additive process (?). Bichrome film (Belgium, date unknown), 55mm positive print, to be projected at 48 fps (courtesy of Laurent Mannoni).

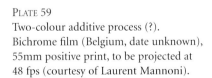

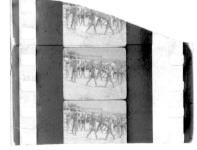

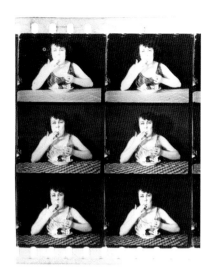

PLATE 60
Three-colour additive process. Unidentified film (Victor Continsouza?, France?, *c.* 1920), 65mm nitrate print and the resulting projected image recreated by a 35mm polyester print made in 1999. The black and white film was run horizontally in front of three lenses with green, blue and red filters (George Eastman House).

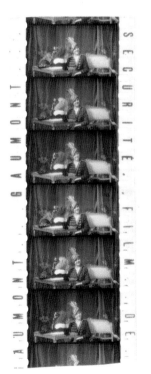

PLATE 61
Chronochrome Gaumont. *Paris Fashion: Latest Sprint Hats* [English release title] (France, 1913), 35mm diacetate print. Black and white panchromatic film, to be projected through a triple lens vertical unit with blue, red and green filters. The lenses were converged in order to produce a single colour image, recreated by a 35mm acetate print made in 1993 (George Eastman House).

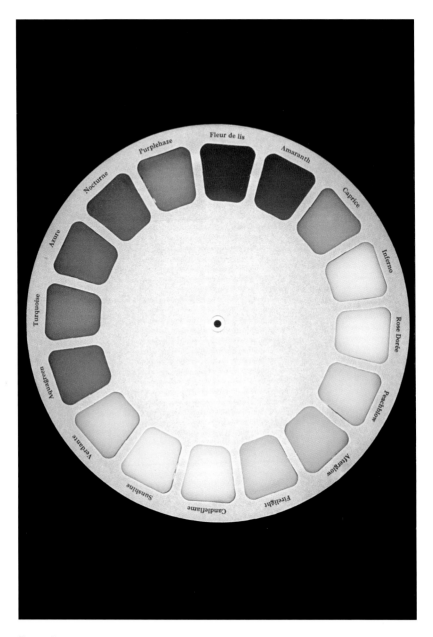

P<small>LATE</small> 62
Kodak Sonochrome (*c.* 1929). Sample plate of tinted film stock from *Eastman Sonochrome Positive Film Tints* (Rochester: Eastman Kodak Company, no date). Actual size, 25.5 cm (George Eastman House).

4
Raiders of the Lost Nitrate

When does posterity begin?

Penelope Houston, quoted by Richard Roud in *A Passion for Films*, 1983

The Pioneers and the Institutions: Collectors, Collections, Archives

Towards the middle of the 30s, with the birth of the cultural movement that was to give rise to an international association of film archives, the wealth of film history already seemed little more than a confused mass of fragments, ignored by official culture and left to moulder in the warehouses. That this was not a universal rule is thanks to those individuals who – investing time, money, and commitment – laid the foundations of the archive collections which we are able to access today.

Their names are known to anyone who has been in contact, even superficially, with the changing galaxy of moving images they created: Henri Langlois in France, Ernest Lindgren in United Kingdom, Jacques Ledoux in Belgium, Iris Barry and James Card in the United States, Mario Ferrari and Maria Adriana Prolo in Italy, Einar Lauritzen in Sweden, and many others. All of them pursued their own particular trajectories, with passion and a sense of adventure, with unstinting opposition to institutional bureaucracy, involved in personal conflicts, great projects and burning defeats.

To understand the story of these people, and the reasons why general access to film archives is a relatively recent phenomenon, one must try to imagine the circumstances in which they had to act. At that time, it was an extremely arduous task to try to persuade most intellectuals that cinema was an aesthetic phenomenon with its own dignity, worthy of being spoken and written about with the same respect given to plays, paintings, architectural structures or musical works. This obstacle has been overcome today, in theory at least. In those days, the only way of prevailing over the general indifference was by relying on one's own initiative: to collect films from everywhere, store them somewhere, ensure, somehow, that they would survive, and screen them. If it were not for the drive and persistence of many an unknown Langlois, of anonymous collectors possessed by the nitrate demon, we would have very little to see today.

To assume that such people no longer exist would be a mistake. Collectors are a secretive breed. They mistrust publicity and prefer sometimes to die with their possessions rather than abandon them to what they consider to be an impersonal institution, lacking the enthusiasm and the protective instinct which made it possible to save the films. Consequently, silent films are not to be found exclusively in the organisational structures called film archives: these are only the relatively better-known sector of a vast, mostly unexplored corpus. A fundamental aspect of archive work is making and maintaining contacts with collectors, in the hope of persuading them one day that bare, aseptic vaults are preferable to the dangerous heat of an improvised projection booth in the domestic living room. It is an exhausting, often fruitless task, which occasionally repays the many failures and endless hours of face-to-face discussions, telephone conversations and letters, though the resulting donation may involve only modest quantities of film. But this contradiction forms the basis of the existence of film archives: those in charge of the collections and their collaborators cannot by themselves search every shuttered cinema and every old house where the last reels of nitrate may lie. So, it is fortunate that this army of explorers exists around them.

There are collectors everywhere, and their number seems to multiply every time one makes contact with a new channel of information such as, for instance, a group of initiates interested only in the films starring Tom Mix, or the Italian comedies featuring Kri Kri. At first, these people tend to adopt an understandably defensive attitude. This can degenerate into an obsession when collectors prefer their films to decay under their bed – thus becoming potentially explosive devices – simply because they cannot bear to be physically separated from them.

But those are the rules of the game. One collector in ten may agree, one day, to deposit his or her copies in an archive while maintaining some kind of legal ownership of them (which is another problem, because nobody wants to let anyone else know how they managed to gain possession of the films). One in a hundred may be persuaded to donate the films altogether, and be content to see them gathered in a collection bearing his or her name, undergoing restoration and finally being returned to the screen and the public. People who find nitrate films in their basement often believe they can make a fortune out of it. Curators must use the most convincing arguments to explain that this is not the case, and that it is in their best interest to let the archive restore it in order to make it accessible. Pointing out that preserving films requires a major financial effort, and offering a viewing print of the restored film in exchange for the generosity of the donor, is often the best approach in the negotiation process.

Because films are to be found everywhere, as are those who look for them and collect them in the most picaresque circumstances, it is impossible to compile a reliable census of what silent films have survived the ravages of time and neglect. We can only presume that there are still thousands of them, hidden in the most unlikely corners of the world, and that – except for some miracle – they will not withstand for long the chemical processes of nitrate decay.

In the mid-80s an American archivist, Ronald S. Magliozzi, prepared a list of every short fiction film of the silent period in the member archives of the Fédération Internationale des Archives du Film. At the time, FIAF had eighty affiliates. Thirty-three film archives were willing or able to take part in the project. Altogether, they admitted to holding a little over 9,000 titles. These were listed by Magliozzi in his *Treasures from the Film Archives: A Catalog of Short Silent Fiction Films Held by FIAF Archives* (1988), one of the books which any serious silent film researcher should always keep close at hand.

So, there are no less than 9,000 fiction shorts still extant, plus an unknown but presumably large number of titles not documented by the book. But what is a short film? Magliozzi's answer is flexible: it is a film no longer than 4,000 feet or some 1,200 metres (if a 35mm copy), running up to an hour on the screen. This is a rather generous definition (it is not easy to call a film on four reels 'short', since each reel can be 1,000 feet or 300 metres long), but there is no point in splitting hairs when trying to collect information on existing films. Fiction features and all non-fiction films are excluded from the list. The latter are as numerous and as precious as the fiction features, but are generally little in demand, regrettably, by collectors and researchers.

It is even harder to say how many feature-length films still survive, but a reasonable (though unofficial) estimate might come close to 8,000 titles. This makes for a total of 17,000 films. In addition, we must consider the material kept in archives which did not participate in the survey. In 1988, there were about fifty other archival institutions, but since then, the number of FIAF members has significantly increased, and in all likelihood will continue to do so. It is true that most of the large archives were represented in the survey, but almost all the other fifty, however small, own collections of a respectable size.

Other prints have come to light since Magliozzi published his inventory, and they probably outnumber the films which have disappeared in the meantime because of chemical decay. All things considered, it is not an exaggeration to suppose that institutions belonging to FIAF own about 30,000 films from the silent period. If the passion we have contracted is not ephemeral, we can relax: a whole lifetime will barely be enough to plough through a corner of this field.

In order to know how large the territory actually is, one must travel. From this point of view, European and North American spectators are in a privileged position: in these two geographic areas there are over fifty film archives of international reputation, various public and private collections which are relatively accessible to scholars, and a number of annual events devoted in whole or in part to the silent film heritage. In other words, seeing films from the first thirty years of the century is much easier in the European Union and the United States than it is in Africa, Asia, South America or Oceania.

This does not mean, however, that silent cinema can be found on any street corner. If we are not satisfied – and we shouldn't be – with a video or digital recording of *Nosferatu* or *The Birth of a Nation* bought in a shop, we have to make an effort, and know where and how to look. Those who have studied silent cinema for an article, a dissertation, or to organise a retrospective, soon learn that the probability of a great discovery increases proportionately to the wish to discover new archives, new collections, and films that have always been there but which nobody has bothered to watch and identify.

RULE 3

Do not limit the scope of your search for prints to
the most obvious sources.
Curiosity will be rewarded in collections outside
mainstream archives.

European and North American archives hold titles from all over the world in quantities sufficient to satisfy most scholars' basic requirements. Sufficient does not mean optimum: as can logically be expected, archives usually offer researchers a large number of films produced within that country's national boundaries, and send them elsewhere if they wish to explore exotic territories. This means that some travel is required. Serious study in silent cinema is not something you can do without leaving your room. If you are a student, or if you have only the standard summer holidays available, every journey to a large city – Brussels, Washington, Prague – offers the opportunity to visit a film archive.

It is not even necessary to spend all day in the archive. Opening times often force or allow you (according to temperament) to begin relatively late in the morning, and to switch off the viewing table in mid-afternoon. The only problem may be the first contact with a collector who invites you to his or her private archive. Once mutual trust has been established, it may not be easy to interrupt the screenings. When they feel like it, collectors have no timetable. They will put you up in their own home, among the film cans, and if you let them, they will bring you sandwiches and beer as you sit in their armchair, in front of the portable screen.

In order to know what is available for viewing, you cannot rely on the subject catalogue often used in bibliographic research. First, you need to know what is likely to be available (which films are in the area, and in which archives) and to build a relationship with the so-called 'milieu': people, clubs, associations, university departments, film journals. In theory, one can manage without the milieu and look up the two or three written sources that signal the existence and availability of films: Magliozzi's book is one, and others are listed at the end of this chapter. But catalogues and lists rapidly go out of date. Dialogue with the people and institutions who inquire into the past of the moving image brings considerable advantages: there is a better chance of seeing the film without waiting for a festival or a video release and a greater possibility of transforming research or simple curiosity into a real intellectual adventure.

The most important of these institutions is the Fédération Internationale des Archives du Film: almost every major film archive belongs to it. Established in Paris in 1938, FIAF was the first formal organisation of disparate and heterogeneous currents which finally coagulated into a structure thanks to the efforts of Iris Barry, John Abbott, Frank Hensel, Henri Langlois and Olwen Vaughan in the name of the following common objectives:

- to coordinate the activity of institutions dedicated to searching for and preserving films in each country;

- to encourage the collection and preservation of materials relevant to moving images (in archive jargon, these are usually called 'non-film' collections);

- to encourage the creation of film archives in those countries where there are none;

- to develop cooperation between film archives, ensuring the availability of films and materials related to film for the Federation members;

- to promote and facilitate historical research on the moving image.

In its founding year FIAF consisted of four members: the Reichsfilmarchiv in Berlin, the National Film Library in London (now called the National Film and Television Archive), the Cinémathèque française in Paris, and the Film Department of the Museum of Modern Art in New York. Since then, the number of institutions joining the Federation has constantly increased to well over a hundred at the beginning of the 21st century. Beyond the size of individual film archives, and the commitment each one shows to collecting, cataloguing, preserving and restoring film, the Federation's fundamental prerequisite is that its members shall not operate for profit. In this they are in line with the ideas of the great national libraries and of the institutions founded to preserve the local and international artistic heritage. From this point of view, FIAF is the equivalent of the United Nations in the field of moving images: it has the same problems where at times very different national realities must reach mutual agreement. But FIAF also has greater power to influence the policy of preservation of the materials collected by its members.

Models of Moving Image Archiving

The Fédération Internationale des Archives du Film has among its affiliates the archives of about forty countries worldwide, whose addresses are listed in Appendix 2. The greatest number are in the United States (a dozen film archives in June 2000); France follows with eleven FIAF archives, Italy with seven and the United Kingdom, Germany and Spain with five each. A few nations have three (Canada, Colombia and Mexico) or two (Austria, Brazil, China, Israel, Luxembourg, the Netherlands, Norway, Slovenia, Uruguay, Venezuela). In each of the remaining affiliated countries there is only one film archive. Other nations, which are currently in the majority, have none.

This outline is necessarily provisional, and somehow misleading. New film archives apply every year to join FIAF, while others leave it, due to financial difficulties or incompatibility with its aims. Most countries have national archives dealing with the moving image in a more or less systematic manner, and you would be surprised to see the amazing results achieved by preservationists operating in countries with financial resources close to nil and challenging climates, such as Papua New Guinea or the Philippines. We shall deal here with the organisations that are connected to FIAF, because their statutes almost always allow researchers to have access to collections, according to regulations under some kind of public control, but we cannot stress enough that the researcher should also turn to archives that do not belong to the Federation, as well as to private collections and in general to all those who collect films. Approaching these institutions and people is at times a challenge (even where you expect to get easy access to well-known collections), but it is no less gratifying than digging in a public archive, once we accept the idea that those in charge of the collections cannot afford to ignore the commercial aspects of their activity.

Most FIAF film archives own important collections of silent films; some are richer than others, but the value of a collection does not depend exclusively on its dimensions. Rather than setting down a list of the 'most important' film archives, which would be as ambiguous as it would be arbitrary, it is better to distinguish their objectives and structures, since these two factors govern access to the collections and the type of material which can be consulted in them. According to this approach, the following models of film archive may be identified. They are not mutually exclusive, in the sense that an institution may well belong to more than one category.

National Film Archives

Most institutions specifically dealing with the preservation of the national moving image heritage are state-controlled. Film producers are sometimes required by law to deposit a negative or at least a positive copy of their work in these organisations. This rule is applied in various degrees by institutions such as the Archives du Film in Bois d'Arcy, the Cineteca Nazionale in Rome, the Suomen Elokuva-Arkisto in Helsinki, the National Film and Sound Archive/ScreenSound Australia in Canberra, the Danish Film Institute/Film Archive in Copenhagen, the New Zealand Film Archive/Ngā Kaitiaki o ngā Taonga Whitiāhua in Wellington, and the Dövlät Film Fondu in Baku, Azerbaijan. The Svenska Filminstitutet/Cinemateket in Stockholm is among the best examples in this category: it has preserved and restored every surviving Swedish film and regularly receives copies of new films produced in Sweden. The Motion Picture, Broadcasting and Recorded Sound Division at the Library of Congress in Washington, DC, operates on a similar principle, even if the huge amount of material produced inside the United States compels it to be selective. The Library's fund of viewing prints may be consulted free of charge by bona fide researchers. From 1895 to 1912, early films were deposited as 'paper prints' (see page 3) which have often been transferred onto standard film stock. Since 1942, a print of each film that is copyrighted must be deposited at the Library of Congress according to specific criteria and conditions (a little-known fact in this respect is that not all the films received are retained, as storage and conservation of every single item would be impossible at the current rate of incoming material).

The preservation of the national heritage of moving images is also the reason for the existence of the National Film and Television Archive in London, which, from 1935 to the present, has collected more than 175,000 titles from all parts of the world. There is at the moment no law in the United Kingdom requiring the legal deposit of films (as is the case, for instance, with books), but priority is given to collecting works produced in the United Kingdom.

The National Film and Television Archive is among those FIAF institutions which adhere to a 'non-restrictive' definition of 'national heritage'; this term indicates not only films produced in the archive's country of origin, but also moving images whose historical identity is tied to their commercial and cultural dissemination within that country's boundaries. This does not contradict one of FIAF's fundamental principles, according to which each member of the Federation undertakes to encourage the return of copies to their respective countries of origin.

Major Collections

Some large archives were initiated by a private organisation or a collector, gaining international recognition over the years. Two typical examples are the Cinémathèque française in Paris and the Cinémathèque Royale/Koninklijk Filmarchief in Brussels. The former, established in 1936, was brought to legendary status by Henri Langlois; the latter, set up in 1938, is a public body whose main aim is to preserve films produced in Belgium but is renowned for its impressive collection of foreign films put together by Jacques Ledoux, another founding father of the international archive movement.

Other archives of this type – particularly well-endowed with silent films – are the Národní Filmovÿ Archiv in Prague, whose treasure of almost 30,000 prints is an endless source of discoveries; the Gosfilmofond in Moscow, whose vaults contain large holdings of Russian, Soviet, European and American silent films distributed in Russia before and after the 1917 Revolution; and the State Archives in Krasnogorsk, Russia, a major repository of non-fiction films.

Regional Film Archives

A number of relatively smaller institutions arise out of political decentralisation, or the growth of autonomous cultural and administrative entities. In some countries, like Italy, these processes have had uneven or contradictory results, leading to the creation of institutes that exist on paper but have little operative or decision-making power. Elsewhere the same circumstances have had better results, with archives far from the capital helping state archives to find films and to spread moving image culture.

Two outstanding examples of this are the Cineteca del Friuli, co-organiser of the Pordenone Silent Film Festival (Le Giornate del Cinema Muto), and the Filmoteca de la Generalitat Valenciana, one of the most active institutions in Spain, a country with no less than ten moving archives, five of which are currently FIAF affiliates, the main one being the Filmoteca Española. Fostering the rediscovery of the local motion picture heritage is also the aim of two archives that are not strictly regional, the Scottish Film Archive in Glasgow and the Kinoteka na Makedonija in Skopje.

Municipal Film Archives

Other public and private institutions were established in a city context, following a similar principle of 'decentralisation'. Among them are the Cineteca del Comune di Bologna in Italy (co-organiser of Il Cinema Ritrovato, a festival dedicated to recent restoration work by film archives); the Cinémathèque de Toulouse, whose instigator was another great theorist of film archiving, Raymond Borde; the Cinémathèque Municipale de Luxembourg, the outcome of Fred Junck's dream of a cinephile sanctuary; the Münchner Filmmuseum/Stadtmuseum in Germany, where the films of Bavarian directors are collected and preserved.

Specialised Collections

An increasing number of institutions are focused not on the 'national cinema heritage' but on specific subjects. Examples are the Cinémathèque de la Danse in Paris, a part of the Cinémathèque française; the Musée du Cinéma de Lyon in Villeurbanne, devoted to the Lumière legacy; the Steven Spielberg Jewish Film Archive in Jerusalem; the Filmoteca Vaticana, dealing with works on religious themes; the Film and Video Archive in the Imperial War Museum, London, where material on the two world wars, produced in Britain, Germany, Russia, Italy and Japan is collected along with moving images of the military operations of British and Commonwealth forces from 1914 onwards.

'Programming' Film Archives

The strength of some institutions lies in their approach to access, which chiefly takes the form of public screenings of films collected and restored by the archive staff, or obtained from other commercial and cultural organisations. Among the most active venues for this kind of activity are the Cinémathèque Québécoise in Montreal, the Cinemateca Uruguaya in Montevideo, the Pacific Film Archive in Berkeley, California, the Cinémathèque française in Paris, the Münchner Filmmuseum /Stadtmuseum in Munich (thanks to Enno Patalas, a prophet of the 'preserve, restore, show' philosophy of moving-image archiving) and the Cinémathèque

Royale de Belgique, the only archive in the world with an auditorium devoted exclusively to the screening of silent films with musical accompaniment.

University Film Archives
Institutions for higher education have established collections of moving images in order to satisfy the needs of academic activity and education practices in general. Two excellent examples are to be found in the United States: the Wisconsin Center for Film and Theater Research in Madison, and the UCLA Film and Television Archive in Los Angeles, whose aims soon broadened to include the restoration of films, just like the other major film archives. Being the result of a fashionable tendency in the 60s, which differentiated between 'film archives' and 'film libraries', the university film archive pays special attention to access to the collections. An increasing number of institutions in this category are providing access to their holdings through electronic and digital formats.

Film Museums
While some organisations are committed to preserving as much as possible (ideally, everything), others take a more selective approach and try to build their collections according to the criteria of historical relevance, cultural interest, and aesthetic excellence. This approach to film archiving is endorsed by the Department of Film and Video at the Museum of Modern Art in New York, active since 1935, and the Motion Picture Department at George Eastman House in Rochester, established in 1947 and opened to the public in 1949. Both institutions – under the impulse of curators such as Iris Barry, Eileen Bowser (at MoMA), James Card and George C. Pratt (at GEH) – have become extremely rich in rare or unique prints of silent films and written documents related to the period. Museums also preserve cameras and projectors, posters, sound equipment, scripts, publicity materials, ephemera, and the objects produced at the time which preceded the invention of the photographic moving image. A spectacular collection of pre-cinema artifacts can be found at the Museo Nazionale del Cinema in Turin; and George Eastman House has an impressive range of film equipment from the first thirty years of cinema, sometimes in prototypes which can no longer be found elsewhere. The Musée Henri Langlois at the Cinémathèque française and the Musée du Cinéma linked to the Cinémathèque Royale de Belgique devote particular attention to education in film history. A similar role is played by the non-FIAF American Museum of the Moving Image in Astoria, New York; while London too had briefly (1987–1999) the imaginative but ill-fated Museum of the Moving Image, again a non-FIAF institution.

Finally, apart from the film archives in developing countries (born from the necessity to stop the systematic destruction of moving images from the colonial and postcolonial eras), there are the so-called 'spontaneous' archives and museums which have arisen from the passion and initiative of individual specialists. Among those institutions closest to FIAF's methods and aims, we should mention at least the Cinémathèque Méliès in Paris, the Cinema Museum in London and the former Barnes Museum of Cinematography in St Ives, Cornwall, whose most important holdings are now divided between the Museo Nazionale del Cinema of Turin and a museum in Hove, England, dedicated to the beginnings of British cinema (in 2000, still nascent). Trying to compile a full list of them would be virtually impossible, but more importantly it would be unfair to those who are not exceedingly active in making themselves known or their collections accessible.

The Searchers

As we said earlier, in order to study silent cinema you must be prepared to travel. Little or no research can be completed in this subject – whether by way of articles, books or theses – without the aid of the archives that hold selections of period films and possess the equipment needed to consult these films. That these archives may be far away from your home is no reason to ignore them and neither should that discourage curiosity. Progress in this field is so fast that almost every film archive in the world is adapting, despite technical and financial difficulties, to the standards of the most prestigious European and American models. Everywhere, from Lisbon to Wellington, from Bangkok to Santiago, there is work enough to last for decades.

Outside Europe and North America, you must first choose the archive which corresponds most closely to your chosen research project. Getting to it will take time and money. If you manage to reach the national archives operating outside the FIAF pantheon, so much the better: the most remote collections hide treasures which few other people have been fortunate enough to see. Much also depends on what one can obtain from the archives that have little or nothing in common with FIAF: private collections and corporate companies. In the former, we shall find the kind of behaviour we have already mentioned: secrecy, suspicion, a personalised relation with the researcher, independence from (or hostility towards) film archives whose activity is controlled by public funds. Making contact with the raiders of the lost nitrate is not easy, but a regular attendance at the Giornate del Cinema Muto in Pordenone and Sacile, Italy, the Cinefest in Syracuse, New York, and countless, though little-publicised collectors' conventions organised yearly throughout the world (as well as reading two periodicals, *The Big Reel* and *Classic Images*, both published in the United States), usually guarantee a wealth of useful information.

There are also commercial companies which exploit the cinema of the past for profit by locating, reprinting and selling moving images. Such organisations may not wish to respond to the needs of the researcher, but nothing is lost by trying. Try, in particular, production and distribution companies. Their archives are sometimes vast and their addresses can be found in national corporate yearbooks. Try also firms specialising in providing stock footage, local historical societies and agencies which lend films for education purposes, where these still exist. In some large corporate firms there is often a historical archive of sorts, and it may be possible to find something useful in their offices. In addition, there are political, military, industrial and trade organisations keeping films (especially non-fiction) which are often impossible to find elsewhere. Access to what could be one of the most important 'specialised' archives in the world, the moving-image holdings of the Pentagon, was virtually impossible until a portion of the collection was transferred to the National Archives in Washington, DC, but elsewhere there are good possibilities for doing research, especially if you have good credentials and a well-defined, realistic project.

Finally, have you ever tried asking your neighbour, relatives in the countryside, former cinema owners, the team working on the demolition or restructuring of your local theatre? Did you know that an extraordinary work such as *Kurutta Ippeiji* (*A Page of Madness*, Teinosuke Kinugasa 1926) was found in 1971, in the garden of the house where its director had once lived?

Further Reading
Collectors
The life and work of the founding fathers of the film archival movement is the object of an uneven literature, ranging from gossip to hagiography, consistent with their eccentric and often flamboyant personalities. A dazzling document on the transition from collecting to restoring silent films is provided by James Card, *Seductive Cinema. The Art of Silent Film* (New York: Knopf, 1994), presented as a book on film history yet to be read as an intellectual autobiography of the first curator at George Eastman House. Jacques Ledoux, curator of the Royal Film Archive of Belgium, is remembered in Anne Head (ed.), *A True Love for Cinema*, (The Hague: Universitaire Pers Rotterdam, 1988) and Dominique Nasta (ed.), *Jacques Ledoux, L'Éclaireur*, special issue of *Revue belge du cinéma*, no. 40, November 1995. Two biographies have been published on Henri Langlois, by far the most written about of the group: Glenn Myrent and Georges P. Langlois, *Henri Langlois, premier citoyen du cinéma* (Paris: Denoël, 1986); translated into English as *Henri Langlois, First Citizen of Cinema* (New York: Twayne, 1995), and Richard Roud, *A Passion for Films* (Baltimore, MD: Johns Hopkins University Press, 1999). *Le Dragon et l'alouette: Correspondance 1948–1979*, edited by Sergio Toffetti (Torino: Museo Nazionale del Cinema, 1992) is a selection of the correspondence between Langlois and Maria Adriana Prolo, founder of a museum of cinema and pre-cinematic artifacts in Turin, Italy.

Moving Image Archives
A fascinating introduction to the world of film archives is provided by Raymond Borde – former curator of the Cinémathèque de Toulouse, and an authoritative voice of FIAF – in *Les Cinémathèques* (Paris: L'Âge d'Homme, 1983), followed by his startling critique of the field in *La Crise des cinémathèques ... et du monde* (Lausanne: L'Âge d'Homme, 1997) written with his colleague Freddy Buache, himself a former curator at the Cinémathèque suisse. *50 ans d'Archives du Film/50 Years of Film*

Archives (Brussels: FIAF, 1988) features descriptions of FIAF and its members (78 at the time): this book is an update of *International Federation of Film Archives* (Paris: FIAF, 1958), published for the twentieth anniversary of the Federation; see also Herbert Volkmann, *Film Preservation. A Report of the Preservation Committee of the International Federation of Film Archives* (London: National Film Archive, 1965), technically outdated yet still valuable as historical document and preliminary reading; Penelope Houston, *Keepers of the Frame: The Film Archives* (London: British Film Institute, 1994); Anthony Slide, *Nitrate Won't Wait. A History of Film Preservation in the United States* (Jefferson, NC and London: McFarland, 1992); David Francis, 'Définition et fonction des archives cinématographiques', in Emmanuelle Toulet (ed.), *CinéMémoire* (Paris: Centre National de la Cinématographie/Ministère de la Culture et de la Communication, 1991), pp. 29–33. Two brief but illuminating accounts of the situation in Europe and in the United States can be found in the report edited in 1991 by Michelle Aubert on behalf of the Association des Cinémathèques de la Communauté Européenne, *Les archives et les cinémathèques européennes: état de leurs activités*, and David Francis, 'Film Conservation Center. A Pioneer in Saving Movies', *Library of Congress Information Bulletin*, vol. 50 no. 1, 14 January 1991, pp. 3–6.

Archival Holdings
Wolfgang Klaue, *World Directory of Moving Image and Sound Archives* (Munich: K.G. Saur, 1993) features a list of 577 non-profit organisations worldwide, from Abu Dhabi to Zimbabwe. A comprehensive index of commercial and non-commercial archives can be found in *Footage. The Worldwide Moving Image Sourcebook* (New York: Second Line Search, 1997), a massive and invaluable research tool for any serious film scholar, also available on CD-Rom (contact: www.footagesources. com). Published lists of archives and viewing prints quickly become obsolete, and can be incomplete or inaccurate; a direct and responsible contact with the institutions relevant to your research is by far the best way to go. However, a limited number of written and electronic sources is likely to make your work easier. Several years after its publication, Ronald S. Magliozzi (ed.), *Treasures from the Film Archives: A Catalog of Short Silent Fiction Films Held by FIAF Archives* (Metuchen, NJ, and London: The Scarecrow Press, 1988) is still a key source on 9,033 silent short films held by thirty-three FIAF institutions. The occasional inaccuracies in filmographic data are mostly due to the inherent limitations in the cataloguing systems of the contributing archives, and by no means affect the importance of this pioneering work. The Federation compiled in 1987 an untitled book (known by the cognoscenti as the *FIAF Black Book*) with information on the archival holdings of 5,899 titles held by forty-seven archives. This document, available exclusively to the staff of the FIAF archives participating in the survey, has been for a long time the Holy Grail of researchers and was circulated for a long time in bootleg copies. The book was the last instalment of a series of indexes and catalogues which became

part of FIAF's Embryo Project, an ongoing census of silent films whose copies were held by the members of the Federation. In the 90s, a portion of the list became public with the *International Film Archive CD-Rom*, a compilation of databases and bibliographies which is an essential working tool for the earnest silent film researcher. While the CD-Rom is revised twice a year, its silent film database (the *Treasures* section) has not been updated since 1995.

Over the years, film archives have published partial lists of their holdings or catalogues of their restorations. Among them are the *National Film Archive Catalogue of Viewing Copies 1985* (London: BFI, 1984); *National Film Archive Catalogue. Part I, Silent News Films, 1895–1933* (1965); *Part II, Silent Non-Fiction Films, 1895–1934* (1960); *Part III, Silent Fiction Films (1895–1930)* (1966); *National Film Archive Catalogue, Volume 1: Non-Fiction Films* (1980); Elaine Burrows, Janet Moat, David Sharp and Linda Wood (eds), *The British Cinema Source Book. BFI Archive Viewing Copies and Library Materials* (London: BFI, 1995); Kemp R. Niver, *Motion Pictures from the Library of Congress Paper Print Collection, 1894–1912* (Berkeley: University of California Press, 1967); *Catalog of Holdings. The American Film Institute Collection and the United Artists Collection at the Library of Congress* (Washington, DC: American Film Institute, 1978); Rita Horwitz and Harriet Harrison (eds), *The George Kleine Collection of Early Motion Pictures in the Library of Congress: A Catalog* (Washington, DC: Library of Congress, 1980); *Restaurations et tirages de la Cinémathèque française*, vols. 1–4 (Paris: La Cinémathèque française, 1986–9); Jon Gartenberg (ed.), *The Film Catalog: A List of Holdings in the Museum of Modern Art* (Boston, MA: G.K. Hall & Co., 1985); *Circulating Film Library Catalog* (New York: The Museum of Modern Art, 1984), updated in *Circulating Film Library Catalog, Volume 2* (1990). Information on surviving Russian and German silent films can be found in Yuri Tsivian *et al.*, *Silent Witnesses. Russian Films, 1908–1919* (Pordenone: Edizioni Biblioteca dell'Immagine/London: BFI, 1989; distributed in the United States by Indiana University Press); Paolo Cherchi Usai and Lorenzo Codelli (eds), *Before Caligari. German Cinema, 1895–1920* (Pordenone: Biblioteca dell'Immagine, 1990, distributed in the United States by the University of Wisconsin Press).

Legal Issues

Birgit Kofler, *Legal Questions Facing Audiovisual Archives* (Paris: UNESCO, 1991); Edith Kramer, 'Should a FIAF Archive ask for Copyright Clearance before Showing a Film?', *Journal of Film Preservation*, vol. 22 no. 17, October 1993, pp. 51–2; Michael Henry, 'Copyright, Neigbouring Rights and Film Archives', *Journal of Film Preservation*, vol. 23 no. 49, October 1994, pp. 2–9.

Festivals

Viewing silent films outside film archives – particularly for those who cannot afford frequent travel – is a rewarding experience at the annual silent film festival – Le Giornate del Cinema Muto – held in Pordenone and Sacile, Italy (contact:

www.cinetecadelfriuli.org), with a focus on history and the dialogue between archives and researchers. Silent cinema is also prominent in the schedule of Il Cinema Ritrovato in Bologna, Italy (contact: www.cinetecadibologna.it), a showcase for European archives and preservation projects. The *Syracuse Cinefest* (contact: Syracuse Cinephile Society, c/o Phil Serling, 215 Dawley Road, Fayetteville, New York 13066-2546), *Cinecon* in Los Angeles (contact: 3405 Glendale Blvd, Suite 251, Los Angeles, CA 90039; website: www.mdle.com/Classic Films/) and *Cinesation* in Saginaw, Michigan (contact: Great Lakes Cinephile Society, PO Box 352, Frankenmuth, Michigan 48734; website: www.cinephiles.org) are the privileged forums of film collectors in the United States, with a strong emphasis on silent rarities and the trade of 16mm prints, posters and memorabilia. Scholarly research is at the heart of Domitor, the international society for early cinema studies (contact: domitor-admin@cri.histart.umontreal.ca) whose conferences take place every two years in different countries, with panels and screenings organised by archives and academic institutions. The above venues (together with Pesaro, Avignon, CinéMémoire in Paris) were for a long time the only places where silent films would see the light. Times have changed, and virtually every festival now features at least one 'special event' or retrospective, often surrounded by the aura of a live music performance. This may be the indication of an encouraging trend, or the evidence that viewing a silent film on a large screen with an orchestra is bound to become a wholly different kind of cultural phenomenon, more or less the equivalent of an opera house event.

The epigraph at the beginning of this chapter is taken from Richard Roud, *A Passion for Films. Henri Langlois and the Cinématheque Française* (New York: The Viking Press), p. 92.

5
F for Filmography

Although our information is false, we do not guarantee it.

Erik Satie

Why Do We Need Written Sources?

A study of film history based exclusively on paper documents is almost bound to remain incomplete unless the subject in question is tangential to the production of moving images, such as distribution, the architecture and design of projection halls, the patent wars, and so on. In any event, even in such cases, it would still be useful to know which films were distributed; what was the relation between the images projected onto the screen and the space that surrounded them; to what model of perception the rival technologies and patented inventions referred. On the other hand, an analysis of silent films that does not take into account the publications available at that time and the in-depth studies derived from them is equally bound to remain inadequate. For research to stand a chance of success, we must have information that only books, articles and magazines can offer. It is true that the skill to identify a film and to recognise the particular style of a production company or a period is acquired only by watching and carefully studying hundreds of films. However, many secrets are buried in the pages of periodicals, catalogues, memoirs and legal documents. Without these, films are silent witnesses of indecipherable projects and ambitions.

Moreover, whenever we study the past, it is useful to have some basic knowledge of other disciplines such as literature, music, architecture, politics and economics relevant to the period. In addition, a familiarity with legal dimensions helps, as does a knowledge of the history of fashion, of uniforms and railway lines, of colonial wars and of car licence numbers. Having seen thousands of films is no reason to underestimate the importance of a wide-ranging general culture; the rest, the so-called 'specialised literature', is little more than a tool of the trade, like the viewing table and a well-organised filing system.

Although they are not always easy to find, the key preliminary texts on early film history are fairly few. A bibliography of about 100 titles published during the silent era, thoroughly examined, guarantees a sound basis. The number of specialised studies from recent times is vast, but on closer inspection of the roughly 500 books currently available on the subject, much fewer are really vital. The others – granted that some may be read simply for pleasure – will be useful mainly or exclusively as a source of inspiration, to find or identify a quotation, for textual details or pointers to other written sources. If you are not a collector – and if you are, the following advice is useless – vast amounts of bookshelf space are not the first requirement. Library collections, in film archives and public institutions, exist precisely for this purpose. On the other hand, you do need the books that you will have to consult continuously, the ones that wear out through use and in which you are likely to find, at some time in the future, precious clues, even though you may have already investigated dozens of different subjects via the most disparate research methods.

At the end of each chapter in this book an attempt is made to provide an outline of a basic bibliography for research into silent cinema. The list of recommended titles for each subject has been kept within manageable proportions so that it will not be necessary to cultivate this interest at the price of abandoning the purchase of other books, listening to music, or subscribing to non-film periodicals. Here we want to concentrate on describing research materials in general: to discover what they are for; to establish what we can draw from them, and, above all, to learn how not to fall into their traps by distinguishing between what they can or cannot tell us.

Primary Sources

With the birth of photography, around 1840, a new form of visual expression announced its existence to the world not only through the objects it produced, but also through the written word. Such a phenomenon was unheard of: it was as if the invention wanted to present and judge itself together with and at the very same time as the rise of the techniques and projects which gave it life. The same phenomenon recurred a few decades later, in the early days of moving photography: scientific publications, theatre magazines, intellectuals and the press all pounced on the cinema, explaining how it worked and how it could work better, on what conditions society could admit it without endangering public morality, and why the world of culture should incorporate or reject it.

The amount of documents produced on this subject in a little over thirty years is so massive that collecting them all is a hopeless task. Many have been lost or destroyed, because few people thought them worth preserving. This should not come as a surprise: civilisation in the late 19th and early 20th centuries was already affected by the frenzy of the ephemeral, throwing away after use works which today we believe to be extremely important: the architecture of the Universal Exhibitions, pulp fiction, the operettas of Meilhac and Halévy. That material, which was mostly considered to be of such low status that even national libraries often disdained to collect it, constitutes the primary source material for studying silent cinema. In this context, 'primary source' does not simply refer to the films, to the surviving 'copies', but includes the written material – whether published or not – from the period of the films' distribution. Finding extant material of this kind is easier today than it was at the time of the great pioneer film historians like Georges Sadoul or Jean Mitry, but what we have is only a tiny part of what we might have had. However, there is no point complaining. Tackling historical research means dealing with some rules of the game, and one of the most important is to take into account, with the necessary perspicacity, the fact that existing information is incomplete. In a way, history has already selected what we shall or shall not be able to know, leaving us the possibility and the responsibility of interpreting the gaps on the basis of surviving fragments.

These fragments are the coordinates of our search for evidence. We can do without many secondary sources, and as a matter of principle we must be very cautious with most filmographies, but we cannot claim really to know silent cinema if we cannot find our way among the vast galaxy of surviving papers: production lists, photographs, actors' memoirs, account books, legal documents, telegrams, reviews, posters, music scores, copyrights and minutes of meetings. Some fragments are even more difficult to access: projectors, cameras, costumes, architectural structures, processing equipment. Film museums exist for their preservation too, and these items should be organised, visited and experienced with the same care and attention one would devote to a rare book.

Trade periodicals, which sprang up a few years after the birth of the moving image, are the sources on which all previous historians have drawn, more or less systematically. By leafing through a volume, it is often possible to establish which magazines were examined by a certain author and which were not, but we would do better to spend our time consulting these journals as often as possible. In some countries, film archives have exhaustive collections or reproductions of such journals, but it is equally important to visit national libraries and, if necessary, to reproduce for everyday use as many pages as possible of articles, lists of film releases and addresses of production companies.

In the English-speaking countries, the most obvious destinations are the British Film Institute in London and the Library of Congress in Washington, DC, which own excellent collections of periodicals published in Britain and the United States. But magazines in English are not enough, and they are not the most important sources of information if one is interested in French, German or Italian cinema. There was a time when anyone wishing to consult foreign periodicals had no alternative but to travel to the country in question, just as one must travel in order to see the films. Things have improved now that several titles are on microfilm or have been stored on other media and can be sent by mail, bought and reproduced (this also enables the original, frequently printed on poor quality paper unfitted to withstand the assault of a platoon of researchers, to be left undisturbed).

If two or three years are to be spent researching French silent cinema, we should certainly consider, for example, buying the relevant volumes of French magazines on microfilm and consulting them in the nearest library that disposes of a microfilm reader. This is not a negligible investment, but it is a wise one: it saves trouble; it provides us with an important research tool, and once the research is finished, we can always sell the microfilm at least for a price close to the one we paid for it. If your interest in film history is a longer-term preoccupation, you might even consider buying a portable microfilm reader which you can carry home in a briefcase and use anywhere, on a corner of your desk or on a shelf: it is more expensive, but still less than one would spend on a modest personal computer.

Film magazines of the silent period are so numerous that they would require a bibliography of their own, and there is no room here to list them all. The names of some, however, crop up regularly and represent the research territory from which we can draw a crucial part of our knowledge. This does not mean that a familiarity with these magazines exempts us from consulting others, but they will do for a start, and one has to start somewhere. For the time being, it is less important deciding whether or not a bibliography is truly exhaustive, than knowing how to work with periodicals on silent film. Working with old magazines is never as simple as consulting a book neatly divided into chapters and with an index, or even as consulting a modern specialised journal. Leafing through an old periodical is both a pleasure and an adventure for the eyes: it is like travelling in a time machine, and reliving – with no filters of any kind – the enthusiasms and tensions of a project in process. But it is an adventure that requires patience, precision and a certain amount of unrelenting stubbornness.

RULE 4

Historical written documents on silent
cinema should be consulted analytically rather
than selectively.

In other words, if we are searching through a silent film periodical to find information about our subject, we should (ideally) go through the whole thing. It seems madness, but we must accept the idea that a piece of essential information could be in a tiny recess of the most insignificant article. Many years ago, American specialists used to ask Italian film historian, Davide Turconi, where he found the cast and credits of films about which little or nothing is known in the United States. Turconi candidly replied that the columns of answers to readers' questions in American magazines include fragments of evidence which are virtually impossible to find elsewhere, and that the names of performers are among them.

If we decide to study the films of Frank Borzage we could be satisfied with the existing filmographies, but a glance at the magazines of the time reveals that the circumstances of his beginnings in cinema are still unclear. Before becoming a director, Borzage acted in several films: some of the titles are still unknown, as are the names of their scriptwriters, technicians and cast members. So, if we want to do things thoroughly, we should use published filmographies as provisional reference points, diving headlong into the pages of *The Moving Picture World* and the other magazines of the time when Borzage had his apprenticeship.

Film titles, patents for new types of film stock, projectors or cameras, companies starting up, winding down or changing name, portraits of forgotten celebrities, embryos of theory, projects for films which would never be released, meetings between directors and producers, dates of birth and death, complaints and denials, debates on political or educational subjects: we can expect to find none of these items if we are content merely to scan the headlines, skipping the often mediocre and repetitive articles, in small print, where for every useful snippet of information one has to sift through thousands of words quite superfluous to our aims. It may be that Borzage's silent films are of interest to us because of what he did as a director, and it may be that these films alone are the subject of our research; however, we may discover that Borzage made a print which is not in any filmography, and that a print still exists. Why deny this possibility? Of course, finding a lost Borzage is a happy, though rare occurrence, but if we lack the means to determine the authorship of a newly discovered film, that is one golden opportunity lost. As François Truffaut used to say, one must deserve coincidences.

A similar argument is true for other primary sources from which any research on cinema, and not just silent cinema, draws its inspiration and substance:

- *books*: projection manuals, histories of the cinema written when cinema did not yet have a history, instructions on how to handle film in the laboratory, first attempts at formulating theories, biographical writings, memoirs, discussions on the morality and otherwise of the moving image, stories and novels based on the production and screening of films;

- *production materials*: contracts, regulations, correspondence between producers, directors, performers, scriptwriters, distributors; scripts, shooting and tinting lists, musical scores, publicity releases, shipment registers, letters to administration offices;

- *production stills*, from which we might be able to identify an otherwise unknown performer, a set component typical of this or that production company, an interesting piece of lighting equipment;

- *film posters*, made by artists who often deserve the same attention that is usually paid to the works they advertised, and whose techniques reflect the relationship between the industry and its audience;

- *unpublished manuscripts*: memos, drafts of projects that never materialised, viewing notes, letters, diaries and many other things, down to scrapbooks of newspaper cuttings and postcards with dedications; cinema programmes; glass slides publicising forthcoming films.

In short, any object connected to the moment when silent cinema entered the lives of spectators from the end of the 19th century to the early 20th century potentially contains historical data. The preferred sources of filmographers such as catalogues, production and censorship bulletins are quite another matter. We shall talk about them shortly. Before doing so, mention must be made of the contemporary evidence which we cannot look for in the library or in the projection room: that is, film equipment. Few people resort to pieces of film machinery as sources of information: it is harder to get access to them, and it is still harder to handle them without some basic technical know-how. Furthermore, many film students are accustomed to the notion that research is an activity done mainly in an area defined by their mind, the computer keyboard, and the library. The idea that it might involve a certain amount of work on the film itself is naturally (though not always) taken for granted, but this fact is often accepted in a rather passive manner: there are scholars who pretend they can manage perfectly well without closely examining a film on the viewing table once they have seen it on the big screen. For others, having to handle the actual print is a nuisance they are happy to avoid, even to the point of giving up any contact with film altogether for a reproduction on a different medium. (A university teacher once expressed exultation at the news that a title on which she had written an entire book but never seen on film had always been available on 35mm at the George Eastman House. That's not a good sign.)

Equipment takes this conflict to its extreme, because it is no longer a matter of seeing a film in the projection room or examining it at close range, but of verifying what has allowed it to exist as a physical and aesthetic object: the camera, the printer, the projector. But getting to know this 'material' aspect is actually decisive, inasmuch as it helps one better to understand why a film was seen one way rather than another, why it was often shown in segments rather than as a continuous flow of images, and why these images appeared more or less clear or more or less steady according to the equipment used.

You may or may not enjoy getting your hands dirty in order to find out how a three-blade shutter or a 'Maltese cross' mechanism works, but there is no doubt that cinema is primarily a mechanical process, and we must understand its rudiments if we do not want our knowledge to be left suspended in an abstract reality, halfway between philosophical speculation and *a priori* judgment. In order to understand silent film we must – from time to time – let our imagination leave the theatre crowded with people and musicians and go to see what is happening in the projection booth, especially when the projectionist is busy changing reels.

Secondary Sources

A primary source provides factual information from the period under study; a secondary source attempts to explain the meaning of this information in relation to other facts. In silent film studies, however, this has sometimes been done in an arbitrary manner, distorting both the primary documents and the research findings. In some cases this distortion has had long-lasting effects: it has been said for forty years that *The Jazz Singer* was the first sound film in the history of cinema, and it may take even longer to erase that misconception from film encyclopaedias, if this ever happens. This is why we distinguish between primary and secondary sources. If someone claims, without adequate proof, that *Das Cabinet des Dr. Caligari* is the first film of German Expressionist cinema, we are left with two options: to accept the claim as correct, because everybody seems to believe it; or to doubt it and not to repeat that assertion next time we write about German Expressionism, at least until primary sources and the films we have seen have been convincing enough to support the claim.

Film history is full of categorical statements such as this on *Caligari*, not because scholars were incompetent or dishonest, but because the discipline has often had to serve the myth in order to acquire dignity in the eyes of those who, for decades, have denied cinema any right of cultural citizenship. Thus it has been written that Georges Méliès made 1,500 films; that *Cabiria* was the first film where the camera was put on rails for tracking shots; that, again, *Das Cabinet des Dr. Caligari* was the first Expressionist film. None of this is true. But when such statements were published for the first time, there was probably a reason – a cultural and ideological reason, at least – for spreading them.

Fortunately, there is continuous and steady progress in cinema studies, and many of these misconceptions have been refuted or reappraised. Similar assumptions – expressed in subtler and more insidious forms – are to be found in highly respected books and articles. And yet we should not disregard these works altogether, unless we want to become ourselves the victims of the determinist attitude for which we too often reproach our predecessors; on the contrary, we should keep in mind the convictions and the 'truths' they set out, and the role they played before their claims were tested by facts. Nevertheless, precautions are in order if past errors are not to endanger future research. The safest precaution is doubt:

RULE 5

Beware of scholarly writings where
no information is given in order to
verify the source of controversial data.

In order to prevent an excessively rigid application of this rule, some distinctions have to be made at this point. The first concerns the right to a margin of error for those who have opened the way for us. Film historians writing in the 1940s might have had at their disposal material which later disappeared, but they certainly did not possess the documentary and operational tools which today are accessible to all. It would have been helpful and would have spared us many false trails and much effort if sources had, in some cases, been identified more carefully. But the kind of cultural struggle which was being fought only a decade or two after the twilight of silent cinema was quite different from today, and – for better or worse – ensuring the kind of objectivity and precision we have a right to expect in a book or an article written today was not the highest priority.

The second distinction concerns the results achieved between then and now in the context of historical, aesthetic and theoretical research about cinema, and the mentality that derives from it. If we had to distinguish what is really invaluable in the huge bibliography of silent film, not very many books and articles would pass the accuracy test. The first victims would be works written without care for precision and detail, hastily published in order to rescue from shameful oblivion many great personalities of the past. To most people, artists such as Lois Weber, Léonce Perret and James Williamson were names without an identity: exaggeration was the price to be paid in order to restore their place in history. It was as if overexposing the negative was the only way to bring out certain details of a photograph, even to the detriment of the chiaroscuro balance. Again, somebody had to start somewhere. Several books written and published in the period between 1930 and 1970, especially in France and the United States, are unreliable in terms of factual accuracy, yet they are of great importance for those who want a vivid impression of the world in which the people who brought cinema to life, and gave it its silent glory, lived and breathed. Besides, some accounts openly based on anecdote and verbal memory may include important truths, confirmed only much later, at the end of long and difficult archive research.

Just as one should not automatically reject 'impressionist' histories of cinema, so it is unwise to place unconditional trust in those who deluge us with superfluous details, vast quantities of footnotes and arcane arguments yielding marginal results. An intricate scholarly apparatus sometimes hides a lack of creativity and insight. We shall return to this problem in Chapter 7. But it must be stressed here that reading theoretically and analytically complex works should not lead us to adopt a passively deferential attitude towards them. Journalists' reminiscences, studies inspired by an uneducated passion, biographies based on faulty memories can be misleading, but never as misleading as an essay that daunts the reader with unnecessary figures, allusions and neologisms. As novelist E.M. Forster pointed out in relation to literary practice, at the end of even the most meticulous search among the events and ideas of the past, comes the responsibility of 'telling a story', that is, making meaning out of our discoveries in a way that may encourage others to listen to the account and go further in analysing its implications. This, too, is a rule which was certainly not invented by film history, but which is vital for its evolution and appeal among future generations.

The Filmographer's Nightmare

With the issue of filmographies we reach the core of the obsessions and frustrations of those who study and examine the industrial and creative output of silent cinema from a scholarly perspective. There are many things we can live without in film history, but we certainly need to know who made which films, when this happened, where and by which production company.

From an analytical standpoint, novelty is only one of a film's relevant features. For example, we may notice that a silent film makes an innovative use of artificial lighting, yet our awareness has little consequence if we do not know when the film was made. If it is a very early film, its importance is likely to increase in the context of our research; if it is a later film, ours is no longer a discovery, but a further proof of what had already been done by someone else. In order to establish or discuss priorities, developments and influences, our knowledge of the essential data concerning each film must be solid and reliable. In brief, we need a filmography.

This need is far from new. However, it has developed over the years in different and sometimes contradictory ways. Every phase in the growth of film studies has had the filmography it deserved: each with its own standards of completeness, its own unanswered questions, its own methods of collecting and presenting data. None is better or worse than the others, because none has survived the tendency which generated it.

The first in chronological order is what might be called the 'cultural' filmography, conceived in order to reinforce with summary information the statements of those who embarked on the rediscovery or the reassessment of a neglected personality, according to the above mentioned 'revisionist' tendency in film history. These filmographies, which were produced towards the end of the 30s (they began to decline only a quarter of a century later), had no claim to scientific accuracy; they often opened with such sentences as: '1910. About forty films, among which . . .' The films were, at best, listed in alphabetical order: incomplete or incorrect titles, confusion with dates, false attributions were common. This, however, was less important than stating that the films made by someone in that year were 'about forty', that is to say, 'many', and therefore that the *auteur* in question had worked hard.

The results achieved thanks to analogical filmographies were less short-lived. They were created by diligently assembling and copying company production lists: praiseworthy work – particularly because these documents were already becoming scarce – but not devoid of uncertainties and errors. The reliability of the filmography was in proportion to the care taken in reproducing the original data, without distortion but also with a minimum of discussion. Starting from this system, the first serious work of filmography began with the Museum of Modern Art monographs on D.W. Griffith and Douglas Fairbanks and the British Film Institute 'Index' series, inaugurated in 1943, including Georges Sadoul's filmography of Georges

Méliès, Theodore Huff's of Charles Chaplin and Seymour Stern's of Griffith – together initiating a historiographical methodology worthy of the name.

A few years later two more models of filmography emerged. The first – credited to Jean Mitry – was the plan for a universal filmography. This soon proved to be a utopian undertaking, but the project at the very least had the merit of finally making clear the scale of the task facing film historians. It was no longer a matter of mentioning 'about forty films, among which …', but of compiling dozens of volumes. The second model, which derived from the first, was the 'authorial' filmography which flourished in French film magazines of the 1960s. These were a wisely revised variation on what had been done via cultural filmographies. The difference lay mainly in an ambition to be scientific which may, at times, have been stated in peremptory terms, but was no less healthy for all that. The problem was that, once the filmography was published, few people dared question it, especially since it was phrased by the historians responsible for compiling the filmography in terms closely resembling a 'take it or leave it' approach. Furthermore, it was difficult to check, even if someone had wanted to, because the sources from which the data were derived were rarely given.

Authorial filmography dominated the field unopposed for almost two decades, barely threatened by a few important exceptions, until the new ideal of the analytical filmography became widespread among those who were fed up with phantom sources and endless (and above all, uncheckable) lists of titles and names which one had to use as if they were definitive filmographies while hoping for the best. The analytical filmography is still the one most often aimed at, at least in intention, but it has already given rise to two collateral phenomena which deserve to be mentioned.

The first is that of not publishing a filmography at all, because it is assumed – often with reason – that it is not yet complete. The author of such a filmography has been the victim of all earlier filmographies, and rather than repeat the mistakes of the past she prefers to wait for some as yet unpublished source to reveal the mystery of what the available documents have not yet made clear. The same attitude is responsible for the opposite extreme, which consists of publishing everything, even the titles of films that perhaps have never been released or were never completed.

One may say that too much is better than nothing, and so it is; however, some filmographies belonging to this category are so labyrinthine that they almost become substitutes for histories of cinema, no longer divided into chapters but into alphabetical, chronological and subject indexes. Every title is described with such precision and such a wealth of detail that actually seeing the film risks becoming a redundant exercise. Each entry can take up scores of pages, betraying one of the main aims of a filmography: to be a flexible, trustworthy and lasting reference tool for study and identification. This kind of monster filmography also has the frequent disadvantage of being 'unfinished'. Indeed, its authors are often exhausted before they complete even a small part of it. But there is no sense condemning these filmographers for following a dream which all silent film historians cherish at least once in their lives. Their unachieved design of an information structure is actually praiseworthy, because it may drive us to explore virgin territories and archives in which few serious researchers have previously set foot. This will always be the case, because there is no such thing as a self-sufficient and ideal filmography. There are, however, many possible models of filmography, all of which suit different purposes, and are not mutually exclusive.

If we are not convinced, we might do well to remember that an 'ultimate' analytical filmography of Charles Chaplin's films has yet to be published. None of the existing ones is free from more or less serious gaps or conceptual flaws, due in part to their authors, and sometimes to the mistakes of earlier filmographies which are repeated simply because the newcomer believes that her predecessors had access to who knows what mysterious source of information. When confronted with any filmography that does not say where the data come from, you must behave as you behave with all secondary sources, and be wary. Always be wary.

Who then should you trust? Above all, your own sense of moral integrity. Just make very clear to yourself and the reader what you wish to achieve in your potential filmography, and how you are going to organise its most essential information:

- the film title, with all its variants;

- the country (or countries) where the film was produced;

- the full names of the production and distribution companies;

- the full names of the filmmakers and their technical and artistic functions, the leading performers and their roles;

- the length (or lengths) of the film;

- a brief (but very accurate) plot summary;

- the date.

Which date? In this book, the year of release has been chosen as a point of reference, but that's only one among many options. Historians have argued about this since the early days of this discipline, and everyone continues to use the system that suits them best. Some stick to the date of shooting, which can be days, months or years before the official release of a film; others give the date when the film was submitted to a censorship board, something that could happen before or after the film had been completed, again within days, months or years. Finally, there is the release date, which corresponds to the day or week when a film or a group of films was made available to exhibitors; this date is usually (though not always) close to that of the first public showing before a paying audience.

There are of course variations on the above criteria: the first date of approval or revision by the censors (when an earlier version of the film was rejected); the date of the beginning or end of shooting; the date of the first public showing, when this does not correspond to the release date; and so on. What matters now is to avoid being trapped by abstract principles; that is, taking a pragmatic approach to the needs of the research being undertaken.

If we want to study the effect a film had on the style of later works, the point of reference should preferably be the release date, or the date of the first public screening: that is the moment in time when a film becomes part of a cultural environment, influencing the expectations and tastes of the audiences, and affecting the style of other filmmakers. If we are interested in knowing whether a performer worked for a production company at a given time, or wish to verify whether or not a certain filmmaker actually did introduce a new technical or stylistic device, it might be better to check the film's production date. Sometimes it is enough to give only the year of release, without further detail. Once you have made up your mind, always specify which kind of date you are referring to, make sure that you know why you have chosen it, and then stick to the rule you have adopted. You are allowed to deviate from such a rule, as long as you explain the reasons for doing so. Take, for instance, a film released on 10 January 1914, probably made at the end of 1913, and passed through censorship sometime in between. If detail helps making your argument clearer and more cohesive, go for it. If it's irrelevant to your hypothesis, just skip it. Whatever you do, do it for a reason.

A similar precaution is necessary when mentioning the length of the film, expressed in metres or feet according to the country of origin. Lengths vary for reasons that would take many more pages than we can afford here. To make a long story short, we do take for granted the length which appears most frequently in the available written sources; if the length is given in reels or acts, we do not attempt to estimate the length of the film from their number. In the United States and many European nations, a reel of 35mm film measured approximately 300 metres (1,000 feet), but in Sweden and Germany it could correspond to more than 500 metres. In some countries, projectionists would designate as a 'reel' what Americans defined as a 'split reel', that is, a reel of approximately 100–150 metres (400–500 feet).

These precautions should be supplemented by two provisos, which concern us as readers and researchers. The first is making sure that what we get from all this work becomes a tool at our service, and not vice versa: a filmography which exhausts in itself our interest in silent cinema does not deserve to be written. The best filmography, even when it deals with only a dozen titles, is the one that provides a source for each piece of information. The entry may be a little longer, but it will have the advantage of giving the reader a chance to verify the accuracy of all references and the use we made of them. Whenever you feel unsure about the accuracy or reliability of information, do not hesitate to add a question mark between square brackets after the name or the date. A true filmographer is not afraid of question marks: and so it should be, for the history of silent cinema is a work in progress which will certainly not be brought to completion by ourselves.

A good filmography need not contain many variables, but each one must be indicated with the greatest care. One day, perhaps, someone will turn to our filmography for the title of an unidentified film (the archivist's dream filmography). As well as a title list, our filmography might include indexes which subdivide films by dates, production companies, names, characters and even lengths and locations of the extant prints. Speaking of lengths, if a primary source says how many metres were in colour and how many in black and white, it costs us nothing to take note of this. The smallest facts are sometimes useful.

We might understand at this point why catalogues, production company bulletins and some specialised periodicals are so precious. They are not totally free from error, and yet we cannot do without them because they contain the best available information in the absence of the actual films. Obviously, conclusive data are derived from film prints, but since many are known to have disappeared, we can only trust what is closest to films, that is to say, a document from those who produced or distributed it. As well as providing the title and a summary of the plot, catalogues and periodic bulletins will often help us – or make our work more challenging – through illustrations and codes (numbers or words) which are potentially useful for purposes of dating.

So, we have before us everything the silent cinema has left as our inheritance, apart from the surviving copies. Film archives, libraries, universities and private collections from all over the world collect and restore this material; meanwhile, they go on looking for more. We who must work on this material are left with one question: since it is unlikely that all these papers and pieces of equipment will be easily at hand, we should at least ensure that some tools essential to research are in our own home. But which ones? Is there an ideal list of the 'necessary' books and magazines?

Clearly, the answer depends on the nature of the research and the kind of passion for silent film which drives us to buy books and periodicals. Whatever the chosen subject, or the depth of our interest, there are certain books which we should definitely read, and which even a broad-minded cinephile should own in order not to restrict his or her competence to contemporary production. Dozens of titles could be listed, but it would be a subjective selection; it is more profitable, perhaps, to take the list of titles at the end of this chapter as nothing more than a comprehensive rough guide to the field. Some of these books may become favourite bedtime reading; others reflect the author's relation to the silent image, or could encourage the reader to explore new horizons, new perspectives, uncharted research areas. Don't treat it as bibliography. It is an invitation to the pleasures of intellectual discovery.

Further Reading
Bibliographies
Hermann Hecht (edited by Ann Hecht), *Pre-Cinema History. An Encyclopaedia and Annotated Bibliography of the Moving Image before 1896* (London: Bowker-

Saur/British Film Institute, 1993); *Union Catalogue of Books and Periodicals Published before 1914 Held by the Film Archives Members of the International Federation of Film Archives* (Brussels: FIAF, 1967), listing 914 titles held in the collections of the twenty-four archives which took part in the project; Emmanuelle Toulet (ed.), *Bibliographie internationale du cinéma des premiers temps: Travaux des membres de Domitor* (Quebec: Domitor, 1987), a survey of international research on film production up to 1915. Her work has been updated by Elena Dagrada in *International Bibliography on Early Cinema* (s.l.: Domitor, 1985). See also Anna Brady (ed.), *Union List of Film Periodicals: Holdings of Selected American Collections* (Westport, CT: Greenwood Press, 1984).

Documents

The direct and thorough knowledge of contemporary written sources is a vital (and sometimes neglected) component of silent film research. This applies to all genres and sub-genres of film literature, from technical manuals to production catalogues, from critical and corporate journals to popular press and theatre programmes. Classics of early literature on film include Bołeslaw Matuszewski, *Une nouvelle source de l'histoire* and *La photographie animée* (Paris: Noizette, 1898), reprinted in Zbigniew Czeczot-Gawrak (ed.), *Bołeslaw Matuszewski i ego pionierska mysl filmowa* (Warsaw: Filmoteka Polska, 1980) translated as 'A New Source of History', *Film History*, vol. 7 no. 3, Autumn 1995, pp. 322–4 and *A New Source of History/Animated Photography. What It Is, What It Should Be* (Warsaw: Filmoteka Narodowa, 1999), which includes an invaluable set of contemporary documents and reviews of Matuszewski's work; Georges Méliès, 'Les vues cinématographiques', in *Annuaire général et international de la photographie* (Paris: Plon, 1907); Eugène Babin, 'Les coulisses du cinématographe', 'Dans les coulisses du cinématographe', 'Le théâtre cinématographique', *L'Illustration* (Paris), 3396, 28 March 1908; 3397, 4 April 1908; 3427, 31 October 1908; Georg Cohn, *Kinematographenrecht* (Berlin: Decker's Verlag, 1909); Victorin Jasset, 'Études sur la mise en scène en cinématographie', *Ciné-Journal*, nos 165–8 and 170, October–November 1911; Emilie Altenloh, *Zur Soziologie des Kinos* (Jena: Verlag Eugen Diedrichs, 1913); John B. Rathbun, *Motion Picture Making and Exhibiting* (Los Angeles: Holmes, 1914); Hugo Münsterberg, *The Photoplay: A Psychological Study* (New York: Appleton & Co., 1916); Austin C. Lescarboura, *Behind the Motion Picture Screen* (New York: Munn, 1919); Homer Croy, *How Motion Pictures Are Made* (New York: Harper, 1918); Terry Ramsaye, *A Million and One Nights* (New York: Simon and Schuster, 1926). Early writings on film are featured in critical anthologies: George C. Pratt, *Spellbound in Darkness* (Greenwich, CT: New York Graphic Society, 1973); Alberto Abruzzese, *Introduzione allo studio delle teoriche cinematografiche americane, 1910–1929* (Venice: La Biennale di Venezia, 1975); Anton Kaes, *Kino-Debatte. Texte zum Verhältnis von Literatur und Film, 1909–1929* (Tübingen-Munich: Niemeyer-Deutscher Taschenbuch-Verlag, 1978); Fritz Güttinger, *Kein Tag ohne Kino. Schriftsteller über den*

Stummfilm (Frankfurt am Main: Deusches Filmmuseum, 1984); Richard Abel, *French Film Theory and Criticism. A History/Anthology, 1907–1939* (Princeton, NJ: Princeton University Press, 1988); Richard Taylor and Ian Christie (eds), *The Film Factory: Russian and Soviet Cinema in Documents, 1896–1939* (Cambridge, MA: Harvard University Press, 1988; reprint edition, London: Routledge, 1994).

Memoirs

Literature on the subject is vast, often unreliable yet fascinating if you wish to get the atmosphere of the times. The most instructive reminiscences are those of Linda Arvidson, *When the Movies were Young* (New York: E.P. Dutton & Company, 1925); Fred Balshofer and Arthur C. Miller, *One Reel a Week* (Berkeley and Los Angeles: University of California Press, 1967); Karl Brown, *Adventures With D.W. Griffith* (New York: Farrar, Straus & Giroux, 1973); Henri Fescourt, *La Foi et les montagnes* (Paris: Publications Photo-Cinéma Paul Montel, 1959); Lillian Gish, *The Movies, Mr. Griffith and Me* (Englewood Cliffs, NJ: Associated University Presses, 1973); Cecil Hepworth, *Came the Dawn. Memoirs of a Film Pioneer* (London: Phoenix House, 1951); King Vidor, *A Tree is a Tree* (New York: Harcourt, Brace, 1952); Edward Wagenknecht, *The Movies in the Age of Innocence* (Norman: University of Oklahoma Press, 1962).

General Histories

Benjamin B. Hampton, *A History of the Movies* (New York: Covici, Friede, 1931); Maurice Bardèche and Robert Brasillach, *Histoire du cinéma* (Paris: Denoël et Steele, 1935); English translation, *The History of Motion Pictures* (translated and edited by Iris Barry, first curator of the Film Department at MoMA, New York: W.W. Norton/The Museum of Modern Art, 1938); Georges Sadoul, *Histoire générale du cinéma. Vol. 1: 1832–1897; Vol. 2: 1897–1909; Vol. 3: 1909–1920* (Paris: Denoël, 1946–52); Jerzy Toeplitz, *Historia sztuki filmowe* (Warsaw: Filmowa Agenca Wydawnicza, 1955; German translation: *Geschichte des Films*, Munich: Rogner & Bernhard, 1973); Jean Mitry, *Histoire du cinéma: Art et industrie. Vol. 1: 1895–1914; Vol. 2: 1915–1925; Vol. 3: 1923–1930* (Paris: Editions Universitaires, 1967–73); Richard Griffith and Arthur Mayer, *The Movies* (New York: Simon & Schuster, 1957); William K. Everson (uncredited) and Joe Franklin, *Classics of the Silent Film* (New York: Bramhall House, 1959); Jacques Deslandes and Jacques Richard, *Histoire comparée du cinéma. Vol. 1: 1826–1896; Vol. 2: 1897–1906* (Paris: Casterman, 1966–68). A non-systematic yet engaging approach to film history is proposed by Francesco Savio, *Visione Privata* (Rome: Bulzoni, 1972). An outstanding synthesis of silent film history is given by Kristin Thompson and David Bordwell in the first chapters of *Film History: An Introduction* (New York: McGraw-Hill, 1994), complemented by David Bordwell and Kristin Thompson, *Film Art: An Introduction* (New York: McGraw-Hill, 1996, 5th edn); see also Robert Sklar, *Film: An International History of the Medium* (New York: Harry N. Abrams, 1993); Geoffrey

Nowell-Smith, *The Oxford History of Cinema* (Oxford: Oxford University Press, 1996).

Pre-cinema and Film Beginnings
David Robinson, *Origins of Cinema: Catalogue of an Exhibition* (London, Cumberland Row Antiques Ltd., 1964); Eric Barnouw, *The Magician and the Cinema* (New York: Oxford University Press, 1981); Franz Paul Liesegang, *Moving and Projected Images: A Chronology of Pre-Cinema History* (London: The Magic Lantern Society of Great Britain, 1986); *The Ten Year Book*, special issue of *The New Magic Lantern Journal*, vol. 4 nos 1–3, 1986; Carlo Alberto Zotti Minici (ed.), *Il Mondo Nuovo. Le meraviglie della visione dal '700 alla nascita del cinema* (Milan: Mazzotta, 1988); David Robinson, 'Masterpieces of animation, 1833–1908', special issue of *Griffithiana*, vol. 14 no. 43, December 1991; Laurent Mannoni, *Le Grand art de la lumière et de l'ombre. Archéologie du cinéma* (Paris: Nathan, 1994); Deac Rossell, 'A Chronology of Cinema, 1889–1896', special issue of *Film History*, vol. 7 no. 2, Summer 1995; Laurent Mannoni, Donata Pesenti Campagnoni and David Robinson, *Light and Movement: Incunabula of the Motion Picture* (Pordenone, Paris and Turin: Le Giornate del Cinema Muto/Cinémathèque française – Musée du Cinéma/Museo Nazionale del Cinema, 1995); Laurent Mannoni, *Trois siècles de cinéma. De la lanterne magique au cinématographe* (Paris: Éditions de la réunion des musées nationaux, 1995); by the same author, *Étienne-Jules Marey, la mémoire de l'oeil* (Milan-Paris: Mazzotta/Cinémathèque française, 1999). The Projection Box (66 Culverden Road, London SW12 9LS; e-mail: s-herbert@easynet.co.uk) has published a series of studies and rare documents on the precursors of film.

Early Cinema
The FIAF Conference of Brighton (1978) marked the resurrection of studies on early films after decades of neglect. The implications of the Brighton experience are discussed by Eileen Bowser in 'The Brighton Project: An Introduction', *Quarterly Review of Film Studies*, vol. 4 no. 4, Fall 1979, pp. 509–38; see also 'The Brighton FIAF Conference (1978): Ten Years After', *Historical Journal of Film, Radio and Television*, vol. 11 no. 3, 1991, pp. 279–91. The Brighton conference resulted in the publication of two volumes by Roger Holman and André Gaudreault (eds), *Cinema 1900–1906: An Analytical Study* (Brussels: FIAF, 1982), including an analytical filmography of the 548 titles screened at the symposium; by the same author, *Ce que je vois de mon ciné* (Paris: Méridiens Klincksieck, 1988). Emmanuelle Toulet, *Cinématographe, invention du siècle* (Paris: Gallimard/Réunion des musées nationaux, 1988); English translation, *Birth of the Motion Picture* (New York: Abrams, 1995); Holman and Gaudreault, *Cinema 1900–1906: An Analytical Study*; John L. Fell, *Film before Griffith* (Berkeley: University of California Press, 1983); Paul C. Spehr, *The Movies Begin. Making Movies in New Jersey, 1887–1920* (Newark, NJ: The Newark Museum/Morgan & Morgan, 1977); Stephen Bottomore, 'Shots in

the Dark: The Real Origins of Film Editing', *Sight and Sound*, vol. 57 no. 3, Summer 1988, pp. 200–4; the same author has edited *Early Cinema*, monograph issue of *Film History*, vol. 11 no. 3, 1999.

Animation
Donald Crafton, *Before Mickey: The Animated Film, 1898–1928* (Cambridge, MA, and London: MIT Press, 1982); by the same author, *Emile Cohl, Caricature, and Film* (Princeton, NJ: Princeton University Press, 1990); Giannalberto Bendazzi, *Cartoons: One Hundred Years of Cinema Animation* (Sydney: John Libbey, 1995).

Avant-garde
Hans Schleugl and Ernst Schmidt (ed.), *Eine Subgeschichte des Films: Lexicon des Avantgarde-, Experimental- und Undergroundfilms* (Frankfurt am Main: Suhrkamp, 1974, 2 vols); Jan-Christopher Horak (ed.), *Lovers of Cinema: The First American Film Avant-Garde, 1919–1945* (Madison: University of Wisconsin Press, 1995).

Non-fiction
The past few years have witnessed a much welcome (and long overdue) growth in early and silent non-fiction film studies, a topic hitherto dismissed in the first few pages of books on documentary (an exception to the rule is Raymond Fielding, *The American Newsreel, 1911–1967*. (Norman: University of Oklahoma Press, 1967). For a discussion on this topic, see the proceedings of the 1994 Amsterdam Workshop edited by Daan Hertogs and Nico De Klerk, *Nonfiction in the Teens* (Amsterdam: Stichting Nederlands Filmmuseum, 1994; distributed in the United Kingdom by the British Film Institute). See also Roger Smither and Wolfgang Klaue (eds), *Newsreels in Film Archives: A Survey Based on the FIAF Newsreel Symposium* (Trowbridge: Flicks Books, 1996; distributed in the United States by Cranbury, NJ: Associated University Presses), based on the proceedings of the FIAF Newsreel Symposium held in Mo i Rana, Norway in 1993; Renzo Renzi (ed.), *Il cinematografo al campo. L'arma nuova nel primo conflitto mondiale* (Ancona: Transeuropa, 1993).

National Cinemas
African continent: To the best of my knowledge, no single African country has been the object of a published history of silent film. Bits of information on the subject can be found in the scarce literature on colonial cinema. For an overview on silent film production in the African continent see Guido Convents, *Préhistoire du cinéma en Afrique, 1897–1918. À la recherche des images oubliées* (Bruxelles: OCIC: 1986) and Alessandra Speciale (ed.), *La nascita del cinema in Africa* (Turin: Lindau, 1998).

Argentina: *Historia de los Primeros Años del Cine en la Argentina, 1895-1910* (Buenos Aires: Fundación Cinemateca Argentina, 1996); AA.VV., *Historia del cine argentino* (Buenos Aires: Centro Editor de América Latina, 1984); AA.VV., *Historia de los primeros años del cine en la Argentina, 1895–1910* (Buenos Aires: Fundación Cinemateca Argentina, 1996).

Australia: Chris Long, 'Australia's First Films', *Cinema Papers*, January (Part I) and March (Part II) 1993; Andrew Pike and Ross Cooper, *Australian Film 1900–1977* (Melbourne: Oxford University Press, 1980); Brian Adams and Graham Shirley, *Australian Cinema: The First Eighty Years* (Sydney: Angus & Robertson/Currency Press, 1983); Ina Bertrand, *Cinema in Australia. A Documentary History* (Sydney: New South Wales University Press, 1989); Lennard Bickel, *In Search of Frank Hurley* (South Melbourne: Macmillan 1980).

Austria: Walter Fritz, *Kino in Österreich: Der Stummfilm, 1896-1930* (Wien: Österreichischer Bundesverlag, 1981). Dejan Kosanović, *Kinematografske delanosti u Puli, 1896–1918* (Beograd/Pula: Institut za Film/Festival Jugoslavenskog Igranog Filma, 1988).

Bolivia: Alfonso Gumucio Dagron, *Historia del cine boliviano* (Mexico: Filmoteca de la UNAM, 1983); Carlos D. Mesa G. (ed.), *Cine boliviano del realizador al critico* (La Paz: Editorial Gisbert, 1979).

Brazil: Maria Rita Galvão, 'Le Muet', in Paulo Antonio Paraganuá (ed.), *Le cinéma brésilien* (Paris: Centre Georges Pompidou, 1987), pp. 51–66.

Canada: Peter Morris, *Embattled Shadows: A History of Canadian Cinema, 1895–1939* (Montréal/Kingston: McGill/Queens University Press, reprint edition, 1992).

Colombia: Hernando Salcedo Silva, *Crónicas del cine colombiano, 1897–1950* (Bogotà: Carlos Valencia Editores, 1981); Hernando Martínez Prado, *Historia del cine colombiano* (Bogotá: Libreria y Editorial America Latina, 1978)

Costa Rica: Daniel Marranghello, *El Cine en Costa Rica, 1903–1920* (San José, Costa Rica: Colección Cultura Cinematografica, 1988).

China: Jay Leyda, *Dianying. Electric Shadows. An Account of Films and the Film Audience in China* (Cambridge, MA., and London: MIT Press, 1972); Li Suyuan and Hu Jubin, *Chinese Silent Film History* (Beijing: China Film Press, 1997).

Cuba: Raúl Rodriguez González, Maria Eulalia Douglas and Héctor Garcìa Mesa, 'Le cinéma muet', in Paulo Antonio Paranagua (ed.), *Le Cinéma cubain* (Paris: Centre Georges Pompidou, 1990), pp. 49–62.

Denmark: Marguerite Engberg, *Dansk Stumfilm* (Copenhagen: Rhodos, 1977); Ron Mottram, *The Danish Cinema, 1896–1917* (Ann Arbor: University of Michigan Press, 1982).

Ecuador: 'El cine mudo en Ecuador', in Héctor García Mesa (ed.), *Cine latinoamericano, 1896–1930* (Caracas: Fundación del nuevo cine latinoamericano, 1992), pp. 169–76.

Finland: Kari Uusitalo, *Eläviksi syntyneet kuvat. Suomalaisen elokuvan mykät vuodet, 1896–1930* (Helsinki: Helsingissä Kustannusosakeyhtiö Otava, 1972).

France: Richard Abel, *The Ciné Goes to Town: French Cinema, 1896-1914* (Berkeley: University of California Press, 1993; updated and expanded edition, 1998); by the same author, *French Cinema: The First Wave, 1915–1929* (Princeton, NJ: Princeton University Press, 1984); Pierre Guibbert (ed.), *Les Premiers ans du cinéma français* (Perpignan: Institut Jean Vigo, 1985); Jacques Kermabon (ed.), *Pathé, premier empire du cinéma* (Paris: Centre Georges Pompidou, 1994). Other useful texts on silent French cinema are published in association with the filmographies listed in the corresponding section of this bibliography.

Germany: Wolfgang Jacobsen, Anton Kaes, Hans Helmut Prinzler (eds), *Geschichte des Deutschen Films* (Stuttgart: Metzler, 1993); Hans-Michael Bock (ed.), *Recherche. Film: Quellen und Methoden der Filmforschung* (Munich: Edition Text + Kritik, 1997); Corinna Müller and Harro Segeberg (eds), *Die Modellierung des Kinofilms: zur Geschichte des Kinoprogramms zwischen Kurzfilm und Langfilm 1905/06–1918* (Munich: Fink, 1998, Mediengeschichte des Films, Vol. 2); Corinna Müller, *Frühe Deutsche Kinematographie. Formale, wirtschaftliche und kulturelle Entwicklungen* (Stuttgart: Metzler, 1994); Thomas Elsaesser, Michael Wedel, Martin Loiperdinger (eds), *A Second Life: German Cinema's First Decades* (Amsterdam: Amsterdam University Press, 1996; German edition, Berlin: Vorwerk, 2000); Martin Loiperdinger, *Film und Schokolade, Stollwerks Geschäfte mit lebenden Bildern*, (Kintop Scriften 4. Frankfurt am Main: Stroemfeld Verlag, 1999, book and PAL videotape with thirty-four Lumière films shot in Germany). Herbert Birett, *Lichtspiele: der Kino in Deutschland bis 1914* (Munich: Q-Verlag, 1994) is worth reading for its offbeat autobiographical overtones.

Guatemala: 'Guatemala: café, capitalismo dependiente y cine silente', in Héctor García Mesa (ed.), *Cine latinoamericano, 1896–1930* (Caracas: Fundación del nuevo cine latinoamericano, 1992), pp. 177–88.

India: Suresh Chabria (ed.), *Light of Asia. Indian Silent Cinema, 1912–1934* (Pordenone and New Delhi: Le Giornate del Cinema Muto/Wiley Eastern Ltd., 1994), pp.

72–235; Ashish Raadhyaksha and Paul Willemen, *Encyclopaedia of Indian Cinema* (London and New Delhi: BFI/Oxford University Press, 1994)

Italy: Aldo Bernardini, *Cinema muto italiano, 1896–1914* (Bari: Laterza, 1980–1982, 3 vols); Gian Piero Brunetta, *Storia del cinema italiano, 1895–1945*, 2nd edn, revised and enlarged (Rome: Editori Riuniti, 1993); Vittorio Martinelli (ed.), *Cinema Italiano in Europa, 1907–1929* (Roma: Associazione italiana per le ricerche di storia del cinema, 1992); Riccardo Redi, *La Cines. Storia di una casa de produzione italiana* (Rome: CNC Edizioni, 1991); Vittorio Martinelli and Mario Quargnolo, *Maciste & Co., I giganti buoni del muto italiano* (Gemona del Friuli: Edizioni Cinepopolare, 1981); Monica Dall'Asta, *Un Cinéma musclé. Le surhomme dans le cinéma italien, 1913–1926* (Crisnée: Editions Yellow Now, 1992); Renzo Renzi (ed.), *Sperduto nel buio. Il cinema italiano e il suo tempo, 1905–1930* (Bologna: Cappelli, 1991); Paolo Bertetto and Gianni Rondolino (eds), *Cabiria e il suo tempo* (Milan–Turin: Editrice Il Castoro/Museo Nazionale del Cinema, 1998); Roberto Chiti, *Dizionario dei registi del cinema muto italiano* (Rome: Museo Internazionale del Cinema e dello Spettacolo, 1997).

Japan: Texts in Japanese. Shoei Imamura *et al.(eds)*, *Nihon eiga no tanjo* [The Birth of Japanese Film], Vol. 1 of *Koza nihon eiga* [Japanese Film] (Tokyo: Iwanami shoten, 1985) and *Musei eiga no kansei* [The Perfection of Silent Film], Vol. 2 of *Koza nihon eiga* [Japanese Film] (Tokyo: Iwanami shoten, 1986); Kenji Iwamoto (ed.), *Nihon eiga to modanizumu 1920–1930* [The Japanese Cinema and Modernism, 1920–1930] (Tokyo: Libroport, 1991); Kenji Iwamoto and Tomonori Saiki (eds), *Kikigaki: Kinema no seishun* [Interviews: Japanese Cinema in its Youth] (Tokyo: Libroport, 1988), pp. 77–100; Yoshishige Yoshida *et al.* (eds), *Eiga denrai: Shinematografu to Meiji no Nihon* [The Introduction of Film: The Cinematograph and Meiji Japan] (Tokyo: Iwanami shoten, 1995); Tadashi Iijima, *Jidenteki essei: Boku no Meiji, Taisho, Showa* [Autobiographical Essays: My Meiji, Taisho and Showa Periods] (Tokyo: Seiabo, 1991); Akira Iwasaki, *Eiga ga wakakatta toki: Meiji, Taisho, Showa no kioku* [When Film was Young: My Memories of Meiji, Taisho, and Showa] (Tokyo: Heibonsha, 1980); Junichiro Tanaka, *Nihon eiga hattatsu shi* [A History of the Development of Japanese Cinema], Vols 1–2 (Tokyo: Chuo koronsha, 1975–6); Tadashi Iijima, *Nihon eiga shi* [A History of Japanese Film], Vol. 1 (Tokyo: Hakusu-isha, 1955); Tsuneo Hazumi, *Eiga gojunenshi* [Fifty Year History of Film] (Tokyo: Masu shobo, 1943); Susumu Okada, *Nihon eiga no rekishi* [History of Japanese Cinema] (Tokyo: Dabiddosha, 1967); Chieo Yoshida, *Mo hitotsu no eigashi* [One More Film History] (Tokyo: Jiji tsushinsha, 1978). Silent screenplays: *Nihon shinario taikei*, Vol. 1 (edited by the Shinario sakka kyokai. Tokyo: Eijinsha, 1973). Studio histories: *Shochiku kyujunen shi* [A Ninety-year History of Shochiku] (Tokyo: Shochiku kabushiki kaisha, 1985); *Nikkatsu yonjunen shi* [A Forty-Year History of Nikkatsu] (Tokyo: Nikkatsu kabushiki kaisha, 1952).Texts in English:

Joseph L. Anderson and Donald Richie, *The Japanese Film: Art and Industry* (1959; expanded edition, Princeton, NJ: Princeton University Press, 1982); Hiroshi Komatsu, 'Some Characteristics of Japanese Cinema before World War I', in Arthur Noletti and David Desser (eds), *Reframing Japanese Cinema: Authorship, Genre, History* (Bloomington: Indiana University Press, 1992), pp. 229–58; by the same author, 'The Fundamental Change: Japanese Cinema before and after the Earthquake of 1923', *Griffithiana*, vol. 13, 38/39, October 1990, pp. 186–93; Donald Kirihara, 'Reconstructing Japanese Film', in David Bordwell and Noël Carroll, *Post-Theory: Reconstructing Film Studies* (Madison: University of Wisconsin Press, 1996), pp. 501–19, a useful reconsideration of Noël Burch's *To the Distant Observer: Form and Meaning in the Japanese Cinema* (Berkeley: University of California Press, 1979); David Bordwell, 'Visual Style in Japanese Cinema, 1925–1945' *Film History*, vol. 7 no. 1, 1995, pp. 5–31.

Latin America: Paulo Antonio Paraganuá, *O cinema na América Latina. Longe de deus e perto de Hollywood* (Porto Alegre: L & PM Editores, 1985); Peter B. Schumann, *Historia del cine latinoamericano* (Buenos Aires: Editorial Legasa, 1986); Héctor García Mesa (ed.), *Cine latinoamericano, 1896–1930* (Caracas: Fundación del nuevo cine latinoamericano, 1992); Guy Hennebelle and Alfonso Gumucio-Dagron (eds), *Les Cinémas de l'Amérique Latine* (Paris: L'Herminier/CinémAction, 1981).

Mexico: 'El cine en México (1896–1930)', in Héctor García Mesa (ed.), *Cine latinoamericano, 1896–1930* (Caracas: Fundación del nuevo cine latinoamericano, 1992), pp. 189–278.

Netherlands: Karel Dibbets and Frank van der Maden (eds), *Geschiedenis van de Nederlandse Film en Bioscoop tot 1940* (Weesp: Het Wereldvenster, 1986).

New Zealand/Aotearoa: Jonathan Dennis, 'A Time Line', in Jonathan Dennis and Jan Bieringa (eds), *Film in Aotearoa New Zealand* (Wellington: Victoria University Press, 1992), pp. 183–219.

Peru: Ricardo Bedoya, *100 años de cine en el Perú: una historia crítica* (Lima: Universidad de Lima/Instituto de Cooperación Iberoamericana, 1995).

Poland: Malgorzata Hendrykowska, *Sladami Tamtych Cieni, Film w kulturze polskiej przelomu stuleci 1895–1914* (Póznan: Oficyna Wydawnicza, 1993).

Portugal: M. Félix Ribeiro, *Filmes, Figuras e factos da história do cinema português, 1896–1949* (Lisbon: Cinemateca Portuguesa, 1983).

Russia, Soviet Union, and Russian exiles: Jay Leyda, *Kino. A History of Russian and*

Soviet Film (London: George Allen & Unwin, 1960; third edition, Princeton, NJ: Princeton University Press, 1983); *Russian and Soviet Cinema: Continuity and Change*, special issue of *Historical Journal of Film, Radio and Television*, vol. 11 no. 2, 1991; Yuri Tsivian *et al.*, *Silent Witnesses. Russian Cinema, 1896–1919* (Pordenone: Biblioteca dell'Immagine/BFI, 1989; distributed in the United States by Indiana University Press); *Le Cinéma russe avant la révolution* (Paris: Éditions de la réunion des musées nationaux/Éditions Ramsay, 1989); François Albéra (ed.), *Albatros, des Russes à Paris, 1919–1929* (Milan-Paris: Mazzotta/La Cinémathèque française, 1995); Aïcha Kherroubi, *Le studio Mejrabpom, ou l'aventure du cinéma privé au pays des bolcheviks*, special issue of *Les Dossiers du Musée d'Orsay*, no. 59 (Paris: Réunion des musées nationaux/Musée d'Orsay, 1996); Denise J. Youngblood, *The Magic Mirror: Moviemaking in Russia, 1908–1918* (Madison: University of Wisconsin Press, 1999).

Spain: Josefina Martinez, *Los primeros veinticinco años de cine en Madrid, 1896–1920* (Madrid: Filmoteca Española, 1992). An inventory of surviving Spanish fiction films has been published in *Cine mudo español. Un primer acercamiento de investigación* (s.1.: Universidad Complutense, 1991).

Sweden: Gösta Werner, *Den svenska filmens historia* (Stockholm: P.A. Nörstedt & Söners förlag, 1978); Jan Olsson, *Sensationer från en bakgård. Frans Lundberg som biografägare och filmproducent i Malmö och Köpenhamn* (Stockholm: Symposion, 1988); Bo Florin, *Den nationella stilen: Studier i den svenska filmens guldålder* (Stockholm: Aura förlag, 1997); Mats Björkin, *Amerikanism, bolsjevism och korta kjolar: Filmen och dess publik i Sverige under 1920-talet* (Stockholm: Aura förlag, 1998); Astrid Söderbergh Widding, *Stumfilm i brytningstid* (Stockholm: Aura förlag, 1998), on the films of Georg af Klercker. John Fullerton, *The Development of a System of Representation in Swedish Film, 1912–1920* (unpublished PhD dissertation, University of East Anglia, 1994); John Fullerton and Jan Olsson (eds), *Nordic Explorations: Film before 1930* (Sydney: John Libbey, 1999).

Thailand: Dome Sukwong, *Prawat phaphayon thai* (Bangkok: Ongkan kha kho'ng khurusapha, 1990); Scot Barné, 'Early Thai Cinema and Filmmaking: 1897–1922', *Film History*, vol. 11 no. 3, 1999, pp. 308–18.

United Kingdom: Rachael Low, *The History of the British Film* (London: George Allen & Unwin, 1948 [Vol. 1: 1896–1906, in collaboration with Roger Manvell], 1949 [Vol. 2: 1906–1914], 1950 [Vol. 3: 1914–1918], 1971 [Vol. 4: 1918–1929]); Richard Brown and Barry Anthony, *The History of the British Mutoscope and Biograph Company* (Trowbridge, Flicks Books, 1995); Stephen Herbert and Luke McKernan (eds), *Who's Who of Victorian Cinema* (London: BFI, 1996); John Barnes: *The Beginnings of Cinema in England* (London: David & Charles, 1976); from the same author, *The Rise of Cinema in Great Britain* (London: Bishopsgate Press, 1983), *Pioneers of the British Film* (London: Bishopsgate Press, 1983 [but 1988]), *Filming the Boer War* (London: Bishopsgate Press, 1991) and *1900* (Exeter: University of Exeter Press, 1997). The five-volume set was republished by the University of Exeter Press in 1999; Martin Sopocy, *James Williamson. Studies and Documents of a Pioneer of the Film Narrative* (London: Associated University Presses, 1998).

United States: Lewis Jacobs, *The Rise of the American Film* (New York: Harcourt & Brace, 1939); Walter Kerr, *The Silent Clowns* (reprint edition, New York: Da Capo Press, 1990); Kevin Brownlow, *The Parade's Gone By* (New York: Alfred A. Knopf, 1969); by the same author, *The War, the West, and the Wilderness* (New York: Knopf, 1979) and *Behind the Mask of Innocence. Sex, Violence, Prejudice, Crime: Films of Social Conscience in the Silent Era* (New York: Knopf, 1991); Tino Balio (ed.), *The American Film Industry* (Madison: University of Wisconsin Press, 1976); William K. Everson, *The American Silent Film* (New York: Oxford University Press, 1978); Lary May, *Screening Out the Past: The Birth of Mass Culture and the Motion Picture Industry* (New York and Oxford: Oxford University Press, 1980); Tino Balio (ed.), *The American Film Industry* (2nd edn, Madison: University of Wisconsin Press, 1985); David Robinson, *Chaplin. His Life and Art* (London: Collins, 1985); David Bordwell, Janet Staiger, Kristin Thompson, *The Classical Hollywood Cinema: Film Style and Mode of Production to 1960* (London: Routledge & Kegan Paul, 1985); Richard DeCordova, *Picture Personalities. The Emergence of the Star System in America, 1907–1922* (Champaign: University of Illinois Press, 1990); Charles Harpole (general editor), *A History of the American Cinema*, Vol. 1: Charles Musser, *The Emergence of Cinema: The American Screen to 1907*; Vol. 2: Eileen Bowser, *The Transformation of Cinema: 1908–1915*; Vol. 3: Richard Koszarski, *An Evening's Entertainment: The Age of the Silent Feature Picture, 1915–1928* (New York: Scribner's, 1990); Tom Gunning, *David W. Griffith and the Origins of American Narrative Film* (Urbana and Chicago: University of Illinois Press, 1991). Eugene Michael Vazzana, *Silent Film Necrology: Births and Deaths of over 9000 Performers, Directors, Producers and Other Filmmakers of the Silent Era, Through 1933* (Jefferson, NC, and London: McFarland, 1995).

Uruguay: *Historia y filmografía del cine uruguayo* (Montevideo: Ediciones de la Plaza, 1988)

Venezuela: José Miguel Acosta *et al.*, *Panorama histórico del cine en Venezuela, 1896–1993* (Caracas: Fundación Cinemateca Nacional, 1997).

Interdisciplinary Studies
Stephen Bottomore, *I Want to See This Annie Mattygraph. A Cartoon History of the Coming of the Movies* (Pordenone: Le Giornate del Cinema Muto, 1995);

Robert C. Allen, *Vaudeville and Film, 1895–1915: A Study in Media Interaction* (New York: Arno Press, 1980); Ben Brewster and Lea Jacobs, *Theatre to Cinema. Stage Pictorialism and the Early Feature Film* (Oxford and New York: Oxford University Press, 1997); Roland Cosandey, André Gaudreault and Tom Gunning (eds), *An Invention of the Devil: Religion and Early Cinema* (Lausanne: Payot, 1992); Dennis Gifford, *Books and Plays in Films, 1896–1915* (London and New York: Mansell, 1991).

History of Television

As we have seen, the beginnings of cinema overlap from a chronological point of view with the origins of the electronic image. A recommended reading on the subject is Albert Abramson, *The History of Television, 1880 to 1941* (Jefferson, NC, and London: McFarland, 1987).

Films, Television Programmes, Video and Electronic Media on Silent Cinema

A filmography on the subject was compiled by Anthony Slide in *Films on Film History* (Metuchen, NJ, and London: Scarecrow Press, 1979). What follows is a selected list of works produced since then: Noël Burch, *Correction, Please; or, How We Got Into Pictures* (Arts Council of United Kingdom, 16mm, 52', 1979); Kevin Brownlow and David Gill, *Hollywood: The Pioneers* (Thames TV, 1980, thirteen episodes of 52'30" each; all sections were cut for American syndication, then restored to their complete length for PBS, laserdisc and video release), *Unknown Chaplin* (Thames TV, 1983, three episodes of 52'30" each), *Buster Keaton: A Hard Act to Follow* (Thames TV, 1987, three episodes of 52'30" each. Episode 3 has been broadcast by Channel 4, only in the United Kingdom), *Harold Lloyd, The Third Genius* (Thames TV, 1990, two episodes of 51'30" each), and *D.W. Griffith, Father of Film* (Photoplay Productions, UK version: three episodes, 156'; US version: six parts, 165'; international version: six parts, 157'); Charles Musser, *Before the Nickelodeon: The Early Cinema of Edwin S. Porter* (Film for Thought/New Hollywood Feature Film, 1982, 16mm, 60'); Werner Nekes, *Was geschah wirklich zwischen den Bildern?* (Werner Nekes Filmproduktion, 1985, 16mm, 83', distributed in the United States by Kino International under the title *Film before Film*). Peter Jackson and Costa Botes, *Forgotten Silver* (WingNut Films/The New Zealand Film Commission/New Zealand On Air, 1996, 35mm, 52'), is an instructive mockumentary on the rediscovery of a neglected pioneer of silent film and the clichés of film historiography.

Filmographies.

An inspiring discussion of the rationale and limits of filmographies is given by Geoffrey Nowell-Smith, 'Filmography', *Screen*, vol. 32 no. 4, Winter 1991, pp. 452–5); see also Stephen Bottomore's discussion of the topic in 'Book Reviews', *Film History*, vol. 11 no. 3, 1999, pp. 387–91. The following is a selected list arranged per country; additional titles can be found in Dorothea Gebauer (edited by Harriet Harrison), *Bibliography of National Filmographies* (Brussels: FIAF, 1985).

Argentina: *La Epoca Muda del Cine Argentino* (Buenos Aires: Centro de Envestigacion de la Historia del Cine Argentino, 1958 [second edition]); 'Filmografia. Películas nacionales estrenadas entre 1896 y 1910 en las ciudades de Buenos Aires y Mar del Plata', in *Historia de los primeros años del cine en la Argentina, 1895–1910* (Buenos Aires: Fundación Cinemateca Argentina, 1996), pp. 113–23.

Australia: Andrew Pike and Ross Cooper, *Australian Film, 1900–1977: A Guide to Feature Film Production* (Melbourne: Oxford University Press/The Australian Film Institute, 1980).

Austria: Walter Fritz, *Die Österreichischen Spielfilme der Stummfilmzeit (1907–1930)* (Vienna: Österreichisches Filmarchiv/Österreichische Gesellschaft für Filmwissenschaft, 1967).

Belgium: Marianne Thys (ed.), *Belgian Cinema: Filmography of Belgian Movies, 1896–1996* (Brussels: Ludion, 1996); *Films Belges: documentaires, films de fiction, dessins animés, films d'archives, reportages* (Brussels: Quatre Bras 2, Ministère des Affaires Étrangères, du Commerce Extérieur et de la Coopération au Dévéloppement, 1974–5).

Brazil: Jean-Claude Bernardet, *Filmografia do Cinema Brasileiro: 1900–1935* (São Paulo: Secretaria da Cultura de São Paulo, 1979).

Bulgaria: Peter Kardzhilov, *Bulgarian Feature Films. An Annotated Illustrated Filmography, Vol. 1 (1915–1948)*, (Sofia: Bulgarska Nacionalna Filmoteka, Peter Beron State Publishing House, 1987).

Canada: D. J. Turner, *Canadian Feature Film Index/Index des films canadiens de long métrage, 1913–1985* (Ottawa: National Film, Television and Sound Archives/Archives nationales du film, de la télévision et de l'enregistrement sonore, 1987); Peter Morris (ed.), *Canadian Feature Films, 1913–1969: Part 1, 1913–1940* (Ottawa: Canadian Film Institute, 1970).

China: Cheng Jihua, Li Shaobai, Xing Zuwen, 'Chinese Cinema: Catalogue of Films, 1905–1937', *Griffithiana*, vol. 18 no. 54, October 1995 pp. 4–77; Sergei Arkadevich Toroptsev, *Ocherk Istorii Kitaiskogo Kino, 1896–1966* (Moscow: Nauka, 1979).

Colombia: 'Indice de peliculas y casas productoras', in Hernando Martínez Prado, *Historia del cine colombiano* (Bogotá: Libreria y Editorial America Latina, 1978).

Czechoslovakia: *Český hraný film I, 1898-1930* (Praha: Národní filmovÿ archiv, 1995); Jan S. Kolar and Myrtil Frida, *Ceskoslovensky Nemy Film 1898–1930* (Praha: Ceskoslovensky Film, 1957).

Denmark: Marguerite Engberg, *Registrant over danske film, 1896–1930*, Vol. 1: 1896–1909; Vol. 2: 1910–12; Vol. 3: 1913–14; Vol. 4: 1915–17; Vol. 5: 1918–30 (Copenhagen: Institut for Filmvidenskab, 1977–82).

Finland: *Suomen Kansallis – Filmografia. Vol. I: 1907–1933* (Helsinki: Suomen Elokuva-Arkisto, 1996).

France: Raymond Chirat (with the collaboration of Eric Le Roy), *Catalogue des films français de fiction de 1908 à 1918* (Paris: Cinémathèque française, 1995); Raymond Chirat, *Catalogue des films français de long métrage: Films de fiction, 1919–1929* (Toulouse: Cinémathèque de Toulouse, 1984); Michelle Aubert and Jean-Claude Seguin (eds), *La Production cinématographique des frères Lumière*, (Paris: Éditions Mémoires de cinéma/Bibliothèque du Film [BIFI]/Centre National de la Cinématographie/Premier siècle du cinéma, 1996, book plus CD-Rom); Henri Bousquet, *Catalogue Pathé des années 1896 à 1914* (Bures-sur-Yvette: Editions Henri Bousquet, 1996 [1896–1906], 1993 [1907–9], 1994 [1910–11], 1995 [1912–14], 1999 [01915–18]; available from the publisher, 31 Avenue Maréchal Foch, 91440 Bures-sur-Yvette, France); André Gaudreault, *Pathé 1900. Fragments d'une filmographie analytique du cinéma des premiers temps* (Ste Foy, Quebec, and Paris: Les Presses de l'Université Laval/Presses de la Sorbonne Nouvelle, 1993); *Gaumont: 90 ans de cinéma* (Paris: Ramsay/La Cinémathèque française, 1986); Éric Loné, 'La production Lux (1906–1913)', *1895*, no. 16, June 1994, pp. 59–76; Youen Bernard, *Les petites maisons de production ciné-matographique française de 1906 à 1914* (filmographies of Le Lion, Lux, Radios, Théophile Pathé and Film des auteurs. Doctoral thesis presented at the University of Paris III, 1994); Juan Gabriel Tharrats, *Los 500 films de Segundo de Chomón* (Zaragoza: Prensas Universitarias, 1988) and *Inolvidable Chomón* (Murcia: Filmoteca Regional de Murcia, 1990); Madeleine Malthête-Méliès, Anne-Marie Quévrain and Jacques Malthête, *Essai de reconstitution du catalogue français de la Star-Film* (Bois d'Arcy: Centre National de la Cinématographie, 1981), integrated by *Analyse descriptive des films de Georges Méliès rassemblés entre 1981 et 1996 par la Cinémathèque Méliès* (Paris: Les Amis de Georges Méliès, 1996); John Frazer, *Artificially Arranged Scenes: The Films of Georges accent Méliès* (Boston: G.K. Hall, 1979); 'Société Française des Films et Cinématographes Éclair (1907-1919): A Checklist', *Griffithiana*, vol. 15 nos 44–5, May–September 1992, pp. 28–88.

Germany: Gerhard Lamprecht, *Deutsche Stummfilme, 1903–1931* (Berlin: Stiftung

Deutsche Kinematek, 1967–70, 10 vols); German and foreign films distributed in the country in the early period are listed in overwhelming detail by Herbert Birett, *Das Filmangebot in Deutschland, 1895–1911* (Munich: Filmbuchverlag Winterberg, 1991), and *Verzeichnis in Deutschland gelaufener Filme. Entscheidungen der Filmzensur 1911–1920, Berlin/Hamburg/München/Stuttgart* (Munich: Saur, 1980), whose symbols and codes give the books – especially the first – the appearance of a massive cryptogram rather than reference tools.

Great Britain: Denis Gifford, *The British Film Catalogue, 1895–1985. A Reference Guide* (New York: Facts on File Publications, 1987); from the same author, *British Animated Films, 1895–1985. A Filmography* (Jefferson, NC: McFarland, 1987); the same author has in preparation a revised edition of the *British Film Catalogue*, and a filmography of British non-fiction films.

Hungary: Ferenc Kovács (ed.), *Magyar Filmográfia, 1901–1961* (Budapest: Magyar Filmtudományi Intézet és Filmarchivum, 1963).

India: Virchand Dharamsey, 'Indian Silent Cinema, 1912-1934. A Filmography', in Suresh Chabria (ed.), *Light of Asia. Indian Silent Cinema, 1912–1934* (Pordenone and New Delhi: Le Giornate del Cinema Muto/Wiley Eastern Ltd., 1994), pp. 72–235; Firoze Rangoonwalla, *Indian Filmography: Silent and Hindi Films, 1897–1969* (Bombay: J. Udeshi, 1970); Ashish Raadhyaksha and Paul Willemen, *Encyclopaedia of Indian Cinema* (London and New Delhi: BFI/Oxford University Press, 1994).

Italy: *Elenco delle Pellicole Cinematografiche approvate dal Ministero dell'Interno* (monthly bulletin issued by the Italian government from 1913 to 1925); Aldo Bernardini (ed.), *Archivio del cinema italiano. Volume I: Il cinema muto, 1905–1931* (Rome: Edizioni Anica, 1991); Vittorio Martinelli, *Il cinema muto italiano* (Rome: Nuova ERI/Edizioni RAI/Centro Sperimentale di Cinematografia, 1996 [1905–9; 1910], 1995 [1911, Part I], 1996 [1911, Part II]; special issues of *Bianco & Nero*, vol 55 nos 1–2, 1994 [1912, Part I]; vol 55 nos 3–4, 1994 [1912, Part II]; vol 54 nos 1–2, 1993 [1913, Part I]; vol 54 nos 3–4, 1993 [1913, Part II]; vol 53 nos 1–2 and 3–4, 1992 [1914]; vol 52 nos 1–2 3–4, 1991 [1915]; vol 51 nos 1–2 3–4, 1990 [1916]; vol 50 nos 3–4, 1989 [1917]; vol 50 nos 1–2, 1989 [1918]; vol 41 nos 1–3, 1980 [1919]; vol 41 nos 4–6, 1980 [1920]; vol 42 nos 1–3, 1981 [1921–2]; vol 42 nos 4–6, 1981 [1923–31]); Carla Manenti, Nicolas Monti, Giorgio Nicodemi (eds), *Luca Comerio fotografo e cineasta* (Milan: Electa Editrice, 1979, pp. 104–6); Aldo Bernardini and Vittorio Martinelli, *Roberto Roberti, direttore artistico* (Pordenone: Giornate del Cinema Muto, 1985); Vittorio Martinelli and Sergio Grmek Germani, *Il cinema di Augusto Genina* (Pordenone: Edizioni Biblioteca dell'Immagine, 1989); 'I film dell'Itala', in Paolo Cherchi Usai (ed.), *Giovanni Pastrone. Gli anni d'oro del cinema a*

Torino (Turin: UTET, 1986), pp. 123–42; Aldo Bernardini (ed.; in collaboration with Vittorio Martinelli), 'I comici del muto italiano', *Griffithiana*, vol 8 nos 24–5, October 1985, pp. 63–134; Aldo Bernardini (ed.), 'I comici del muto italiano. Aggiunte e correzioni', *Griffithiana*, vol 9 nos 26–7, September 1986, pp. 99–101; Aldo Bernardini and Vittorio Martinelli (eds), *Francesca Bertini, 1892–1985* (Rome: Centro Sperimentale di Cinematografia, Cineteca Nazionale, 1985); Riccardo Redi, *La Cines: storia di una casa di produzione italiana* ([Rome]: CNC Edizioni, 1991), pp. 13–76.

Japan: *Nihon eiga sakuhin jiten senzenhen (1986-1945/8)* [Complete Dictionary of Japanese Movies from 1896 to August 1945]. (Tokyo: Kagaku shoin, 1996, 5 vols, including a filmography of foreign films released in Japan).

Mexico: Federico Dávalos Orozco and Esperanza Vázquez Bernal, *Filmografía general del Cine Mexicano (1906–1931)* (Puebla: Universidad Autónoma de Puebla, 1985); Aurelio de Los Reyes, *Filmografía del Cine Mudo Mexicano 1896–1920* (Mexico, D.F.: Filmoteca de la Unam, 1986); Vol. 2, *1920–1924* (1994).

Netherlands: Geoffrey Donaldson, *Of Joy and Sorrow: A Filmography of Dutch Silent Fiction* (Amsterdam: Stichting Nederlands Filmmuseum, 1987).

New Zealand/Aotearoa: *Aotearoa and the Sentimental Strine. Making Films in Australia and New Zealand in the Silent Period* (Wellington: Moa Films, 1993; available from the publisher, 14 Edge Hill, Wellington, Aotearoa New Zealand).

Norway: Leif-Erik Bech (ed.), *Norsk Filmografi, 1908-1979* (Oslo: Norsk kino-og Filmfond/Norsk Filminstitutt, 1980); Øivind Hanche (ed.), *Register over Norske Langfilmer 1908–1.4.1990* (Oslo: Norsk Filminstitutt, 1990).

Poland: Jadwiga Bochenska and others (eds; compiled by Jerzy Toeplitz), *Historia Filmu Polskiego*: Vol. 1: *1895–1921* [with a filmography of silent fiction films produced between 1911 to 1929] (Warsaw: Wydawnictwa Artystyczne i Filmowe, 1966).

Portugal: José de Matos-Cruz, *Prontuario do cinema portugues, 1896–1989* (Lisbon: Cinemateca Portuguesa, 1989); from the same author, *O cais do olhar. O cinema portugues de longa metrageme e a ficçao muda* (Lisbon: Cinemateca Portuguesa, 1999).

Rumania: *Productia Cinematografică din România, 1897–1970; Filmografie Adnotată*, Vol. 1: *Cinematograful Mut (1897–1930)*; Vol. 2: *Filmul de Ficţiune* (Bucharest: Arhivă Nationala de Filme, 1970).

Russia and the Soviet Union: Veniamin Vishnevskij, *Sovetskie Hudozestvennye fil'my. Annotirovanny katalog*. Vol. 1: *Nemye fil'my, 1918–1935* (Moscow: Iskusstvo, 1961); *Hudozestvennye fil'my dorevolutzionnoj Rossii. Fil'mograficeskoe opisanie: fil'my do 1917 goda* (Moscow: Goskinoizdat, 1945); A.A. Chernyshev, *Russkaia dooktiabr'skaia kinozhurnalistika* (Moscow: Moskovskogo Universiteta, 1987); Veniamin Vishnevskij, *Dokumental'nye filmy dorevolutzionnoj Rossii 1907–1916* (Moscow: Muzei kino, 1996).

Spain: Palmira González Lopez and Joaquín T. Cánovas Belchi, *Catálogo del cinema español, vol. F2: Peliculas de ficción, 1921–1930* (Madrid: Filmoteca Española, 1993).

Sweden: *Svensk filmografi* (Stockholm: Svenska Filminstitutet, 1986 [Vol. 1: 1897–1919], 1982 [Vol. 2: 1920–9], 1979 [Vol. 3: 1930–9]).

Turkey: Agah Özgüc (ed.), *Türk Filimleri Sözlügü, 1914–1972* (Istanbul: Cahit Poyraz, 1963).

United States:

GENERAL FILMOGRAPHIES: *The American Film Institute Catalog of Motion Pictures Produced in the United States. Vol. A: Film Beginnings, 1893–1910. A Work in Progress*, compiled by Elias Savada (Metuchen, NJ, and London: The Scarecrow Press, 1995); *Vol. F1: Feature Films, 1911–1920* (Berkeley: University of California Press, 1988); *Vol. F2: Feature Films, 1921–1930* (New York: R.R. Bowker, 1971). The subtitle of *Volume A* should be taken literally, as its author has pointed out that a large amount of information was not included in the book. The *Film Beginnings* section contains inconsistencies and potentially confusing editorial decisions, such as the inclusion of foreign films distributed in the US and the fact that virtually all the films referred to are said to have been made in black and white, which is evidently not true. A practical companion to the AFI filmography is the two-volume set compiled by Einar Lauritzen and Gunnar Lundquist, *American Film Index, 1908–1915. Motion Pictures, July 1908–December 1915* and *American Film Index, 1916–1920. Motion Pictures, January 1916–December 1920* (Stockholm, Film Index, 1976 and 1984; distributed by Akademibokhandeln, Stockholm Universitet); the two volumes have been indexed by Paul C. Spehr in *American Film Personnel and Company Credits, 1908–1920: Filmographies Recorded by Authoritative Organizational and Personal Names from Lauritzen and Lundquist* (Jefferson, NC, and London: McFarland, 1996). The *Catalog of Copyright Entries: Motion Pictures, Vol. 1: 1894–1912*; *Vol. 2: 1912–1939* (Washington DC: Library of Congress, Copyright Office, 1951–3; the first volume is now available from the US Department of Commerce, National Technical Information Service, Springfield, VA 22161) is not a filmography in the strict sense of the term, but stands out as an invaluable source

of information. See also *The WPA Film Index* (New York: The Museum of Modern
Art Film Library/The H.W. Wilson Company, 1941 [Vol. 1]; White Plains, NY:
Kraus, 1985 [Vols 2 and 3]).

PRODUCTION COMPANIES, GENRES, AND INDIVIDUAL ARTISTS (IN ALPHABETICAL
ORDER): Denis Gifford, *American Animated Films: The Silent Era, 1897–1929* (Jefferson, NC, and London: McFarland, 1990); Steven Higgins, 'American Eclair,
1911–1915: A filmographic chronology derived from the pages of the Eclair Bulletin and the trade press of the day', *Griffithiana*, vol. 15 nos 44–5, May–September
1992, pp. 89–129; Davide Turconi, *Monty Banks. Biofilmografia* (Cesena: Quaderni
del Centro Cinema, 1987); Davide Turconi, 'The Silent Films of Frank Borzage',
Griffithiana, vol. 15 no. 46, December 1992, pp. 44–58; Brian Anthony and Andy
Edmonds, 'Charley Chase: Filmography' in *Griffithiana*, vol. 16 nos 48–9, October
1993, pp. 34–53; Len D. Martin, *The Columbia Checklist: The Feature Films, Serials,
Cartoons and Short Subjects of Columbia Pictures Corporation, 1922–1988* (Jefferson, NC, and London: McFarland, 1991); Karel Čáslavský, 'American Comedy
Series: Filmographies, 1914–1930', *Griffithiana*, vol. 17 nos 51–2, October 1994, pp.
9–168; Robert Farr, 'Max Davidson: Filmography', *Griffithiana*, vol. 19 nos 55–6,
September 1996, pp. 126–49; 'Walt Disney Silent Filmography (1921–1928)', in *Nel
paese delle meraviglie/Walt in Wonderland. The Silent Films of Walt Disney* (Porde-
none: Le Giornate del Cinema Muto/Edizioni Biblioteca dell'Immagine, 1992), pp.
174–230; Charles Musser, *Edison Motion Pictures, 1890–1900: An Annotated Fil-
mography* (Pordenone and Washington, DC: Le Giornate del Cinema
Muto/Smithsonian Institution Press, 1997); Cooper C. Graham, Steven Higgins,
Elaine Mancini and João Luiz Vieira (eds), *David W. Griffith and the Biograph
Company* (Metuchen, NJ, and London: The Scarecrow Press, 1985); Paolo Cherchi
Usai (ed.), *The Griffith Project, Vol. 1: Films Produced in 1907–1908*; *Vol. 2: Films Produced in January to June 1909*; *vol. 3: Films Produced in July to December, 1909*
(London: BFI, 1999. Further volumes are scheduled to appear on an annual basis,
covering the period 1910 to 1931, with a final volume of essays and integrations to
the previous volumes); Davide Turconi, 'Another Griffith: Filmography of Raymond Griffith', *Griffithiana*, vol. 14 nos 40/42, October 1991, pp. 22–46; Robert Farr,
'Lloyd Hamilton Filmography', *Griffithiana*, vol. 15 nos 44–5, May-September 1992,
pp. 217–30; Diane Kaiser Koszarski, *The Complete Films of William S. Hart: A Pictorial Record* (New York: Dover, 1980); Steven Higgins, 'I film di Thomas H. Ince',
Griffithiana, vol. 7 nos 18–21, October 1984, pp. 155–203; Davide Turconi, 'Filmografia di Larry Semon', *Cinegrafie*, vol. 1 no. 2, 1989, pp. 35–70, plus a page of
addenda; Kalton C. Lahue, *Continued Next Week. A History of the Moving Picture
Serial* (Norman: University of Oklahoma Press, 1964); Q. David Bowers,
Thanhouser Films:An Encyclopedia and History, only on CD-Rom (Portland, OR:
Thanhouser Company Film Preservation, Inc., 1997; available through the pub-
lisher: www.teleport.com/~tco/); Anthony Slide, *The Big V: A History of the*

Vitagraph Company (Metuchen, NJ, and London: The Scarecrow Press, 1987 [revised edition]); Davide Turconi, 'Filmografia. La produzione Vitagraph dal 1905 al 1916', in Paolo Cherchi Usai (ed.), *Vitagraph Company of America. Il cinema prima di Hollywood* (Pordenone: Studio Tesi, 1987), pp. 443–634, plus a page of addenda.

Uruguay: 'Filmografia de largometrajes', in *Historia y filmografia del cine uruguayo* (Montevideo: Ediciones de la Plaza, 1988), pp. 63–84.

Venezuela: Ricardo Tirado, *Memoria y Notas del Cine Venezolano 1897-1959* (n.s.[Caracas]: Fundación Neumann, n.d.).

Periodicals of the Silent Era.
Denmark: *Filmen* (1911–18).

France: *Ciné-Journal* (1908–37), *Ciné pour tous*, which later became *Cinéa-Ciné pour tous* and finally *Cinéa-Ciné pour tous réunis* (1919–32); *Le Cinéopse* (1919–67), *Le Courrier cinématographique* (1911–14; 1917–36), *Phono-ciné-gazette* (1905–9).

Germany: *Erste Internationale Filmzeitung* (1907–20), *Der Film* (1916–43), *Filmkurier* (1919–44), *Der Kinematograph* (1907–35), *Lichtbild-Bühne* (1908–39).

United Kingdom: *The Bioscope* (1908?–32); *The Era*, 'British variety artists' trade paper, [containing] the most information on films in the period when music halls were the main screening venues' (letter from Ben Brewster to the author, 26 February 1992); *The Optical Magic Lantern Journal* (1899), which became *The Optical Lantern and Kinematograph Journal* (1904), was later renamed *The Kinematograph and Lantern Weekly* (1907) and finally became *The Kinematograph Weekly* (1919–60).

Italy: *La Cine-Fono* (1908–27), *L'illustrazione cinematografica* (1912–16?), *Lux* (1908–11?), *La Rivista Cinematografica* (1920–42), *La vita cinematografica* (1910–34). A list of film periodicals published in Italy was compiled by Davide Turconi and Camillo Bassotto, *Il cinema nelle riviste italiane dalle origini ad oggi* (Venice: Edizioni Mostracinema, n.d. [1972]; revised and updated edition: Riccardo Redi (ed.), *Cinema scritto. Il catalogo delle riviste italiane del cinema, 1907–1944* (Rome: Associazione Italiana per le Ricerche di Storia del Cinema, 1992).

Japan: *Kinema Record* (originally *Film Record*, 1913–17). Available for purchase in reprint editions: Kenji Iwamoto and Makino Mamoru (eds), *Fukkokuban: Kinema junpo* [reprint edition of *Kinema junpo, 1919-sgg.*] (Tokyo: Yushodo, 1994–6, 19 vols); Makino Mamoru (ed.), *Nihon eiga shoki shiryo shusei* [A Collection of Research Material from the Early Days of Japanese Film] Fascimile edition, *Katsudo shashin zasshi*, June-December 1915 [vol. 1–2]; *Katsudo no sekai*, January-December 1916 [vols 3–5]; *Katsudo gaho*, January–December 1917 [vols 6–9]; and *Katsudo kurabu* (originally *Katsudo hyoron*, December 1918–December 1920 [vols 10–14] (Tokyo: Sanichi shobo, 1990–1).

Russia and the Soviet Union: *Kinezhurnal* (1910–17), *Kinofot* (1922), *Kinoteatr i zhizn'* (1913), *Sine-fono* (1907–18), *Sovetski ekran* (1925–9), *Vestnik kinematografii* (1910–17).

Sweden: *Filmbladet* (1915–25 ca.).

United States: *Nickeodeon* (1909–11), later renamed *Motography* (1911–18), *Exhibitors' Herald and Motography* (1918–1919) and *Exhibitors' Herald* (1919–27); *Moving Picture News* (1908–13), *The Moving Picture World* (1907–27), inventoried by Annette D'Agostino in *An Index to Short and Feature Film Reviews in the Moving Picture World, The Early Years 1907–1915* (Westport, CT and London: Greenwood Publishing Group, 1995) and *Filmmakers in the Moving Picture World: An Index of Articles, 1907–1927* (Jefferson, NC: McFarland, 1997), *Views and Film Index* (1906–8), *The Film Index* (1907–11), *Motion Picture News* (1913–30), *The New York Clipper* (1853–1923), *The New York Dramatic Mirror* (1879–1922). Two vast collections of reviews from the period have been published in facsimile editions: *Variety Film Reviews: Vol. 1: 1907–1920*; *Vol. 2, 1921–1925*; *Vol. 3: 1926–1929*; *Vol. 16: Index to Titles* (New York: Garland Press, 1983); *The New York Times Film Reviews, 1913–1968* (New York: The New York Times/Arno Press, 1970).

Scholarly Journals.
1895 (Association Française de Recherche sur l'Histoire du Cinéma, c/o Jean A. Gili, 15 rue Lakanal, 75015 Paris; website: www.dsi.cnrs.fr/AFRHC/AFRHC.html); *Archives* (Institut Jean Vigo, 21 rue Mailly, 66000 Perpignan, France); *Archivos de la Filmoteca* (Filmoteca de la Generalitat Valenciana, Valencia, Spain; see the address in Appendix 2); *Bulletin Domitor* (website: http://cri.histart.umontreal.ca/ Domitor/); *Cinema Journal* (University of Texas Press, Journals Division, 2100 Comal, Austin, TX 78722–2550); *Cinémathèque* (c/o Cinémathèque française, 29 rue du Colisée, 75008 Paris); *Cinémathèque Méliès* (Les Amis de Georges Méliès, 11 rue de Belzunce, 75010 Paris; e-mail: MélièsStar@aol.com); *Film History* (1987–90); new series (1993–seqq, London: John Libbey & Company Pty Ltd, Level 10, 15–17 Young Street, Sydney, NSW 2000, Australia; e-mail: jlsydney@mpx.com.au); *Griffithiana* (Cineteca del Friuli, Palazzo Gurisatti, via G. Bini, 33013 Gemona del Friuli [Udine], Italy; website: www.cinetecadelfriuli.org); *Historical Journal of Film, Radio*

and Television (Carfax Publishing Ltd., PO Box 25, Abingdon, Oxfordshire OX14 3UE, UK; website: www.carfax.co.uk); *Immagine* (Associazione Italiana per le Ricerche di Storia del Cinema, via Villafranca 20, Rome, Italy); *KINtop* (01992-seqq, Stroemfeld/Roter Stern, Oetlingerstrasse 19, CH–4007, Basle, Switzerland, and Holzenhausenstrasse 4, D-6000 Frankfurt am Main, Germany; e-mail: stroem feld@t-online.de); *Living Pictures* (2001–seqq., Flicks Books, 29 Bradford Road, Trowbridge, Wiltshire BA14 9AN, United Kingdom, e-mail: flicks.books@dial. pipex.com). The *International Index to Film Periodicals* (New York: R. R. Bowker, 1972–73; London: St James Press, 1974–8; Brussels FIAF, 1979–seqq) and the *Film Literature Index* (Albany, NY: State University of New York at Albany, 1973–seqq) provide bibliographic information drawn from an extensive list of film magazines and journals on a yearly basis.

6
Histoire de Détective

What an unreasonable request! Ten films! ... No, Sir, we are still not
equipped to grant access to that kind of stuff ... The library would look
as if it has been infected by some kind of tapeworm.

An employee of the Bibliothèque Nationale in Paris
answering Guillaume Apollinaire, 1910

How to Contact Moving Image Archives

Once we have identified the object of research, it is time to knock on the doors of
the archives where the films that interest us are kept. There is nothing special about
this stage: you write letters (no phone calls, please) specifying the nature of the project, and ask about the conditions under which it is possible to see the copies you
need. At this point, the really important decisions have been made already; that is
to say, the methodological questions, which the archives are not responsible for
solving in your place, have been addressed and you are now in a position to inquire
about procedures such as the conditions of access to the viewing material. In return
for the services and the access you are requesting, the least you can do is to treat the
collections respectfully and, if possible, to give practical help if the archivist needs
to clear up any doubts about the identity of the films you wish to see or about any
other aspect of your request.

RULE 6

Work in a film archive involves an agreement
over the mutual rights and duties of
the researcher and the archivist.
Both must ensure that the act of consulting the film
will contribute to a better knowledge of the work
and to its material preservation.

Putting it as clearly as possible, we should acknowledge that the archivist is some-body who is paid to increase, protect, improve and make known the property of the film archive. If the archive's rules provide for part of the collection to be open to the public, it has a duty to facilitate the viewing of this material and to provide the most suitable research tools for this purpose. Some archives are poorer than others and, therefore, not equipped with some of the technical means necessary for the study of film: one or more viewing tables, a projection room, a library, a catalogue open to the public, a collection of photographs, posters, screenplays and other material concerning the production and distribution of films.

The researcher must keep in mind the financial limits within which some film archives are forced to struggle. This does not mean that the archivist is entitled to make life impossible for the well-intentioned visitor. If the archive is a public insti-tution, the people in charge of it accept the duty of performing a specific public service. If the archive is private, and if its mission statement says that access is one of the reasons for its existence, it is probable that the archive receives private or pub-lic contributions towards its operations. In that case, viewing a film may cost more, but that is all the more reason why the paying visitor should be treated with respect and cooperation, not as an intruder. If the latter happens, the best answer is to turn to the public or private organisation to which the film archive belongs. Those who give financial support to a moving image archive must know what use is being made of their money.

This is not to say that the scholar is an absolute and unquestionable judge; quite the contrary. A researcher's responsibilities are even greater, because it is on the basis of your behaviour and according to the behaviour of those who preceded and will follow you, that archives will take a defensive or an open attitude towards the user. The policy of inaccessibility or diffidence which characterised some film archives in the past was due to the cumulative effect of a number of factors. The first was the difficulty or impossibility of ascertaining the legal status of films, often acquired without the rightful owners' knowledge (although most owners in the past lost interest in their films after their commercial exploitation.) In many countries the archive's concern was, and often still is, compounded by the fact that there was no copyright law, or if there was, it was not applied. The second factor was the des-perate struggle to save images which were of little or no interest to anyone, or were at best simply regarded as the object of a collector's obsession; but it is precisely thanks to the thousands of people who contracted this virus that film archives came into existence. The third variable is the lack of manners of some people who, once they have gained access to the films, tend to abuse their own rights. If curators had not reacted to their excesses with a severity which may at times have seemed unpleasant, film archives today would have very little left to show.

When making contact with any archive, it is imperative to be honest, tactful and tenacious. You must gain the trust of the archive staff, and that is not always easy, even when inquiring about such elementary rights as:

1 the right to information about the films owned by the archive, in line with the
   state of the catalogue (that is to say, its relative completeness and reliability), and
   the right to know about any technical or legal limitations affecting their availability;

2 the right of access to viewing material;

3 the right of access to supplementary information relating to objects held by the
   archive (for example, the dates of restoration, whether something came from
   another archive or belongs to a special collection);

4 the right to carry out research, whenever possible, on copies of a quality as close
   as possible to that of the originals.

For their part, visitors should make it clear that they are fully aware of their duties,
and that they intend to respect them. These duties may be summarised under the
following headings.

Clarity

Requests should be phrased simply and clearly – the ideal is a list of films in alphabetical order by title, with some basic filmographic information: the date, the
production company, the director. Let's make this point clear: if we ask to see 'that
American film with John Gilbert where the protagonist goes to war and loses a leg',
we shall at best receive a polite letter asking for further explanation, but we should
not be surprised if we receive no answer at all. Our correspondent may be an authority on silent cinema (and may therefore know that you are referring to *The Big
Parade* by King Vidor, 1925), but it is totally unreasonable to expect archive staff to
remember everything we have not taken the time or trouble to find out for ourselves.

Precision

The archivist is not a researcher in the user's service. Before applying to the archive
you must be as sure as possible of what you want. However sophisticated the cataloguing system, and however much it may allow quick cross-referencing (rare even
in the most organised departments), archive staff have neither the duty, the right
nor the time to do work on behalf of the scholar.

   Therefore, you should not assume that a request, for instance, for films from 1906
containing point-of-view shots can be considered precise. Let us assume that the
archive's computerised catalogue allows you to search by key words (which is highly
improbable), and let us assume that the cataloguers have been able to remember
which of the films from 1906 in the archive's collection might include point-of-view
shots. The question then remains: what definition of 'point-of-view' are you talking about? There are many, and it is possible that the cataloguer's opinion is
different from the scholar's. Besides, is it right to conduct research on point-of-view

shots in early cinema without viewing examples of films in which there are no such shots in narrative patterns which might have justified their use? This is a problem for the researcher, not for the person who makes the material available. Nobody in their right mind would dare ask a librarian to point out all the books deploying first person narration.

Care

The objects the archive puts at our disposal must be treated in such a way that their integrity is not threatened: restoring a film is very expensive, and sometimes the copy which is entrusted to us is difficult to replace (for example, the print may have been derived from a negative owned by another archive).

Notice

Requests for films and related materials must take account of the workload for the archive where you intend to work. Pulling an archive print from the climatised vaults is absolutely not like taking a book from the shelf, as each reel must go through a complex and time-consuming process of retrieval, storage in a cool area and inspection before being put in your hands. Any plan for large-scale viewing (anything over twenty or thirty titles) should be presented with the maximum notice, thus allowing technicians to find and verify the physical condition of the prints before making them available.

Moderation

An 'average' day's work at the viewing table allows you to consult, at a reasonable pace, two full-length films of five or six reels, or about ten shorts of a reel each. This is only a rough guide, because it is certainly possible to spend a week on a five-minute trick film, and to exhaust our interest in a single sequence of a two-hour fiction film in less than fifteen minutes. When organising a work plan, you need to take into account the time that may be necessary for repeated viewing; for setting up the reel; for putting it back in its container; for stopping the viewing machine to take notes or frame enlargements (if taking photographs is allowed by the rules of the archive); for making sure that a research assistant is available to repair any possible damage to the film; and so on. Asking for many more films than may usefully be consulted in the allotted time involves a useless and expensive workload for the archive staff and encourages a hurried and superficial viewing experience.

Respect

If the material we wish to see is subject to legal restrictions concerning access, it is better not to insist that the archivist break any agreement made with the holders of the rights or the collectors who have deposited their copies. Understandably, researchers feel a sense of deep frustration knowing that the films they want are near at hand and that they cannot see them. Fortunately, this does not happen often when you are dealing with silent cinema. If it does happen, we must not take it out on the archivist, who can do nothing about it (we are assuming here that the archivist is in good faith, and not using this as a pretext for denying us access to the material).

Discipline
Handling original nitrate copies (and all film prints in general) requires a certain amount of experience and manual dexterity. In general, nitrate films are not available to the researcher for the obvious reason that copies must be protected against damage inevitably entailed by repeated access. Only after several visits, and after demonstrating with convincing arguments your absolute need to consult the original, will some archives (and only some) be responsive to your request. If all goes well, we will be given a viewing table with manual controls where the image is not projected, but seen against a source of 'cold' light. In this context, it cannot be stressed enough that examining a nitrate copy is a privilege which is earned by showing a flawless rigour in the implementation of research methods and practices.

Feedback
The results of research should be made available to the archive for internal use by the staff. This applies particularly to filmographic data, which cataloguers are always eager to have, and to information about the condition of the copy. If a print seems in extremely poor shape, of if we know that the original has wonderful colours while the viewing copy is a faded black and white, we might tactfully point this out, ask when the print was struck (it is nobody's fault if this happened fifty years before), and enquire if anything can be done to have a better one in future. If the copy is excellent, and you tell the archivist, she will be encouraged to keep up with these high standards. An archivist knows very well that a properly printed viewing element contributes to the reputation of the archive which produced it.

The Tools of the Trade
This section deals with the equipment used to see films, and both the active (at the viewing table) and passive (in the screening room) use of archival prints. In either case we might want to ask to handle – or we might be given the opportunity to examine – the film print itself directly, for its images as well as for any other kind of information it may contain. This is particularly relevant for copies printed during the silent era, but it also holds true for any duplicate derived from them. Therefore, we shall not consider here films which are reproduced on media other than photographic motion picture film stock. A rationale for this decision will be provided later in this chapter and at the end of the book. If you do consult films via other media – out of necessity or choice – you can skip the following pages and go straight to the last section of this chapter. Before doing so, however, it might be worth at least having a look at the arguments set out on pages 166–7.

So here we are: we have the film in front of us and we are about to examine it. If we are allowed to touch and handle the print itself, we have to keep in mind a number of things and have at hand some useful items which any archive worthy of the name should have:

- *Gauze gloves.* If the copy has been printed recently, you should wear them to avoid fingerprints and dirt on the film stock. If the copy dates from the silent era, the gloves will primarily protect your fingers from scratches and dirt resulting from the film's condition (broken perforations, dust, chemical substances emanating from the nitrate). If the gloves are not next to the manual rewinder or the viewing table, always remember to ask for a pair. Technicians usually have whole boxes of them available.

- *A magnifying glass.*

- *A micrometer gauge.* This is used for measuring the frame's aspect ratio, the size of the perforations, the dimensions of the frame line and, occasionally, the thickness of the celluloid.

- *A comparative table of lengths and projection speeds* (Appendix 1), to be used for calculating running times.

- *One or more tables of edge codes* (Appendices 3, 4 and 5) for dating copies.

Some archives also have a microscope with a cold light source (to avoid damaging the print). Such a microscope allows you to discover details which are otherwise invisible on the screen and which at times increase our knowledge of the film's identity and state of preservation. It may seem an exaggeration to insist on the need for such an instrument, but you will soon realise by using it that a small semi-transparent surface like the frame is actually a vast visual universe. Some equipment has a variable direction light source which allows you to distinguish the trade marks embossed on the film by producers and distributors (see Plate 18), the traces left by printing machines, and other characteristics which are difficult to recognise with standard examination practices.

The Viewing Experience

The fate of a silent film and its fortune with today's audiences are decided at the moment the film passes through the mechanisms of an optical projector. The projector in question is most likely to be set up for showing recent sound films. The gate behind the lens is different from the full aperture gate (the one used for screenings of silent films in a museum context) used in the silent era, in which the aspect ratio is generally about 1:1.28 to 1.31 (see pp. 4 and 61). You will soon notice whether the wrong type of gate is in use because, for example, the heads and feet of the characters may not appear in full on the screen, or portions of the intertitles are cropped. In many early films the performers are so far from the camera that the edges of the frame seem to be intact; but with some experience and a sense of proportion it is fairly easy to work out whether the aspect ratio is correct. In any case, an intertitle filled with text will reveal any possible mistake: you will not be able to read it in its entirety, and then someone will have to remind the projectionist that it only takes a few moments to change the gate. (We assume here that the film was properly printed during the preservation process. If it wasn't, there's nothing you or the projectionist can do about it. This point has already been discussed in Chapter 3, p. 60.)

It is slightly more difficult, but certainly not impossible (at least from a technical standpoint) to ensure that the projection speed is suited to the movements of the characters. For a long time, 16 frames per second was the most common speed. As we have pointed out on p. 9, the adoption of the standard speed of 24 frames per second is the result of a long evolution which ended just at the twilight of silent film. Before then, speeds could be much higher (for some experiments with colour cinematography) or as low as 14 or even ten frames per second (for the amateur Oko film, 1913), and sometimes they could even vary within the same film.

It may be too much to ask the projectionist to change the speed during a screening (even if some archives and festivals do this on special occasions). It is, however, quite correct to ask that a silent film be shown at a speed other than 24 frames per second when this is necessary. Many modern projectors have built-in speed controls, in which case it is only necessary to establish what the appropriate projection speed is and adjust the projector accordingly. But even if the projector is not one of these sophisticated models, a variable speed control attached to the motor with diode connectors will fulfil its task quite adequately. It is neither cumbersome nor expensive, and can be plugged in and removed quite easily. If projection takes place in a commercial auditorium, the owner should not be allowed to get away with saying that adjustments to the projector require too much time and money.

What cannot be installed at a moment's notice (but is just as necessary) is the three-blade shutter, a device which remedies the so-called 'flickering' of the image projected at a speed lower than 22 frames per second. Anyone who understands a projector and has a little practical know-how will be able to make the modification without too much trouble: the image will now seem to benefit from a more continuous flow of light, instead of appearing intermittent and a source of eyestrain, as would be the case with a standard two-blade shutter installed on most optical projectors.

Then there is music, which was almost always an integral part of the cinema experience in the silent period, and which a number of festivals and some film archives entrust to orchestras, chamber groups, organ players and pianists. At this point the needs of the scholar and those of the general audience part company. If silent cinema is the object of a study with ambitions of objectivity, it is important to know what kind of music was performed at the time. Extant scores from the period are usually for piano, sometimes for instrumental groups and occasionally for full orchestras (see p. 7). Easier to find are the cue sheets instructing the pianist or the conductor as to which classical or popular pieces had to be performed during the show.

These were actually more suggestions than instructions. Simple improvisation and variations on tunes in the public domain were the mainstay of musical accompaniment. Some theatre owners even gave up having musicians in the auditorium and replaced them with sometimes exceptionally complex equipment for the mechanical reproduction of sound: gigantic carillons with a much varied acoustic range, pianolas with multiple rolls, string and wind instruments driven by a pneumatic apparatus. Few of these precious objects are preserved, and only in extremely rare cases can you see them at work in a projection room; a specimen of extraordinary beauty is held by the Nederlands Filmmuseum in Amsterdam.

Some archives have restored silent films by recording a soundtrack onto them (ranging from a specially composed score to the reproduction of phonograph records made at the time of the film's original release, or an arrangement of the original music). The aim of this practice was to encourage the commercial distribution of films which otherwise would have been seen by only a very few. The system has some advantages, but it falsifies the nature of a performance based on a clear distinction between an equipment producing images and a sound source in front or behind the screen.

This practice lies at the heart of a debate between 'purists', for whom it makes no sense to show films in conditions that do not respect the original spirit of the medium, and 'reformers', who are ready to accept compromises so long as it is to the benefit of the film. Everyone, however, is agreed on one rule. With very few exceptions, justified by specific historical circumstances, musical accompaniment should be intended as a complement to the film, not vice versa. Peter Konlechner and Peter Kubelka, co-directors of the Österreichisches Filmmuseum in Vienna, have repeatedly argued against any musical accompaniment at all, in the name of the quintessential purity of the silent image. Their position goes consciously against historical evidence and is an easy target for charges of critical idealism. (Incidentally, they are also wary of colour, remaining faithful to the abstract stylisation of black and white and deliberately ignoring that a silent film is often in black and white just because that is the way a silent film in colour happens to have been preserved in the archive.) Their protest is far from being naïve, though. It is the expression of a legitimate desire not to overload the film with embellishments under the pretence of making it attractive to the public, as well as a reminder that these additions and alterations betray the nature and atmosphere of the original film experience.

The fact remains that an honest musical accompaniment – neither 'wallpaper' music nor, at the other extreme, a virtuoso recital – is without doubt more faithful to the film than an auditorium plunged in aseptic silence. Especially when a silent screening lasts several hours, nobody will deny that music puts the audience at their ease, whatever the reasons that prompted them to attend. And the student who has the chance of hearing a pianist who discreetly underlines some dramatic passage or stresses an unusual gag may rest assured that her role as careful interpreter or casual witness is not in danger.

In the archive's film study centre, whether we like it or not, the interpreter prevails over the witness. There is no music, no sense of community with the people in the next seats, and usually no big screen: the film is like an ancient painting, or a statue protected from the weather, whose viewing is permitted only under specific (and definitely artificial) conditions. Respecting these conditions guarantees the survival of the object and facilitates the release of some of its secrets.

Most archives have equipment for the individual viewing of films: viewing tables for safety copies, hand-cranked viewing tables and rewinders for nitrate and, in general, for all films requiring special care. The most common viewing tables come from Germany (Steenbeck and KEM-Elektronik Mechanik GmbH), the United States (RGI), Italy (Prevost) and France (CTM). When an employee in the Library of Congress (Washington, DC) escorts the researcher to the viewing room, her first question is: 'Do you know how to use the Steenbeck?' But there is no great mystery about its use. Structurally, the Steenbeck viewer resembles any other flatbed viewing table. The instructions we are about to give therefore apply to the Steenbeck as well as to every other machine (whether vertical or horizontal) which operates on similar principles.

First, however, it would be useful to recall a couple of general principles on how films should be treated. Not all archives allow researchers to handle 35mm reels: this is a pity, since physical contact with films is a significant element of research. Where there are no such restrictions, and whatever the format with which you are working, there are two things you should never do: take hold of a reel lightly, by the edges only, as if it were a phonographic record; and unwind a film by hand. The first mistake will cost you dear. The middle of the reel will slip down to form a funnel which is impossible to flatten. The second will damage the film in the area most vulnerable to dust and scratches.

In the best organised archives an assistant will show us the films, how to handle the containers (the metal ones are sometimes a little hard to open), how to hold the reel and place it on the viewing table or rewinder. If the assistant is in charge of putting the film on the equipment, the responsibility is hers alone: we shall only have the bother of waiting while reels are changed. If we are alone, on the other hand, first make sure that the film can actually be seen and has not been damaged since last it was checked. If you are consulting a nitrate copy, and if the print shows one of the stages of decay described on pages 12–14, do not try to unwind the film. Stop everything, return the reel to its container (or better, don't even touch it) and call the assistant.

As for safety copies, the assistant will show us how to thread the film through the mechanisms of the viewing table. It is very simple – especially since we almost never have to put the film through the optic cell or the magnetic head that reads the sound

– and we shall soon learn to cope by ourselves. The things we have to know and which the assistant might not necessarily tell us can be summed up as follows.

Speed

The viewing table has a control which advances the film at the standard speed of 24 frames per second (in some models the running speed can be modified). The same control usually allows the film to be wound or rewound at higher speeds, but it is better not to use it for such a purpose, especially with 35mm copies. The faster the film goes through the gears, the greater the damage it suffers. Winding and rewinding a film is not like using a remote control to rewind a magnetic tape or to move the digital reader on a video disc.

Some researchers suppose that, in order to 'see' several films quickly, it is enough to run them at great speed to obtain the information needed at that particular time. This procedure is of doubtful value as a research practice, even when our object of research may perhaps be a single shot from each of the chosen films. A film cannot be 'scanned' like a book; this applies particularly to a silent film, the analysis of which requires greater attention.

Tension

If you must go backwards and forwards while viewing the reel of film, activate the control gently. Avoid sudden changes of direction: the film suffers and too much tension in one direction or the other can break it.

Breaks

If for any reason the film should break, or if we find it broken, stop the viewer and call an assistant. If no assistant is available, you could splice the two ends of the film with joining tape (there should always be some at hand); otherwise, you can simply put the two ends of the film together, winding the reel on in its direction of travel and insert a piece of paper so that the technician can find the break and put it right.

Rewinding

When you have finished examining a reel, do not rewind it: the technician whose job it is to verify the state of the copy after viewing will deal with that. It may happen that the reel has not been rewound after an earlier viewing: the image will then appear upside down. Do not try to rewind the film: the technician will do this. Meanwhile, you can look at the next film on your list, or sort out your notes.

Reelholders

35mm and 16mm films are wound around plastic cores or reelholders of various sizes. It is good practice to make sure that there is a core or reelholder of the same size on the side of the table where the film collects (the take-up spool): this will simplify the job of inspecting the print and avoid the problem of the film not fitting back in its container because the core is too big or the reelholder is larger than the box.

Adhesive Tape

When starting to watch a film, never use adhesive tape to stick the leader (the 'head', sometimes a strip of green film) of the film to the core: this risks causing dangerous tension in the film when it is rewound. Moreover, the glue on the tape can be transferred to the film itself, damaging it and getting dirt on the gears of the viewing table through which the film will go next time. On the other hand, when viewing is over, fasten the end of the film (the 'tail', sometimes a strip of red leader) to the outside of the reel. This will prevent the coils of the film from loosening and will ease the job of checking. In general, remember that a reel should not be rewound too tightly, but neither should it be wound round the core too loosely: excessive tightness causes scratches on the base and the emulsion, while too much looseness makes it easier for dust to penetrate and for the film to curl up.

When you have almost reached the end of the reel (that is to say, when you have reached its protective leader), stop the viewer. Despite the previous rule, many reels are still attached to the core by adhesive tape. If this is so, remove the film from the viewer track before the taped end reaches the mechanisms.

Caution

If, while viewing, your experience leads you to realise that this particular copy is rare or unique, or if you recognise that it is a nitrate film or a safety film in urgent need of restoration, do not be foolish. Stop the viewer immediately and call an assistant. In that way, you will also gain the esteem and trust of those responsible for the archive.

Safety

Finally, although it may seem unnecessary to mention it, no smoking, no drinking and no food are permissible near the viewing table. Everyone likes a coffee after three solid hours of work, but – for our own good as well as the good of the film – it is better to sip it at leisure, in a room set aside for this purpose (the better organised archives always have one not far from the viewing room). If the film is on a nitrate base, smoking in its vicinity would be extremely dangerous, for you, for the film itself and indeed for the whole building.

Never Trust a Film That Says 'Trust Me'

The list of practical advice is now complete and it is time to start exercising the brain, always keeping in mind the clues and pitfalls which may influence the understanding of the film we are about to see and avoid false trails and hidden traps. One could ask: why isn't it simply a matter of 'trusting' the film itself? Isn't it enough to have struggled to obtain access to the copies, learned how to organise a viewing session and to have taken every precaution to get the best out of a film without con-tributing to its destruction? What's the matter now?

The matter is that we have to choose. We can take the film for what it is, or for what it is said to be, and try to make it 'speak' to our sensibilities: this is our right, after all. But since we have reached this point, why not do things properly? We should not stand before the film as if we were about to begin an autopsy. However modest its aesthetic value, however massacred by time and manipulated by theatre owners, distributors and zealous archivists, a print in a moving image archive is more than ever a living object which asks to be examined sympathetically and respectfully as well as with objectivity. If the print being viewed turns out to be a discovery, our efforts will be amply rewarded. But because moving images are enti-ties which did not crystallise materially at the time when they were produced, films from the silent period have a history, and history is an endless minefield.

The first trap is a very treacherous one: however much a film may look complete, some parts of it may not belong to the 'original' work. They may have been inserted for a later distribution of the film, or even borrowed from other titles. The practice of recutting a film, still fairly widespread at the end of the silent era, was routine during the first years of the 20th century. Distributors, theatre owners and projec-tionists used to cut, splice and re-edit films for the most varied reasons: because a reel had been lost or had deteriorated, and had to be replaced; because the dramatic effect of an episode was considered weak, and it was deemed appropriate to make it conform to what the public expected; a censorship cut may have made the con-tents of a sequence so obscure that it became necessary to re-edit the rest of the film, and so on.

But this is nothing compared to the surgical operation a film underwent when, some years after it first came out, somebody decided to put it back into circulation (the alterations suffered by Stellan Rye's *Der Student von Prag*, 1913, are notorious in this respect). It may have been felt that the original intertitles were out of date, but the new ones sometimes had nothing to do with those they replaced, either in style, content or graphics. We have already mentioned (p. 9) that at the beginning of the 1930s sound was added to many of Larry Semon's comedies: it is easy to recognise that the music does not belong to the original films, but who can say how many other amendments were made?

Two copies of Irvin V. Willat's *Below the Surface*, produced by Triangle in 1920, are preserved in the Library of Congress in Washington, DC: in one of them, a French narrator reads a heavily ironic commentary on a grim anti-German propa-ganda story, which is hard to follow unless you have seen the other print or you know the original story. All the intertitles have been cut from the sonorised version, and someone viewing this print as their first encounter with *Below the Surface* might mistakenly believe that the film never had intertitles of any kind.

But prints which have survived without intertitles are in this condition for one or another of various reasons. For example, because the copies have been taken from original negatives. Instead of intertitles, one can sometimes see, for a fraction of a second, two diagonally crossed lines on the frame, or words written in ink, embossed or 'scratched' on to the negative, which are illegible on the screen (see Plate 39). In many instances, this writing refers to the text of the intertitle (which was printed separately and inserted at the marked place), the colour to be used for tinting and/or toning, and the sequence number of the shot. Sometimes the intertitle appears for a brief moment; one has enough time to realise that it is there, but not enough to read it. This is known as a flash title, and is common in copies destined for distribution outside the film's country of origin. Production companies often sent their film negatives abroad without intertitles, but accompanied by precise instructions on their number, placing and content. The camera negatives kept by companies in case of any possible further commercial exploitation were often without intertitles as well. Some years after the Russian Revolution of 1917, when the vaults of most large companies came under the direct control of the state (and later of Gosfilmofond, the national film archive of the former Soviet Union), the films produced by Aleksandr Khanzhonkov were confiscated just as they were, that is, as negatives without intertitles. Most copies of films by Khanzhonkov which can be seen today are struck directly from a first-generation negative, and if the positive prints have intertitles it is very likely that they have been reconstructed at a later date on the basis of scripts or other contemporary material.

Telling the difference between original intertitles, those remade at a later date and those reconstructed in the archives requires a careful eye for graphics and style, and a thorough knowledge of 'original' prints. Archives sometimes try to reproduce the intertitles by using the same typeface as the original, or printing a surviving legible frame several times until the intertitle reaches the required length. The difference is noticeable because the text will not show the slight scratches and printing defects which characterise a complete intertitle, but will appear instead as a 'frozen' image (hence the term 'freeze frame').

Given these practices, two challenging issues recur: is the print complete, and is the film close to its 'original' condition? The first question can be answered satisfactorily, although not definitively. To the second, however, we can only say: we shall never know, especially if the print in question is unique. The margin of doubt is very wide with films of the 20s; there is no definite answer for copies printed before then, even if all contemporary documents agree on a film's length, and a list of shots and a tinting and toning record is available. We might find three prints of a film which are apparently identical, but such an occurrence is in fact so rare that archivists take for granted that every copy of a given title has its own distinctive look.

Between the time when an employee of a production company noted down the order of the shots and the time when the audience saw them on the screen, anything could (and often did) happen. Directors and producers had second thoughts; something did not suit the censor, who demanded changes; distributors received a negative produced abroad and did not bother – because they were in a hurry or short of money – to follow the instructions for colouring the film at the printing stage; the laboratory ran out of a certain dye and had to print some parts of a scene in which interior shots (in ochre yellow) alternate with night-time exteriors (in cobalt blue) with the only dye left, ochre yellow. The next day supplies of cobalt blue arrived, and the prints produced from then on had the exterior and interior colours in the right place (among the smaller companies, the idea of stopping work while waiting for deliveries was not even considered).

From the screening event, when the projectionist could cut a section of film containing an awkward pause in the action, we have thus gone back to the moment of printing; and the closer we get to the origin of the copy, the more the idea of an 'original' print loses its meaning. It is a mistake to believe that a film is an abstract, immutable entity and that, once we have seen one copy, we have seen them all. This illusion, which is common even among experts, stems from misconception and ignorance. The former lies in believing that film is an art of reproduction, and that there is an ontological identity between the matrix and the duplicate. Ignorance derives from a refusal to acknowledge that the history of the production of moving images and its wider cultural effect is inextricably bound up with the history of the individuals who have been the direct cause of everything which constituted the 'internal' history of the print.

Each print has in fact its own history, and we must unravel it to understand that the alterations which a film has undergone are not just the result of random circumstances, but of projects, compromises and accidents which involved, as well as the object itself, the people who conceived, made and saw it. You should be aware that the analysis of a film's 'internal' history (misleadingly defined by some as its 'editions', a term borrowed from literary practice with little or no theoretical justification) can appear to be a pointless exercise in splitting hairs which those who regard the cinema as an instrument serving their ideas, rather than the other way round, may greet with a dismissive shrug. However, behind the discrepancy between the different prints of a film there are multiple influences, pertaining to different cultures and professions. These shaped the film in the course of time, turning it into the object before us. Moreover, the life of that object does not end with the process of preserving the film or with its showing in an archive: restoration, too, is the expression of a project, a declaration of intent, a relationship between the film and the people who 'saved' it or thought they did. A film is never completely finished nor restored once and forever: there is always 'work in progress' around it.

Splices

All those who handled prints of silent films (for editing, censorship, or projection purposes) have almost always left traces of their passing, which can be interpreted. An original nitrate copy usually shows several splices, made for at least three different reasons: the film broke, and had to be mended; the contents of the film were altered; the finished product could not be obtained without separating and joining different parts of a print.

The first reason is self-explanatory: every handling of a print involves the risk of breaking it. That risk was particularly high at the beginning of the century, when film technology was still in its infancy, but even today films continue to be scratched, broken, deformed by those machines which Vincent Pinel, former curator of the Cinémathèque française, called – in a rough but effective phrase – 'film manglers', that is to say, film projectors. It is also obvious that, if someone does not like a film, or if part of it is the source of aesthetic, political, economic or moral concerns, the simplest way of modifying its contents is to tamper with the shot continuity by suppressing, interpolating or adding bits of film.

The practice of editing for creative purposes is less obvious. In the period of the so-called 'early cinema', the idea of splicing together different shots in order to obtain a sequence with its own meaning was a real revolution which met with perplexity and resistance before becoming common practice. Until the time when cutting techniques became an art in themselves, complete with rules and tools for the job, the pioneers of cinema resorted to the most bizarre methods for making splices. All sorts of things were used, from sewing thread to metal staples (see Plate 21). Very soon, however, people learned that the most practical way of joining two ends of a film was to glue together the ends of each section.

Thus, even when it became easy to get several metres of continuous positive film (which did not happen immediately, since the processing equipment at the beginning of the 20th century had only a limited capacity), splices fulfilled two other fundamental functions. These were not directly linked to the principle of 'editing' in the current meaning of the term, but were somehow related to it. The first was typical of the 'artificially arranged scenes' of Georges Méliès, dominated by sudden substitutions of objects and people and by extraordinarily complex visions of fantasy. In his memoirs, Méliès writes that he discovered the secret of these 'special effects' in Paris, on the Place de l'Opéra, when his camera malfunctioned while a carriage was in front of the lens. When the machine started cranking again, a hearse had replaced the carriage on screen: this 'transformation' looked like an amazing optical effect.

The anecdote may or may not correspond to the truth, but Méliès cannot have taken very long to learn that the trick of 'stop camera and substitution' could not be produced successfully by simply interrupting the shooting in order to change the position of performers and objects: at least one over-exposed frame, corresponding to the pause, would have appeared on the print, to the detriment of the effect: instead, it was better to develop the film, cut the blank frames and join the two pieces of negative exactly at the desired point (during the first decade of the cinema's existence, the same result was often obtained by repeating the same join on all positive prints).

As well as being motivated – particularly in non-fiction film – by the necessity of reducing or concentrating the duration of a natural event or a human action at the moment of projection, the presence of splices is also associated with the colouring of the film stock by tinting, toning or mordanting. The film segments were divided according to the colour that had to be applied to them: all shots to be treated with red were immersed in a tank containing liquid mixed with red dye, all shots meant to be blue were put in another, and so on. Innovative filmmakers could create effects of changing colour within the same shot through ingenious systems which, however, could not be applied on an industrial basis; as a rule, a team of women would work with splicers and film cement, placing every shot in the right place according to precise instructions. A curious German short comedy, *Tragödie einer Uraufführung* (O.F. Maurer 1926), also known as *Wenn die Filmkleberin gebummelt hat . . .* (When the Film Editor Got Confused . . .), describes the distractions of a female cutting worker and the consequences of her daydreaming (upside-down intertitles, pieces of film that have nothing to do with the story, disrupted time sequences).

For those not present at that time who still want to know whether a peculiar editing strategy is due to experimental daring, to a projectionist's carelessness in 1918 or to the cavalier attitude of a film curator in 1954, there is nothing for it but to examine these joins directly, and to try to interpret them. How? First, by looking at their shape. For example, if all the joins of a 1907 nitrate print appear as straight lines, except for one where the corners of the film have been cut (the joint has then a trapezoid profile), and if things do not tally precisely at that point (the editing seems too audacious for the time, or the story becomes confused), then you can bet that the problem does not lie with whoever assembled the copy in 1907, but with someone else at a more recent date.

It is fairly easy to check the difference on a modern 35mm viewing print as well: the profile of a splice made on the negative always appears as a thin light line, along the upper or lower edge of the frame (see Plate 23B); a splice made on the positive copy of a former 'generation' will show up as a dark line (see Plate 23A). The difference is unmistakable even when the print is a third- or fourth-generation duplicate – that is to say, if other negatives have been printed in order to reach the copy on which we are working. Of course, this is not the solution to all our problems related to the study of editing practice in early cinema, but it is definitely something.

Identification Clues

Apart from splices, a nitrate copy always has something to tell us if the print is closely examined.

- The space between one frame and the next (the frame line): the thickness and shape of this segment are very variable and are sometimes characteristic of a specific production company. It may happen that the frame line is the only use-ful element for a preliminary identification of the film;

- The shape of the frame itself may also be characteristic of a particular produc-tion company;

- The inscriptions along the edges of the print, between the perforations: some companies fought the illegal duplication of their films by printing their names or initials in characters and wordings that could change according to the time of production (see Plates 51, 52, 61 and Appendix 5). The same technique was used by manufacturers of raw film stock, who resorted to codes identifying the year when the print had been made (see Plates 22, 47, 54 and Appendix 4);

- The dark area marking the distance between the profile of the camera (or nega-tive) aperture and the shape of the positive aperture: this is visible in the photo on page 49, especially on the right side of the frame;

- The 'shadow' of the perforations from the positive or negative copies from an earlier generation (page 49): when such detail is visible on the edges of the frame, next to the perforations of the copy being viewed, one may be able to establish whether a print has been derived directly from the camera negative or whether it is the result of one or more 'transfers';

- The number, width and shape of the perforations, as described in Chapter 1, are also characteristic in the films of the early period.

We must add to these elements the thickness of the print itself, although variations in this respect between one manufacturing company and another are negligible after 1915. It is worth pointing out that details like the frame line and the inscrip-tion between the perforations must be examined on prints made at the time of their release. Archival duplicates reproduce – in whole or, unfortunately, only in part – merely the frame, not what is around it. Other details, like the actual shape of the negative's perforations, are sometimes visible on copies from a later generation, but it is very difficult, if not impossible, to decipher them. If the copy available is a smaller format than 35mm it is better to give up, because none of the features described above can be examined closely enough. One last recommendation: For example, the presence of the edge mark used by the Pathé company in 1907 is

---

RULE 7

Identification clues inside or outside the frame are
indicators to be used comparatively, and are not
conclusive proof of the print's identity.

---

no guarantee that the film we are examining was shot around 1907. All we know is that the film was not printed in 1906 or earlier. There is a good probability that the film was actually made in 1907, but for the moment we are far from having proved it beyond reasonable doubt. In other words, the material information derived from the print is useful above all for ruling out other possibilities, but not for indicating the identity of a film beyond all doubt. The greater the variety of clues confirming a hypothesis, the smaller the number of alternative hypotheses. An inference appears to be all the more plausible the more different tracks, when jointly verified, lead to the same solution.

We shall have the opportunity of experiencing this on countless occasions, such as when looking at a nitrate reel held by the George Eastman House with a patchwork of shots from Charlie Chaplin's *The Face on the Bar Room Floor*, *Caught in a Cabaret*, *Gentlemen of Nerve* and *Recreation*, all produced by Keystone in 1914, or when struggling with a print of the Pathé film *Vie et Passion de N.S. Jésus-Christ* in which, during the Crucifixion sequence, Jesus reaches the top of a Golgotha from the 1902 edition, is nailed to a cross from the 1914 remake and dies in front of a backdrop from the 1907 version, all made by the same company: the whole in a single sequence (with two splices). This fascinating puzzle is not imaginary: something very similar to it is to be found, in a colour viewing print, at the Museum of Modern Art in New York.

These are extreme cases, of course; but extreme cases thrive in film archives, and we shall never exhaust them all in our lifetime. If we wish to go looking for trouble, all we need to do is ask to consult an anthology of early films. Archives have plenty of them, surviving from the times when curators used to put together on a single reel everything that seemed old and which they were unable to identify after the corresponding nitrate prints had been lost (or had been deliberately destroyed since they were believed to be chemically unstable, and therefore dangerous). Have fun!

Viewing Notes

At this point, all that remains is to write down in a concise but complete form the information derived from the examination of the copy. It is important here to be vigilant, and keep a sense of balance: the amount of work involved should be geared to our needs and to the results we wish to achieve. Such a requirement applies to any kind of intellectual work, and the methods to be used in this context are not very different from those of other disciplines. But the unique nature of the object we are dealing with is such that a methodic organisation of the data is essential, especially when it is a matter of assembling notes about films lasting only a few minutes, or even a few seconds. While the tradition of impressionist criticism may have yielded many benefits, it also caused the film scholar to overlook the habit of applying some elementary procedures based on fact rather than memory: perhaps because taking notes is considered rather pedestrian for those who cultivate the dazzling intuition that arises out of the very act of looking, or perhaps out of sheer laziness.

The activity of one of the founding fathers of film history, Jean Mitry, is a paradoxically brilliant result of the former attitude. Helped by a phenomenal memory and a remarkable talent as a film *connoisseur*, Mitry used to amaze his listeners by remembering in detail shots he had allegedly seen fifty years before and were now apparently missing from the print that had just been screened. Quite often it was no longer possible to check his claims, but their imperiousness and precision – together with the occasional checks which could still be made – had the power to sway even the greatest doubters. On this matter, what we have said about 'cultural' filmographies holds true: when the fertility of the interpretation clashes with the data's reliability, interpretation takes over. Putting the blame on Mitry for having misremembered the development of a sequence or the text of an intertitle, at a time when historiography and militant criticism were the only way of legitimising film as an art, would be like blaming Vasari for not having used infra-red rays to analyse Michelangelo's second thoughts and corrections in the Sistine Chapel.

Today, the means for analysing second thoughts and corrections do exist, and it would be foolish not to use them. Some scholars, accustomed to following in Mitry's footsteps (though with none of his genius), are hardly inclined to stringent reasoning and may try to persuade us that taking notes and cataloguing them is a waste of time, maintaining that hundreds of file cards and long days spent describing in detail scraps of nameless films are no use for understanding the inner meaning of a narrative pattern or a technical innovation. The recurring accusation will be to compare this kind of empirical caution to the barren meticulousness of the encyclopedist who pays more attention to the names of things than to their intrinsic value.

The only reply to these criticisms is to prove they are meaningless, by showing that names and things do not count for what they are but for what they stand for. Some film historians may wrangle over the spelling of a director's name, and stop, satisfied, once the precise spelling has been established. Anyone might be annoyed at reading 'Seastrom' in the first chapters of a book on Victor Sjöström, who worked in Sweden from the early 1910s and later emigrated to the United States, where Hollywood immediately adapted his name to its own commercial requirements and to the simplifying power of the English language. It is, however, one thing to ensure that Georges Méliès is written with the accents in the right place, and another to believe that inquiry into a film is over the moment one discovers the name of the leading performers. Knowing that a film by Méliès was made with a prototype derived from Robert W. Paul's Animatograph, rather than with the Cinématographe Lumière, is useful to us not because we may like anecdotes, but because it is important to relate the formal and technical characteristics of a film to the equipment which was used to produce it and which contributed to its commercial success.

The viewing notes are neither equivalent to a dictionary entry nor to an untouchable formula. They are a working tool subject to constant revision and updating; their value is never absolute, but it will last all the longer the more we endeavour to add to them information compatible with the working hypothesis we have adopted for our research (even if it is true that its formulation can in turn be influenced by the process of collecting data). Nothing prevents us from noting details we believe to be of potential relevance or useful for jogging our memory. We may be studying lighting methods for interior scenes in Italian films of the 1910s: our notes will include information on the use of low-key light; but why not spend a few words on the fact that Francesca Bertini was in the film and that her acting seems to be more restrained than usual? Obviously we cannot know whether in future that detail will be valuable or not, but it is worth remembering that no technical characteristic is an end in itself, and that there is a relationship between the positioning of light sources, the movements of the actress within the scene, and her performing style.

It is up to us to decide how we wish to record our notes: on file cards, in notebooks or on a computer. What really matters is that the system should be followed methodically. It should allow you to make corrections easily, and carry out quick cross reference. The content of the notes depends, of course, on our research and the ideas and methods we intend to pursue, and that is up to us. However, some basic information is important for everyone. Before listing this information, and the order in which it might appear on the viewing notes, it is necessary to state once and for all a rule to be followed not only on file cards, but every time one happens to name a film or use a piece of information:

The first line of our 'ideal' notes is reserved for the film's official title, which is often not on the print, but which in any case is our first filmographic reference point. On the second line write the title as it appears on the copy, or, in its absence, in the avail-

---

RULE 8

Always keep clear the distinction between evidence found in the print and information drawn from written sources.

---

able written sources. Whatever your preferred system of notation – asterisks, numbers or letters – you must ensure that every indirect piece of information is accompanied by a bibliographical reference. If you suspect that the title on the print was added at a later date, take note of it and perhaps find the date this occurred. Of course it is a great deal of trouble, but this is the only way to avoid what happened to many scholars forced to use incomplete, distorted or even wrong information because they had no choice but to trust those who went before them.

In general, archives include the titles given to unidentified films in round or square brackets. It is not necessary to follow this system to its extremes, but it is sensible to distinguish those films which as yet do not have a title from those whose identity is suspect or uncertain. *[SOME ARGUMENT]* is the archival title of a print at the National Film and Television Archive in London, and about which only the content is known: two passers-by start to quarrel because of an article in the newspaper. The fact that such a title is in English does not necessarily mean that the film was produced in the United Kingdom or the United States, but only that it is preserved in an archive where English is the official language. *(BOTSCHAFT DES PFEILES)* is the probable German title appearing on a print of a Danish film produced around 1906. The film has not yet been definitely identified, but a German trade periodical of that year mentions a film with this title – whose plot corresponds to the content of the archive print – among the new Danish releases of the week. On another part of the file card write in parentheses: (Denmark), so that we may have a firm starting point for our research. Somewhere else note the name of the periodical, its issue number and page, or the archive that has catalogued the film with these brief details. The same applies to the date, which can be entered in the right-hand corner of the file card: in round brackets if you doubt the archive information, with a question mark or a 'ca.' if the date given is a matter of conjecture. Next to the date, for convenience, you could mention whether the film is a comedy, a drama or a trick subject, though this does not commit us to providing definitions which, especially with early cinema, may be misleading. A title defined as 'trick film' in a turn-of-the-century catalogue can also be a comedy, perhaps of erotic nature, and can therefore belong in three different categories: the distinction between genres could change from year to year, at least in the advertising and in the production company catalogues.

Speaking of ambiguities, let us briefly return to the problem of dates (see pages 101–2). Which date is the most valid when we are faced with conflicting documentary evidence? This question triggers endless quarrels. Filmographies most often use that of a film's first public screening. However, filmographers often use the term 'release' for the date on which the film was made available to the exhibitors, which is not always the same as the date of the first public showing. Strictly speaking, the fact that a film was released on 12 January 1911 does not necessarily mean that spectators would have been able to see it on that same day. Sometimes it is enough to know the year of first public showing (or release); more precision means more trouble. Any official report on the release date of a film is a worthwhile piece of information; but this may not be always found in the trade press, in which case we have to rely on the earliest report of the film's public screening or (as far as we can tell) the earliest published review.

Another common practice is to mention the date on which a film was passed by the censors. This usually preceded the release date by a few days or weeks. However, certain titles may have been approved by the censors months or even years before their commercial distribution (in which case the censorship date is useful in determining when a production was completed). A film may also have gone through the censorship procedure after it had been seen by the public. This was often illegal, of course, but legality does not always regulate events (and more confusion arises). It may also be the case that a censorship board had to examine films released a long time before it was itself established, or that a producer waited a while before making up his mind to present the film to the censors or to the judgment of the public. We should also watch out for the unfortunate possibility that a film which went through the board of censors and was announced, complete with date and reviews in the newspapers, may never have been released at all. It happened every now and then.

In order not to fall victim to chronological obsession (or to an obsession for any film data), a reasonable question we could ask ourselves is: what is the use of the date? If we only need it to provide a legitimate reference point in time, it will be enough to specify that we are referring to the year the film passed through censorship or the year of general release (usually the same, except for films examined in December and perhaps released in January the following year). If knowing whether a film was distributed in January or in December is really important to us (for example, because a rival company may have plagiarised its contents), then it is advisable to make a further effort in detail. Finally, if we need to know who was the first to use a technical innovation, it might be more useful to establish the period when the film was made rather than the date of release or first showing.

As every historian learns sooner or later, exceptions and anomalies are so numerous that any attempt to rationalise events is bound to encounter serious difficulties: luckily, life is more complex than filmographies. But since studying cinema also involves dealing with dates and names, there is no choice. To avoid paralysis, always measure the effort against the result. You certainly must aim towards perfection in everything you do, but in this case the foreseen outcome should at least be worth the effort.

Thank goodness, not every aspect of the viewing notes raises such ethical problems. And even the scholar most reluctant to engage in empirical analysis cannot afford to ignore the following items:

- the place (archive, town, private collection) where the film comes from, or the circumstances (a festival, a conference, a seminar) in which you saw it;

- the nature of the medium (safety, nitrate, magnetic or digital reproductions);

- the format of the film or the medium carrying the images;

- the presence or absence of colour, and the colouring technique used, if any;

- the presence (if necessary, the number) or absence of titles and intertitles, the language in which they are written, and their nature (original release, foreign distribution, reissue, archival reconstruction);

- the type of equipment used in the viewing session;

- the date on which the film was seen;

- the number of reels, compared to the overall number in the complete copy;

- the length and screening time, compared to the projection speed;

- the archive location or accession number;

- marks, symbols and letters on the intertitles or elsewhere in the copy (names of actors, catalogue numbers, trademarks and producers' logos).

In that order, these collected data on the file card could look like this:

GEH 35 S bw (nt), viewing table, 29 aug 1970, r.1, 3 of 3, 1640 ft, 18′ (24 fps), FAB 7591.

This breathtaking sequence of letters and numbers is not attractive to look at, but it offers a great deal of information, saving effort and possible future mistakes. The film was seen at the George Eastman House in Rochester, New York, (GEH), on a 35mm safety (S) copy, in black and white without titles (nt) on a viewing table (we need not specify the type). On 29 August 1970, the day we consulted the copy, the film was incomplete (we saw only the first and third reel of a three-reel film); it was 1,640 feet long (the viewing table uses this unit of measurement in that archive), and ran about 18 minutes when projected at 24 frames per second. The location code used by the archive (copied from the box containing the film) was FAB 7591.

Why is it so important to know all this? Let's go through the list again. The archive source is an essential document of identity: we must quote it whenever we mention the film (if the film was shown during a festival, ask the organisers which institution lent it); this is something we owe to those who wish to check a statement we made about the film and establish the source on which such a statement was based. Not quoting it is a negligence one can barely forgive a manic collector. People who proudly claim to have seen a copy of a rare or unknown film without pointing out its source are dishonest towards themselves because they contradict their own desire to let their discovery be known and appreciated; the childish privilege of not letting others see the object they are talking about is not even justified by the presumed respect towards the private collector who allowed them to examine the print, unless collectors specifically declare they do not want publicity.

Those who are reluctant to say where a print was viewed are dishonest towards others as well, because they do not allow anyone else the chance to confirm or disprove the conclusions they have reached. Leaving aside any malicious intent, stating from which archive a film comes avoids confusion and possible mistakes. Remember that having seen a silent film during a festival, in a film archive or a collector's home does not necessarily mean that one has seen the film in question in the form which is known to others. In writing about our sample film, we shall say, therefore, that the copy belongs to the George Eastman House collection and is 1,640 feet long, that the second reel is missing, and so on.

RULE 9

Every print of a film is a unique object, with its own
physical and aesthetic characteristics, and should not be
treated as identical to other prints with the same title.

We should bear in mind that the film seen in an archive often originated from a
place other than the one where it was found; the collection of the Swiss abbé Joseph
Joye, for example, a huge repertory of world production from the early period, was
found in Zurich, then partially duplicated in Italy and finally deposited at the
National Film and Television Archive in Berkhamsted. Moreover, the 'internal history' of a copy depends, at least in part, on the country (or countries) where it was
originally shown, and the print in question – whose original area of commercial
use should therefore be stated in the viewing notes – can differ significantly from
those shown during the same period in other countries.

The importance of knowing which print we are referring to becomes clearer still,
even to the enemies of close analysis, when the format of the film is at issue. Did
we see a copy in 8mm, 16mm, 35mm or video? It can make a world of difference.
On a tenth-generation copy, *Un Chien andalou* (Salvador Dalí and Luis Buñuel,
1929) is not an avant-garde film: it is an indecipherable ectoplasm which some
people have ended by accepting as such only because the inscrutability of the image
can intuitively be associated with the unusual nature of its contents. We only have
to look at a gorgeous print held by the Münchner Filmmuseum to realise how
approximate are duplicate elements from printing elements of poor quality.

As a general rule, if you have a choice between a 35mm and a 16mm copy, choose
the former. There is no assurance it will be the better or more complete of the two,
but there will certainly be less likelihood of finding yourselves confronted with the
blurred moving shadows which, for a long time, collectors and archives handed out
as viewing copies. If possible, and if the research requires it, the ideal is to see every
available print: they may have come from different sources and may therefore reveal
significant differences.

To note the physical nature of what we saw is also of great importance. Unless
you intend to study the optical quality of images printed on different film stocks
(diacetate, triacetate, polyester), it is enough to differentiate the original nitrate
prints from reproductions on safety film. We have often mentioned that, ideally,
consulting nitrate copies is the ultimate goal of many research projects on silent
cinema; but because access to a film on nitrate stock is so difficult, you have to make
the most of the circumstances which allow you to do so. A nitrate copy has a distinctive sharpness and texture that cannot be reproduced on other carriers despite
all the progress in laboratory technology. Moreover, the original allows you to
analyse aspects of the film which a duplicate distorts or wipes out altogether: colour

(tinting, toning, dyeing by hand or mechanical means), perforations, frame line, edge inscriptions.

The importance of making a note on whether the print viewed is in black and white (as in our sample entry, where we used the abbreviation 'bw') or colour is self-explanatory. Knowing what colour technique, if any, was used in the source elements is no less crucial, and helps avoid hasty judgments: for instance, a 1906 Pathé *féerie* can tell us very little about its charm if the viewing copy does not reproduce the amazing stencilled dyes of which the French company was so proud. Nor should you rule out the possibility of coming across two or more copies of the same film with different colour schemes and systems (see p. 27).

For the same reasons, you should specify which equipment was used to view the film: in a projection room, on a viewing table (as in almost every major film archive), or on a hand-cranked rewind bench. You may wish to mention a sequence which included consecutive panning shots to the right and to the left. If the film was shown on the big screen, perhaps after several shorts, you should be cautious in trusting your own memory: even an expert researcher can lose concentration for a few seconds. If your notes make a clear reference to three consecutive panning shots, and if you have seen the film on a viewing table, you have every right to feel safe. By the same token, the credibility of your assertions on tinting and toning is likely to be greater if you say that you were given access to a nitrate print on a manual rewind table.

Between the note on the film format and the equipment used for viewing is some information on the intertitles. In our sample entry we find 'nt', meaning the print had no titles at all. If there are intertitles and they are written in, for example, French or German, the letters 'F' or 'G' for will remind us of this. If the film was produced in a country other than the one in which the copy was distributed, the translation of the intertitles may not have been accurate, or the text may have been modified. The number and position of the titles may have been changed, perhaps to suit local taste or censorship requirements.

The date of viewing is, among other things, a useful reminder of our current competence. Due to inexperience, some entries in our files may contain only scant observations and approximate remarks. In August 1970, for example, we may not yet have learned how to evaluate high-angle shots or rapid alternating cuts. If these are matters which now concern us, we would do well to see the film again (and until then include it only provisionally among our research sources). If the file card dates from last year, we may perhaps be more confident that we took note of high-angle shots and alternating cuts, if we found examples of either. It may also be that since we last saw the film, the nitrate has started to decay and the archive staff had to discard some footage in order to save the rest of the print. If other people notice discrepancies between our description and theirs, the date we wrote down may help us to find an explanation for this.

Make sure to note the length of the print: in metres or feet and in reels (ideally, the note should make a distinction between the total footage and the segments added to the film after its period of commercial release, such as archival titles). Saying that a film in two reels is incomplete is not enough: we should specify which reel is missing, and keep that in mind if some aspect of the plot is unclear from the notes taken at the time of screening. Most viewing tables have a footage counter; some, like those at the Library of Congress, can measure the film to the frame and calculate its running time at 24 or 18 frames per second.

Working in a projection room is a different matter. All we can do there is to view the film with a stopwatch in hand. But this is distracting, impractical and, most importantly, inaccurate, especially if we do not know what the correct projection speed is. It is better to approach the projectionist and ask if the cans containing the reels bear any indication of the film's length. Be careful: the label often carries only approximate information, useful as a reference point but not uncontestable data. And in an early film the difference of half a metre can mean a lot, both for the narrative structure and for such technical and stylistic aspects as cutting and camera movement.

The last item in our sample entry is the location number of the print. That's easy if you are working on a viewing table in the archive's premises; if you are in a projection room, all you can do is try to meet the projectionist and ask to write down the location code and number of the reel being shown. It is extra work, but before considering it useless and finicky, it is worth listening to the following cautionary tale. Among the countless treasures of the National Film and Television Archive in London there is a film probably directed by Phillips Smalley (perhaps in collaboration with Lois Weber, or perhaps by Lois Weber alone) called *Suspense* (1913). According to a friend, it is an extraordinary film, and on our first trip to London we manage to see it. Our friend was right. *Suspense* is an amazing display of technical innovation and genuine narrative tension: shots divided into three triangular sectors (with a different action taking place in each), bold positioning of the camera, a breathtaking editing style. There is, however, a wrong note: about halfway through the film, during a car chase, a man stands in the middle of the road and lights a cigarette. Surely he is about to be run over. But nothing happens: in the following shot the chase continues and the passer-by has crossed the road safe and sound. How could a remarkable film like this be spoiled by such a gross oversight? Maybe the film is incomplete. We go home, talk about it with people who have seen it, and our accounts do not tally. Somebody gives a different account of the story: the passer-by was run over, and the chase went on. We seek assistance from the Cataloguing Department and the mystery is revealed: NFTA has three copies of *Suspense*, but only one of them is complete. We saw the most incomplete one, while our friend saw a version which was not quite complete. The truth is that one of the cars brakes and is unable to avoid the crash, yet the passer-by does not get more than a few scratches and a fright. The police help him to stand up and go to one side, and the race carries on. Clearly, it is not our fault that the copy we saw was not the most complete, but once we know which one is, when we next want to see it or show it to someone, it will be essential to ask for the archive number corresponding to the complete version. Perhaps five years ago the only copy available was the incomplete, and later a better one was found: when writing about that film, which copy shall we refer to? The only solution is, again, to clarify the identity of the copy in question.

Now that we have dealt with the source, the carrier and its format, the length, the date and the equipment used for viewing, the presence or absence of colour and intertitles, the archive number and the screening time, we have just one line of notes in front of us. But a wealth of information is concentrated into that single line, and many issues have been raised in this simple attempt at putting together the precise details of the object we have examined. It may have seemed an onerous job, but we are now in a much stronger position. With these notes at hand, we can launch into the most daring interpretation knowing that our feet are firmly on the ground. The notes must now be integrated by our own ideas (whatever they may be), and ideas directly reflect our critical skills, but everybody is now given the opportunity to check them against the evidence that has been provided.

Ideally, a film should first be seen on a big screen (that is to say, in the conditions closest to those for which it was designed), and then on a viewing table. There is an instructive qualitative difference here. In the first instance, the experience is 'synthetic', its purpose being an acquisition of the 'global' sense of the work. In the second it is analytical. At the viewing table, the film ceases to be a homogeneous flow of images and becomes instead something we can fragment, concentrate or distort every time we decide to stop at a certain shot, examine the reels out of order, or study a particular sequence for perhaps a whole afternoon. Such distortion cannot be eliminated altogether, but it can be brought into proportion. If we have no opportunity to see the film on the big screen, we should first watch it on the viewing table without interruption, and then start again. In doing so, we must always be aware that this way of looking at films has little to do with the experience of an audience in the projection hall. We can stop, fast forward, and reverse the course of time for study purposes, and that's fine, but this is a luxury (or a curse) that viewers of the silent film era could not afford.

However artificial it may be, viewing a film in the form of a 35mm or 16mm print is definitely preferable to watching it on other kinds of media, either magnetic or digital. The eye does not 'see' the electronic image in the way it sees the photographic image; the brain decodes it, memorises it and understands it differently, both in relation to time and space and in a wider psychological sense. A non-photographic carrier can be a very helpful *aide-mémoire* after a repeated, thorough analysis of the projected image, but it does not replace work on the print itself.

Those who oppose this principle are keen to point out that alternative formats are practical and economical. They challenge – in the name of a misplaced sense of democracy – the so-called 'purist' attitude of those who demand to see images on a photographic carrier. (According to this opinion, the fact that digital or magnetic reproduction is cheap and available to all makes it more useful than material of better quality available only to the few, and subject to wear and tear). But this argument is more authoritarian than the assumption it is supposed to challenge, since it takes for granted that the distorted imitation of a work of art is more or less as good as the work of art itself.

For a completely different reason – that is, the understandable effort to reduce the costs of replacing worn-out copies – some institutions tend to support this serious prejudice, taking as an alarming justification the fact that most users are not as committed to analysing the formal qualities of the moving images as their narrative, psychological and socio-cultural implications. In ethical and intellectual terms, this is an unacceptable position, which is bound to have a devastating influence on the future development of film studies; it places the film archive on the same level as an imaginary museum whose curators may decide to show the visitor photographic reproductions of its paintings, maintaining that most of the public is solely interested in what appears in the paintings themselves, rather than in their formal values. The fact that archives will soon be likely to have no other choice than to show films in the form of non-photographic duplicates is not a good enough reason to justify the passive acquiescence to a practice which is morally questionable, and indefensible from a philosophical standpoint.

Since we spoke of 'ideas' about films, it is worth saying a few words on the best ways of gathering these ideas. Everyone knows about taking notes by the light of a pen-torch, one of those which do not disturb the person in the next seat. But when the film only lasts a few minutes, or even a few seconds, everything happens very fast, and note-taking may not be enough. For setting down momentary impressions in the auditorium or at the viewing table, a small portable tape recorder is of undeniable value. Instead of the effort – in the dark, with the film rolling – of finding the right words to describe what you have seen, all you have to do is whisper some words into the microphone; later, these intuitions can be properly developed in written form. You should be guided here by practicality and good manners: a mumbled sentence will be difficult to puzzle out when replayed; in order to speak quietly but clearly, tactful viewers try to find places a little way from the rest of the audience, far from those who want to enjoy the film in peace.

If it is used unobtrusively (it is never pleasant to be sitting next to someone who is muttering esoteric remarks into a plastic box, all the more so if there are several whispering voices polluting the silence in the theatre), a tape recorder can save us from creative paralysis: the brain always runs faster than the pen, and it is sad to stop at the second film because scribbling in the notebook has reached an impossibly frantic pace. Two important objections to this method ought to be mentioned here. The first is a technical limitation: if the film is shown with music in the auditorium, you are in serious trouble, and there is nothing left for you to do except leave the front rows of the auditorium, sit as far as possible from the screen, and speak a bit louder into your recording machine. If the music is being performed by a large orchestra you may as well give up, and it is better not to take out the tape recorder if the theatre is crowded and your activity is bound to annoy nearby spectators.

The other problem has consequences which can last long after the moment of projection. Listening to your taped observations in the comfort of your own home is very sensible, but if you do not deal with the tapes as soon as possible, you will end up cursing yourself for having used this method at all. Written notes, even when laconic or scrawled, can usually be deciphered. But a tape is a piece of plastic with a limited lifespan, labelled with ambitious yet anodyne titles such as 'Danish films seen in Pordenone 1986' or 'Brighton 1978/Pathé'. Before the tapes pile up – and they do – you must transcribe them immediately. You will not regret it. If you cannot keep pace with the taped notes (a whole afternoon is not enough to transcribe and develop the contents of half an hour of tape accurately), it is better to forget the tape recorder and revert to pencil and paper. We may take fewer notes, but we won't run the risk of being unable to use them when needed. Even if they have not been reworked or copied out into a more legible form, we can keep them in folders; our only worry will be whether we can read our own handwriting months or years later.

The swift progress in digital technology suggests other methods and possibilities of recording and organising your notes. Copying the recordings directly to the computer by means of voice recognition programmes will help you to get rid of all the hassles described above. Still, you will need to disentangle your improvised prose and make things clear to yourself through some sort of editing process. Do it right after your viewing session; if you don't, even your computer screen will be a disheartening mess of textual fragments.

If this issue has been resolved, all that remains to be done is to decide how to manage the different files you have set up for comparative analysis. You may have, for instance, one main file for each film and a set of subject files (for example: films with onscreen depictions of physical violence; panoramic shots of 360 degrees; films with the German actress Anna Müller-Lincke; prints coloured with a combination of different techniques) on which the titles of the corresponding films have been entered. According to the scope of the project, and to the extent of our interest in silent cinema, this data archive may include a few dozen or several hundred files.

Frame Enlargements

With the curator's permission, we may want to bring a camera suitable for making frame enlargements from the films being viewed. Basically, it is a slightly modified version of a slide duplicator which can be connected to the lens by means of an adjustable fitting (there are several models available, including some reasonably priced ones). Learning to use it does not take long. You need to know the optimum distance between the frame and the light source (a lamp next to the viewing table may be suitable for black and white photography, otherwise a flash gun will be required for colour duplication), and the exposure time in relation to the sensitivity of the film you are using. More sophisticated equipment is available for those making frame enlargements frequently, or by digital means. It is expensive, but relatively easy to operate, and satisfactory results can be obtained even when dealing with poor quality 16mm film. The most advanced portable model is currently produced by Canon. Some archives are equipped to make frame enlargements with computer scanners. Ordering them may be an expensive (because of staff labour) and time-consuming affair (allow several months for delivery), but this option can sometimes be the most practical solution to your problems.

Don't get upset, though, if your inquiry gets a negative response. Handling film for a frame enlargement may endanger its physical integrity, and institutions just can't afford the risk of having their work ruined by a careless treatment of their holdings. It is also very unclear whether or not the publication of a frame enlargement requires copyright clearance. That's not a problem if the film is in the public domain (as are most silent films made until 1923 under the current laws in the United States), but it definitely is a potential one in all other cases according to some very cautious curators.

As for the management of photographic files, improvisation is out of the question: with ten rolls of negatives which have not been catalogued, memory is not enough. To save our memory for better use, try the following.

- Note the photos on the viewing file cards, and give a number to the negative film and the pictures taken;

- Once the negatives have been printed, keep them in numbered envelopes;

- Make a list of negatives, with the photo numbers and the titles of the corresponding films;

- Whenever you print a photo, write the negative number on the back. In that way, you will be able quickly to locate the photo from the film you are after and it will be easy to retrieve the title of an image that slipped out of your file or that you lent to someone. It is not necessary to print all photos immediately; in fact, it could be enough to have a contact print of the negative and stick the small-scale reproductions on each folder.

Similar rules will apply in the event that you decide to download frame enlargements in your computer (printouts are still recommended for quick reference). No matter how you collect information, you must do it in a way that makes long-term retrieval a smooth, painless procedure. Here lies the advantage of having frame enlargements in paper form: since you might find more documentation on a film tomorrow or in the distant future, and since the photos, once they are printed, should be next to the relevant file, it is best to devote a folder to each title in which you can insert clippings, further notes, photocopies of articles, and so on. Even if you are interested in silent cinema as a whole, and not just in some particular aspect of it, there is no need to worry: the set of files obtained in this way will be of a respectable, but not a daunting size. And when data are easily accessible, you will have more time available to elaborate useful ideas, without which all this preliminary organisation is nothing but a wilderness of meaningless codes, words and images. Adopting and implementing a research method is only a matter of discipline; bringing the method to its creative outcome is a whole different matter. Making sense of history is a much larger endeavour than organising research files, and the responsibility it entails is not something that can be taught in a research manual. From now on, you must be your own teacher, and quite a demanding one.

Further Readings

Despite the flourishing of silent film studies in recent years, literature on the subject of viewing practice is still scarce. A general outline of the problems of access to film collections can be found in *Documents That Move and Speak. Audiovisual Archives in the New Information Age* (Munich: K.G. Saur, 1992). The problem of identifying early films has been addressed by Harold Brown, *Physical Characteristics of Early Films as Aids to Identification* (Brussels: FIAF, 1990); Suzanne Richard, 'Pathé, marchio di fabbrica', *Segnocinema*, vol. 6 no. 23, 1986, pp. 74–7 (a revised, French version of the essay was published in *1895*, no. 10, 1991, pp. 13–25); Jacques Malthête, 'Pour une véritable archéologie des premières bandes cinématographiques', *1895*, no. 24, June 1998, pp. 9–21. (Many more studies of this kind are needed, but few scholars have taken the challenge so far.) Ethical problems of research in film archives are confronted in Paolo Cherchi Usai, 'Archive of Babel', *Sight and Sound*, vol. 59 no. 1, 1990, pp. 48–50; *Film Preservation and Film Scholarship*, special issue of *Film History*, vol. 7 no. 3, Autumn 1995, and the *FIAF Code of Ethics* (Brussels: FIAF, 1998); *Guidelines Dealing With Misuse/Use of Film and Video Archive Material* (Stockholm: FIAT/IFTA, 1998, with accompanying VHS/PAL videotape). The Fédération Internationale des Archives du Film has published a *Manual for Access to Film Collections* in the *Journal of Film Preservation*, vol. 26 no. 55, December 1997. Ironically, the framework adopted for the manual is the opposite to that described in this chapter: active access is defined from the viewpoint of the archive, 'the selection of films put together according its own agenda (programming)', while 'passive access means that the archive generally waits until an individual or a group approaches it with with a list of requests' (p. 6). Most of the texts on film preservation listed at the end of Chapter 3 include a wealth of suggestions and insights which are germane to the methodology of the silent film experience; sorting them out and making good use of them is another question, as the information they provide may seem haphazard and often contradictory even to the experienced reader.

The Apollinaire quote at the beginning of the chapter is from Pascal Hédegat (pseu-
donym for Guillaume Apollinaire), 'Le cinéma à la Nationale', *L'Intransigeant*, 1
March 1910, pp. 1–2. My thanks to Stephen Bottomore, who located the article and
brought it to my attention.

7
Film History Pursued by Other Means

All in all, the creative act is not performed by the artist alone;
the spectator brings the work in contact with the external world
by deciphering and interpreting its inner qualifications.

Marcel Duchamp

Film Spectatorship as an Art Form

Spectators who know what they are doing pay attention to the content of every film they watch, but also to the technical and environmental conditions of the film's presentation. This holds true in all circumstances: during an evening at the movie theatre, in the course of a festival, in front of the video. When it is a matter of watching a film made in the early 20th century, you need to make an extra commitment: you must try to imagine the effect of the film when it was first distributed and how that differs from the event you are witnessing.

This problem can be examined from two points of view. On the one hand, there is what we have called the 'internal history' of the copy, that is to say, the alterations which the print has undergone over the years. On the other, there is the historical, psychological and cultural distance between ourselves and, say, an audience of the year 1910. No historical enquiry will ever be able to bridge it completely. This is no excuse to abandon the attempt. We should try to imagine ourselves as the people in the period when the film was made, yet be aware that we are definitely not those people, without veiling our experience with a conceptual apparatus which distorts the object rather than bringing it closer to our understanding.

From the first point of view, knowing how to watch a silent film involves realising how it has been presented to us and possibly modified in order to make it available. At the end of the first chapter we reviewed some of the most typical errors made in the past by technicians and archivists in their efforts to duplicate 'original' prints. Now it is time to delve further into what was outlined in Chapter 3: restoration, the synthesis of every modification to the original print according to a coherent vision of what the film would have been originally and how it 'should' appear to a modern audience. This does not mean that every film you see in an archive is always the result of carefully conceived actions and strategies. Having to deal with staggering amounts of decaying film and insufficient human or financial resources, film archives are forced to set a minimum standard for what is considered an acceptable level of intervention, and must apply this standard systematically without discussing individual cases except those that present especially challenging problems or are seen as being of exceptional aesthetic and historical relevance.

The restoration of a film is often the result of individual tenacity (or obsession): after all, that is how a monumental opus such as Abel Gance's *Napoléon* has been brought back to a condition relatively close to the original. Whatever the starting point, there are usually two aims connected to this goal: theoretical consistency, sometimes misnamed 'textual integrity', and entertainment. In various ways and with different degrees of scientific accuracy, almost every so-called film restoration has gone to one extreme or the other, or looked for a synthesis of the two.

According to the consistency principle, a restoration is complete when the final result reveals what is supposed to have been the original concept of the film along with the incongruities and gaps shown by the copy that has come down to us. If, for example, it is certain that the second-to-last shot of a film is missing, the restorer might come to the extreme solution of pointing this out by inserting a piece of dark or blank film, perhaps describing the missing shot in an intertitle, or by inserting a production still of the shot, as we have seen in Chapter 3. In that way, the viewer is informed that the object of restoration is incomplete and that the lacuna has affected a significant part of the work. Similarly, if research shows that shots or intertitles in a 1914 film were added after its first commercial distribution (and if the purpose of restoration is to reconstruct the film to the form in which it was presumably shown to audiences in 1914), the additions will have to be removed. If the text of lost intertitles has been recovered, curators may try to reproduce the original typeface and the original designs; or they may do without the designs and use modern lettering, but in either case it will have to be pointed out that this is a reconstruction, not a reproduction.

The sum of these precautions is meant to confirm the curator's integrity towards the film and towards its eventual audience. We have been deceived too often by prints which we thought were conceived in a certain way but which turn out to have been modified in recent times. These alterations were made not by those who exploited the films for profit – as might have happened even many years after their first showing – but by those who had undertaken to hand down the work to posterity without the competence to do so, nor an awareness of the ethical issues involved.

There is a problem, though: don't all these precautions form a palimpsest of codes, emendations and interruptions which deny the non-specialist public the sheer pleasure of watching a film? And don't they deprive the informed spectators of that aesthetic pleasure which they could derive from a copy which might not be flawless from the point of view of its fidelity to the 'original', but which is, nevertheless, perfectly coherent in terms of narrative structure and image quality?

Curators who have taken this approach may answer that a beautiful but unfaithful copy is to be preferred to a print which conforms to a presumed 'original version' but which in some way disrupts the very emotional impact that won the film acclaim in the first place and on which its reputation is founded; or which makes this emotion disappear by reducing it to a sterile intellectual exercise. Saving and preserving films in order to show them as dissected corpses rather than living memories is – according to this philosophy of restoration – a blatant contradiction in terms. A paradigm of this approach is represented by the 1999 showing in Paris of *Enoch Arden* (W. Christy Cabanne, 1915) with live music and a recital of the poem by Alfred Lord Tennyson, the literary source of the film. The screening was often interrupted so that the performer could read the poem, and the ending was left out because it did not correspond to the original text. The problem here is not the experiment as such, but the fact that a historical document was deliberately mutilated and used as a background for an event where cinema had to be excused for not being interesting enough in itself.

Another telling example is provided by the three versions of D.W. Griffith's *Intolerance* (1916) which followed each other at almost yearly intervals between 1987 and 1989. The first, based on a copy from Raymond Rohauer's collection, was screened at the Avignon Festival in France with an orchestral accompaniment composed for the occasion by Antoine Duhamel and Pierre Jansen. The second was the result of a joint effort by Thames Television, film historians Kevin Brownlow and David Gill, and the American composer Carl Davis, to whom we also owe a new score for the reconstruction of Gance's *Napoléon*. The third was presented by the Museum of Modern Art, New York, in collaboration with the Library of Congress in Washington.

The Museum of Modern Art restoration project was prompted by two extraordinary events: the discovery of instrumental parts of the score for the first 'official' public screening of *Intolerance* on 5 September 1916 (other unofficial screenings had been held in California in the preceding weeks), and the retrieval of a notebook containing the first frame of every shot in the film, in the order designed by Griffith three months before the official premiere. Thanks to these frames and the detailed instructions on the score, it was possible to work out what was apparently missing from the many copies which were then available and which had been so modified over the years that each print seemed part of an intricate puzzle of versions, amendments and additions. Curators tried to imagine what *Intolerance* might have looked like on that evening in September 1916, and attempted what nobody had so far managed: assembling every shot in the right order, and inserting freeze frames (taken from the notebook) for the missing parts, the shot lengths being determined by the score.

When this version of *Intolerance* was shown to the audience of the New York Film Festival on 2 October 1989, a fierce debate mingled with applause: the film had substantially 'changed' from what had been known until then. New ideas and narrative digressions were recognisable; some episodes, which in earlier versions were so brief that they seemed to have been extensively cut, appeared to be better motivated; and

Griffith's controversial political opinions gained complexity and depth. Missing, in contrast, was the kind of emotional involvement which in a film like *Intolerance* can lead to genuinely thrilling moments. These were precisely the aspects which had been prioritised in the version from the series 'Thames Silents', thanks above all to the rhetorical impact of Carl Davis's score; they also re-emerged at each showing of the Rohauer/Duhamel-Jansen version, enhanced by a sophisticated musical accompaniment which often helped to highlight the dramatic peaks of each episode.

The orchestral music of the reconstructed *Intolerance* from the Museum of Modern Art was from Joseph Carl Breil's own score. It was written in 1916, under the supervision of Griffith himself, and followed the current conventions of musical accompaniment for silent films. It had plenty of ambition, and several quotations from material in the public domain, from Wagner to what would soon become the American national anthem. It is not great music, but it is the music which viewers actually heard in 1916 at some American showings of the film. Nothing to do with the freely recreated scores by Davis or Duhamel and Jansen.

Deliberately or not, all of the above projects take into account the fact that Griffith himself had decided – at various points in his life – to make further amendments to his film. In a way, the various stages in this process are worth documenting as much as their starting point. The question would perhaps lead us too far, but is germane to the issue of intellectual consistency in film studies. What option should be preferred when watching and studying silent cinema? Incomplete authenticity or artificial beauty? There is no hard and fast solution to this dilemma, but several options are correct and plausible, partly because they are culturally inevitable and partly because all we ask is that in each case the objectives should be clearly defined. When an institution presents a silent film which it claims to have restored, the result may fall into one of the following categories:

1   The film is being shown just as it was found, with all the gaps and imperfections it had when the copy became part of the archive's collection. Here the only action taken by the technicians has been to duplicate the film onto another carrier and to eliminate the most noticeable flaws. Even in the case of more thorough intervention, curators will ensure that creating a new version will not destroy the preceding one, of which at least a negative and the 'original' will be kept.

2   The film is being shown in the version which comes closest to the one that is believed to have been shown for the first time, or at a certain moment in its commercial distribution. If this cannot be achieved, the copy may be supplemented with inserted visual information explaining the distortions or incompleteness.

3   The intentions of whoever made the film are known, and the copy restores the film to the state it should have been in before other material, historical and/or economic factors altered it. Sometimes this operation may have been carried out

by the authors themselves, and if so it should be respected. However, the result does not necessarily correspond to what viewers of the time actually saw on the screen.

4 Somebody got hold of a print of the film and manipulated it in order to create a new work, with or without taking responsibility for such an action. Whether we should accept or reject this intrusion depends on value judgments which change according to cultural standards and with the passing of time, but it is essential that this manipulation (by an archive or an author) should not be confused with the historical identity of the object. When the alteration is intended to create an entirely new work (as happened in 1984 with *Metropolis* by Giorgio Moroder, made with footage from the 1926 film of the same title by Fritz Lang), it is important that the intervention should not involve the destruction of the archive material.

When looking at a silent film being projected in a theatre, or being analysed at the viewing table, always remember that a different film was actually seen at the time of its commercial release. We can get close to this condition only if we have the rare opportunity of seeing the nitrate copy; but the equipment and the auditorium, the screen, the audience's psychological expectations, the cultural and economic conditions of the time cannot be reproduced nor recalled, even approximately. Aside from the fact that it may be worn and incomplete, the 'original' print is not the same document it was in the past: on the contrary, it is simply one of the many faces the work has assumed in the course of time.

RULE 10

The 'original' version of a film is a multiple object
fragmented into a number of different entities
equal to the number of surviving copies.

The multiplicity of 'original' prints is a fact which we must recognise whenever we analyse a film. Still, this awareness should not become an obsession: excessive caution can at times be more paralysing and destructive than a careless methodology.

As pointed out earlier, silent films were usually printed on cellulose nitrate stock, while we get access, in the best of cases, to a 35mm acetate or polyester copy. Apart from the fact that any reproduction necessarily involves a loss of visual information one way or another, we know that the clarity and the contrast which were typical of a nitrate copy can be imitated but never reproduced perfectly on a different carrier. We also know that the 'original' prints were often in colour, while many of those available to us today are in black and white. If they are not, it means almost always that the colour has been reproduced with modern techniques (the experiments in colouring copies according to the techniques from the silent period described in

Chapter 3 are admirable, though sporadic, exceptions), and it is certain that these techniques are as yet unable to render with absolute fidelity the subtle chromatic variations and light effects of the source material. But complaining because the best restored copy is shown through a projector which, even though it has a three-blade shutter and variable speed, does not use carbon lighting, reminds us of Theodor W. Adorno's comment about the 'resentful listener': some orchestral scores by Johann Sebastian Bach required, among other instruments, a hunting horn whose performance was so uneven that it could not be played with precision even by a proficient musician. What sense would it make then, nowadays, to feature an early eighteenth-century hunting horn in a performance for original instruments? In our case, this would be like demanding a projector which could not guarantee the steadiness of the projected image or an even intensity of light on the screen.

The progressive deterioration of the film print after repeated showings was taken for granted by the pioneers of cinema and by the industry which succeeded them a decade later, and was even considered desirable as an extra guarantee of the obligation upon producers and exhibitors to return or destroy copies after use. Cinema has always been an art of the ephemeral. It is still so today, but it was even more so in 1905, when the demand for new moving images had become so intense that films which could no longer be commercially exploited were thrown away without a second thought. The operetta scores by Jacques Offenbach, today considered of outstanding historical and aesthetic value, suffered a similar fate: when a certain piece of music had gone out of the repertory, the score could be used to wrap fish in the market of Les Halles. That some of these old films have survived, and can still be seen, is a very fortunate occurrence in itself. Their permanence in time was neither foreseen nor believed to be necessary. As we have seen, the differences between these films and their modern duplicates are numerous and far from superficial. Recognition of these differences does not mean that we should ignore their implications: after all, we know that many of the statues from ancient Greece were brightly coloured when new, yet the sculptors who worked on the temples of the Acropolis are judged great artists even though their work is now identified with the whiteness of marble. The same goes for classical Greek tragedy. It was certainly not performed originally as it is today; but it is not rejected as 'false' by modern specialists because of that. If we accept this standpoint, MoMA's *Intolerance* should be called a 'study version' or a 'reconstruction', aimed at understanding the original design of Griffith's work.

The Ethics of Research

The rules of intellectual work are learned by observing how research grows and evolves, by recognising our own and other people's mistakes, and by adopting a respectful attitude towards those who will use our work. In part, we can demonstrate this respect by refusing to use shortcuts or to resort to methods which sacrifice the value of the result to the ease with which it can be achieved. Remember this when studying a silent film, because the temptation to interpret it according to familiar precepts is strong, at times hard to resist. Yet resist we must: while early cinema certainly requires methods of analysis which are compatible with it, at times you must adopt an attitude of both detachment and identification, being wary of passively adopting present-day criteria for the aesthetic and ideological evaluation of a visual message presented in the form of projected images. The reason why people so often laugh when watching a silent film, even when it's a heart-wrenching drama, is that the narrative conventions, the visual and verbal signals of expression, the techniques for reproducing reality and the abstractions of meaning are so markedly different from our own. To regard them with an assumption of condescension and superiority is the equivalent of the unsophisticated or ignorant laughing at people of a foreign country because their manners and language are different from their own.

Instead, we should try to identify with a public for whom the moving photographic image was, and continued to be for several years, a real miracle, and with the rhetorical strategies being used at the time to communicate the meaning and the possibilities of film. Today, we take for granted that a hectic montage of shots belonging to different contexts should be immediately understandable. But can we really imagine how difficult and deeply felt the decision to place one piece of film next to another in order to produce the effect of continuous action may have been?

The average length of a feature film is now over ninety minutes, but there was a time when cinema owners resolutely opposed showing a story which lasted that long. Fifteen minutes were believed to be more than enough. Increasing the duration of a story to thirty minutes, and then to fifteen, was a possibility only achieved with great difficulty after harsh conflicts between directors, distributors and production companies. At times, films from the beginning of the century, lasting no longer than fifteen minutes, today seem so packed with action and incidents that they are very difficult to follow, but the 1908 audience was so used to it that they noticed with great precision details of gesture and décor which are barely recognisable to us after repeated viewings.

Early cinema audiences perceived the sequence of time on the screen differently from us. It was far from rare – and for at least seven years, from 1900 to 1906, it was common practice – to show two consecutive actions without worrying about establishing a direct visual connection between them: the causal connection was judged quite sufficient. (For instance, a shot would show a man wearing woman's clothes in order not to be recognised by his fiancée's lover, and in the next shot the same man would be seen in a grocery store, being forced by circumstances to behave like a housemaid.) This pattern of representing events is based on the concept of *time lapse*: an action was shown underlining its possible consequences, and then the next shot followed, presenting the consequences already in operation, even if the action does not start exactly where it ended in the preceding image. The passing of time was taken for granted, therefore it was not shown.

A parallel but contrasting case is the use of *time overlap*: a series of events is described and then, in the next shot, some actions from the previous shot are repeated from another point of view, reinforcing the continuity between the two segments. (For example, a burglar would be seen breaking the window of an apartment and entering the bedroom from the outside, and in the next shot the breaking of the window would be seen again from inside the house.) As time went by, these techniques fell into disuse. In the end, they came to be considered editing 'mistakes' (unless they occurred in an experimental film); nevertheless, for almost a decade, such narrative devices were considered perfectly legitimate, at least until Griffith and his contemporaries developed what we call today 'continuity' editing.

These are only a few examples among many. The same holds true for all instances of unfamiliar cinematic devices: they should not be judged according to today's criteria. They did not 'anticipate' more sophisticated techniques, nor were they 'late' compared to more contemporary stylistic parameters. It has taken years to persuade scholars not to label this period of cinema as 'primitive', with its derogatory connotations. Now and then, some specialists revive this definition claiming they have found new reasons to justify it. But before we follow their example, let us consider what definitions are actually for. Some help us identify a technique, a visual constant or a narrative model and recognise their meanings. Others force the film into straitjackets modelled on reductive categorisations, fashionable theories or tenuous intuitions. To make films say what one wants them to say, as if they were objects one can manipulate at will, is a petty exercise carried out at the expense of images which have been ripped out of the context which gave them life. Since early cinema (and silent cinema in general) have become areas of academic interest, they have given rise to illuminating theoretical constructions, but also to conceptual scaffolding which has no justification other than its own existence.

When countering this danger, one runs the risk of applying a remedy that is worse than the original evil: that is to say, we could turn 'historical fact' into the self-contained icon of the Filmography of all Filmographies. Adopting this fetish at its face value, with its high concentration of simplistic positivism, means turning silent cinema into a dry catalogue of names, dates, patents and events, mercilessly yoked together into chronicles totally devoid of life. In the past, this reductive notion of history as an expanded filmography has given rise to a paradoxical search for technical records: who made the first tracking shot, which is the first full-length feature, which was the first camera capable of holding more than forty metres of film, who shot the first views of microbes through a microscope.

Underpinning this antiquarian's approach to scholarship is a two-fold prejudice. On the one hand, it is the belief that putting fragments of evidence in neatly serried ranks is the essence of historical research, and that these pieces of information should be 'confirmed' by documentary proof, the mere existence of which is mistaken for relevance. On the other hand, it is implicitly claimed that research on silent cinema should exclude any kind of aesthetic or political appraisal on the works created with those machines, or by the men and women and production structures which made them possible. Thus a dual negative effect is produced in the name of 'historical accuracy': either silent cinema is left to the most gratuitous speculation, or it is treated as an object of study comparable to naval engineering or to the tobacco trade.

In doing so, the above attitude towards silent cinema disregards the fact that we are talking about artifacts endowed with an inherent artistic and cultural value: all silent films are such, from *The Birth of a Nation* to the humblest chase comedies. That the creators of the latter were generally motivated by intentions which do not wholly correspond to the kind of things usually analysed in books of art history does not prevent us from comparing their works to the music, painting and literature of the time when they were made. It is right, therefore, that the Musée d'Orsay in Paris, which is devoted to the arts of the late 19th and early 20th centuries, has dedicated exhibition space to silent cinema. Doing otherwise would have been to deny what has been repeated since the days of critics and theorists like Louis Delluc and Ricciotto Canudo, but which is too often taken for granted without putting the idea into practice: cinema, as a whole, is an aesthetic phenomenon.

Such are the principles. Now it is time to suggest ways to put them into practice without betraying the object's specific nature. We have already made some formal suggestions in the preceding pages about the principles to be followed in our endeavour. Having stated them as 'rules' and set them out in a way that they can be easily noticed has nothing to do with authoritarian didacticism. On the contrary, it is intended to stress their problematic nature. The other suggestions scattered throughout this book are mostly bits of advice to be recalled when a project seems to be running along the rails of predictability, or convenience, or when we fall prey to the ambition to say new things at any cost. It is inevitable that from time to time laziness gets the better of us, but the quality of our research and our pleasure as spectators can be lastingly enhanced by the ability to apply these principles systematically:

1 Whenever possible, see the greatest possible number of prints of the same title, especially if the film is the subject of a case study or of a carefully designed theoretical or historical hypothesis. Always make sure that your notes on the titles you consult are full and detailed. Clearly, it is often impossible to comment on every print shot by shot, but sometimes the important differences between two prints are also the least striking, and a set of good viewing notes – in addition to a well-trained, focused mind – is often a decisive resource for making the most exciting and unexpected discoveries.

2 When consulting information sources, never trust data implicitly. This is equally true for film credits, actors' faces, primary and secondary sources. Film journals of the silent period may be wrong as much as any other printed document. Reasonable explanations, contributory circumstances, causal links which seem

perfectly plausible can lead to resounding errors in judgment. The following example may clarify the point. A modern source claims that Danish director Holger-Madsen's first name was Forest. In doing so, the author accepted the information given by another text, whose author read the caption of a group photograph in an old corporate journal ('. . . Forest Holger-Madsen') and interpreted the Danish word 'forest' ('in the foreground') as a Christian name. The mistake was further reproduced by other authors, and is now widespread among writers on Danish silent cinema.

The opposite case also holds true: things that appear inconsistent but are not, coincidences which are believed impossible, dates and lengths of films that 'do not fit', styles that seem too old-fashioned or too advanced for the time may have a reason, and the fact that we can't detect it does not necessarily mean that one of the sources is mistaken. In their memoirs, film directors of the silent era could sometimes exaggerate their merits, or mix them up with other people's, precisely as happens today, and their attitude was often amplified by the journalists who interviewed them. Embellishing the truth was also common with some producers who were used to attributing to themselves the authorship of other artists' work. We are reminded here of a warning to researchers dear to Davide Turconi, who once said that studying the history of cinema is like venturing into quicksands. One wrong premise, one misleading or unverified piece of information is enough to change research into a hopeless tangle of fictional histories.

3   Part of the time spent visiting a film archive should be devoted to exploring its catalogue. If this is allowed, it can lead to the discovery of recently acquired titles or titles unknown to us. Time should be allowed for assessing any supplementary information about known copies (donors, date of finding, to which specific collection the film belongs).

4   Archive rules permitting, it is always best to consult an 'original' print of the film we are studying. One may think the advice in the preceding pages about the usefulness of examining nitrate copies and the extreme difficulty of gaining access to them are at odds with each other. In fact, there is no contradiction between the two claims. For those who watch silent films for research, and who want to make sure that their hypotheses are well-founded, a quick look at a vintage print can dispel many doubts. It is sometimes useful to explain to those who are in charge of preservation that the purpose of the request is not to see the film but, for example, simply to look at the print in order to check the inscriptions along the edges of a Pathé film (see Appendix 5) or the shape of the splices in a sequence with parallel editing.

5   Non-fiction titles deserve the same attention and respect normally given to fiction films. This advice would be quite redundant if scientific and industrial films, travelogues or newsreels items were privileged objects of aesthetic and historical

research, but they are not: scholarly attention is still focused mostly on fiction films. This seems easier to analyse because it is 'narrative' (as if 'narrating' concerned only what belongs to the world of the imagination) and more suitable as a testing ground for theories derived from literary practice, auteurism, and the cult of screen performers. And yet it is well known – and worth repeating – that many technical and stylistic resources acquired by cinema over its first thirty years arose and developed within this galaxy of images overlooked by most film histories.

6 Thousands of films held by moving image archives are unidentified. This is inevitable. Some of them were already incomplete when they became part of collections, which can make it hard to find their titles, directors or production companies. This is also their misfortune, since archives usually do not like restoring films with no name. When they must allocate money for restoration, curators want to be sure that the funds have been spent well, on 'important' films which are in demand from researchers and appreciated by the public as well as by the institutions making the necessary funds available. The imperative of film archives is 'preserve everything', but since resources are always limited, harsh decisions on selection must be made.

Unidentified films pay the price for this, and treasures of extraordinary value lie buried for decades and disappear through decay before somebody is able to bring them back to light. Some institutions at the forefront of the archive movement try to restore these films as well, and we can help them by integrating our planned viewing with the appraisal of nameless prints belonging to the period we feel we know best.

Film History Without Film

Whatever archive we have decided to visit or conceptual tool we have adopted, the one thing which should never be questioned is that films are given a chance to speak for themselves. While being projected, films can confirm or deny the ideas and causal connections we may have suggested in order to draw out deeper layers of their meaning. A film can tell a contemporary spectator much more than its creators meant to imply: each image is the mirror of a society and a culture, and because of our position in history we may know the consequences of these momentary images, and maybe understand better the circumstances which shaped them. But we must not exploit this advantage. There is a gap between the producer of silent motion pictures, the contemporary viewers of these images, and today's audiences. We may well attempt to fill this gap, but the fractures and absences are very deep in the case of silent cinema: too many material and historical variables separate us from it, and our patterns of perception of moving images have remarkably changed in the meantime. Herein lies the fascinating challenge of studying silent cinema: both the greatest discipline and a visionary mind are needed in order to bring back to life something which is relatively close to us in time. It is closer than prehistoric art or the music of ancient Egypt, but it can be no less mysterious and elusive.

To prevent this historical and psychological distance from becoming unbridgeable, it is better to watch silent films in a form which is most similar to the original one, that is to say, as a projection of light through a semi-transparent photographic base. There is a reason for insisting on this point. The industry is being very forceful in proclaiming that film is no longer necessary to cinema, and that may be fine in a commercial context, but not in a museum, nor in any other venue where history and cultural heritage are being preserved. One may argue that other systems are more practical and less expensive than film. Others could claim, with some reason, that viewing film on film is rapidly becoming a luxury that even archival institutions will no longer be able to afford in the near future. Both points of view are acceptable. We may first examine the photograph of a painting instead of the actual canvas, or study music by means of a recorded performance, or understand an architectural work through drawings or models. But sooner or later we will have to take the next step, and attend the concert hall, walk through the cathedral at different times of the day, observe the painting at close quarters, see frames of a film (as long as film exists as a photographic carrier) projected in quick succession on a clear surface. The sooner we decide to do so, the better we shall understand why cinema came into being and how, among the many possible patterns of evolution, its existence has become entwined with that of millions of viewers who laughed and suffered, followed their dreams and drew in the dark, in front of the screen, a new image of the world.

Further Reading
Textbooks and Surveys
Richard Abel (ed.), *Silent Film* (New Brunswick, NJ: Rutgers University Press, 1996) has established the record of having published the first (and, so far, the only) academic textbook specifically dedicated to this area. *Early and Silent Cinema: A Source Book* (London: BFI, n.d. [1995]), is good for quick reference but also marred by factual errors (beware of the bibliography!); see also Marshall Deutelbaum (ed.), *'Image' On the Art and Evolution of the Film* (New York and Rochester, NY: Dover Publications/George Eastman House, 1979). Although not exclusively dedicated to silent cinema, the special issue of *Film History* on *The Philosophy of Film History*, vol. 6 no. 1, Spring 1994, deals with many of the issues addressed in this book.

Scholarly Studies
The overwhelming surge of studies in early and silent film since the 1978 FIAF Brighton Conference has produced a vast corpus of research on a wide spectrum of topics, ranging from the shape of film perforations to animal rights, railroads,

and male hysteria. Richard Abel (*Silent Film*) has almost 200 titles in his selected bibliography of recommended readings. The following is a much shorter list, representing a reference sample of the most recent intellectual currents in the field and a complement to the scholarly texts mentioned at the end of the previous chapters. In chronological order: Barry Salt, *Film Style and Technology: History and Analysis* (London: Starword, 1983; 2nd edn, 1988); Fritz Güttinger, *Der Stummfilm im Zitat der Zeit* (Frankfurt am Main: Deutsches Filmmuseum, 1984); Tom Gunning, 'The Cinema of Attraction: Early Film, Its Spectator and the Avant-Garde', *Wide Angle*, vol. 8 nos 3–4, 1986, pp. 63–70; André Gaudreault, *Du littéraire au filmique. Système du récit* (Paris: Méridien Klincksieck, 1988); Noël Burch, *Life to those Shadows* (Berkeley: University of California Press, 1990); Thomas Elsaesser (ed.), *Early Cinema: Space, Frame, Narrative* (London: BFI, 1990), with two film compilations on VHS PAL videotapes compiled by the National Film Archive, London (*Early Cinema. Primitives and Pioneers*, 70′ and 95′); Tom Gunning, 'Film History and Film Analysis: The Individual Film in the Course of Time', *Wide Angle*, vol. 12 no. 3, 1990 pp. 4–19; Heide Schlüpmann, *Unheimlichkeit des Blicks. Das Drama des frühen deutschen Kino* (Basle-Frankfurt: Strömfeld/Roter Stern, 1990); *Early Cinema. From Origins to 1913*, special issue of *Persistence of Vision*, no. 9, 1991; Roland Cosandey and André Gaudreault (eds), *Images across Borders* (Lausanne: Payot, 1995); David Bordwell, *On the History of Film Style* (Cambridge, MA: Harvard University Press, 1997); Claire Dupré la Tour, André Gaudreault and Roberta Pearson, *Le Cinéma au tournant du siècle/Cinema at the Turn of the Century* (Québec and Lausanne: Éditions Nota Bene/Éditions Payot, 1999); Hiroshi Komatsu (ed.), 'Film and History I', special issue of *Iichiko* (Tokyo), no. 64, Autumn 1999, with contributions (in English, French and Italian) by Henri Bousquet, Jan Nielsen, Roland Cosandey, Vittorio Martinelli, Geoffrey Donaldson, William Uricchio and Hiroshi Komatsu; Noël Burch has produced a television series in six parts, *What Do Those Old Films Mean?* (Channel 4 TV, 1985; distributed in the United States by Facets Multimedia, 1989), dealing with Denmark (1910–12), France (1905–22), Germany (1925–32), Great Britain (1900–12), the Soviet Union (1924–8) and the United States (1902–14).

Silent Film as Seen through the Electronic Image
The experience of film in other media is discussed by Dimitri Balachoff, 'Psycho-Physiology of Film and Video', *Bulletin de la Fédération Internationale des Archives de la Télévision/International Federation of Television Archives Newsletter*, special issue, nos 7–12, January 1986 reprinted in *The Perfect Vision*, vol. 2 no. 5, Fall 1989; John Belton, 'Pan and Scan Scandal', *The Perfect Vision*, vol. 1 no. 3, Indian Summer 1987, and 'The Shape of Money', *Sight and Sound*, vol. 57 no. 1, Winter 1987–88; Paolo Cherchi Usai, 'The Unfortunate Spectator', *Sight and Sound*, vol. 56 no. 3, Summer 1987, pp. 170–5; Tom Mann, 'High Definition Television as It Stands Today', *The BKSTS Journal*, September 1981; Harry Mathias and Richard Patterson, *Electronic Cinematography: Achieving Photographic Control over the Video Image*

(Belmont, CA: Wadsworth, 1985); Timothy Palmer-Benson, 'What's Wrong with Video', *The Perfect Vision*, vol. 1 no. 1, Winter 1986–7. The use of viewing materials other than film in cinema studies was confronted by the Society for Cinema Studies Task Force on Film Integrity (John Belton, Tom Doherty, Ellen Draper, Christine Holmlund and William Paul) in its 'Statement on the Use of Video in the Class-room', *Cinema Journal*, vol. 30 no. 4, Summer 1991, pp. 3–6 and by the contributions of Bill Nichols, Royal S. Brown and John Belton to this debate, published in the same issue, pp. 60–72. See also John Belton, 'Looking through Video: The Psychology of Video and Film', in Michael Renov and Erika Suderburg (eds), *Resolutions: Contemporary Video Practices* (Minneapolis: University of Minnesota Press, 1996), pp. 61–72; Todd McCarthy, 'Digital cinema is the future ... or is it?', *Daily Variety*, 25 June 1999; Dan Sweeney's 'Electronic Cinema: A Parricide's Progress', *The Perfect Vision*, vol. 22 no. 5, July/August 1999, pp. 23–7; Jean-Fabien Dupont, 'Film and the Future of Imaging', *SMPTE Journal*, vol. 108 no. 10, October 1999, pp. 710–12.

Appendix 1
Film Measurement Tables

35mm metres	35mm feet	16	18	20	22	24	16mm metres	16mm feet
		\multicolumn{5}{Projection speed (frames per second)}		
		\multicolumn{5}{Running time}		
0.3	1	1″	1″	1″	1″	1″	0.1	0.4
0.7	2	2″	2″	2″	2″	1″	0.3	1.0
1.0	3	3″	3″	2″	2″	2″	0.4	1.3
1.2	4	4″	4″	3″	3″	3″	0.5	1.6
1.5	5	5″	4″	4″	4″	3″	0.6	2.0
1.8	6	6″	5″	5″	4″	4″	0.7	2.4
2.0	7	7″	6″	6″	5″	5″	0.8	2.7
2.3	8	8″	7″	6″	6″	5″	0.9	3.0
2.7	9	9″	8″	7″	7″	5″	1.0	3.3
3.0	10	10″	9″	8″	7″	7″	1.2	4.0
3.3	11	11″	10″	9″	8″	7″	1.3	4.4
3.8	12	12″	11″	10″	9″	8″	1.5	5.0
4.0	13	13″	12″	10″	9″	9″	1.6	5.3
4.3	14	14″	13″	11″	10″	9″	1.7	5.6
4.6	15	15″	13″	12″	11″	10″	1.8	6.0
5.0	16	16″	14″	13″	12″	11″	2.0	6.5
5.1	17	17″	15″	14″	12″	11″	2.0	6.6
5.3	18	18″	16″	14″	13″	12″	2.1	7.0
5.8	19	19″	17″	15″	14″	13″	2.3	7.6
6.0	20	20″	18″	16″	14″	13″	2.4	7.8
6.1	20	20″	18″	16″	15″	13″	2.4	8.0
6.4	21	21″	19″	17″	15″	14″	2.6	8.4
6.7	22	22″	20″	18″	16″	15″	2.7	8.8
7.0	23	23″	21″	18″	17″	15″	2.7	9.0
7.3	24	24″	22″	19″	17″	16″	2.9	9.6
7.6	25	25″	22″	20″	18″	17″	3.0	9.9
7.6	25	25″	22″	20″	18″	17″	3.1	10
8.0	26	26″	23″	21″	19″	18″	3.3	11
8.2	27	27″	24″	22″	20″	18″	3.3	11
8.5	28	28″	25″	22″	20″	19″	3.4	11
8.8	29	29″	26″	23″	21″	19″	3.5	12

| 35mm | | Projection speed (frames per second) | | | | | 16mm | |
metres	feet	16	18	20	22	24	metres	feet
				Running time				
9.0	30	30″	27″	24″	22″	20″	3.6	12
10.0	33	33″	30″	26″	24″	22″	4.0	13
10.7	35	35″	31″	28″	25″	23″	4.3	14
12.2	40	40″	36″	32″	29″	26″	4.9	16
12.5	41	41″	36″	32″	30″	27″	5.0	16
13.7	45	45″	41″	36″	32″	30″	5.5	18
15.0	49	49″	44″	39″	36″	32″	6.0	20
15.2	50	50″	45″	40″	36″	33″	6.1	20
16.8	55	55″	50″	44″	40″	36″	6.7	22
18.3	60	1′00″	54″	48″	43″	40″	7.3	24
19.8	65	1′05″	59″	52″	47″	43″	7.9	26
20.0	66	1′05″	59″	53″	48″	44″	8.0	26
21.3	70	1′10″	1′03″	56″	50″	46″	8.5	28
22.9	75	1′15″	1′08″	1′00″	54″	50″	9.2	30
24.4	80	1′20″	1′12″	1′04″	58″	53″	9.8	32
25.0	82	1′21″	1′13″	1′05″	1′00″	55″	10.0	33
25.9	85	1′25″	1′17″	1′08″	1′01″	56″	10.4	34
27.4	90	1′30″	1′21″	1′12″	1′05″	59″	11.0	36
28.9	95	1′35″	1′25″	1′16″	1′08″	1′03″	11.6	38
30.0	98	1′37″	1′27″	1′18″	1′11″	1′05″	11.9	39
30.5	100	1′40″	1′29″	1′19″	1′12″	1′07″	12.2	40
35.0	116	1′55″	1′43″	1′32″	1′24″	1′17″	14.1	46
38.1	125	2′05″	1′51″	1′39″	1′30″	1′24″	15.2	50
40.0	131	2′10″	1′56″	1′44″	1′35″	1′27″	16.0	52
45.0	147	2′26″	2′11″	1′57″	1′46″	1′38″	17.9	59
45.7	150	2′30″	2′15″	2′00″	1′48″	1′40″	18.3	60
50.0	164	2′43″	2′25″	2′11″	1′59″	1′49″	20.0	66
53.3	175	2′55″	2′37″	2′20″	2′06″	1′56″	21.3	70
55.0	180	2′59″	2′40″	2′25″	2′11″	2′00″	21.9	72
60.0	197	3′16″	2′54″	2′38″	2′23″	2′11″	24.0	79
61.0	200	3′20″	2′58″	2′40″	2′25″	2′13″	24.4	80
62.5	205	3′25″	3′02″	2′44″	2′29″	2′17″	25.0	82
65.0	216	3′35″	3′12″	2′53″	2′37″	2′24″	26.3	86
68.6	225	3′45″	3′22″	3′00″	2′42″	2′29″	27.4	90
70.0	230	3′49″	3′24″	3′04″	2′47″	2′33″	28.0	92
75.0	246	4′05″	3′38″	3′16″	2′59″	2′44″	30.0	98
76.2	250	4′10″	3′41″	3′19″	3′01″	2′47″	30.5	100
80.0	262	4′21″	3′52″	3′29″	3′10″	2′54″	31.9	105
82.3	270	4′30″	4′00″	3′35″	3′16″	3′00″	32.9	108
83.8	275	4′34″	4′08″	3′40″	3′18″	3′02″	33.5	110
85.0	286	4′45″	4′13″	3′48″	3′28″	3′10″	34.9	114

| 35mm | | Projection speed (frames per second) | | | | | 16mm | |
metres	feet	16	18	20	22	24	metres	feet
				Running time				
90.0	295	4'54"	4'22"	3'55"	3'35"	3'16"	36.9	118
91.4	300	5'00"	4'27"	3'59"	3'38"	3'20"	37.0	120
95.0	316	5'15"	4'40"	4'12"	3'50"	3'30"	38.5	126
100.0	328	5'27"	4'51"	4'22"	3'59"	3'38"	40.0	131
106.7	350	5'49"	5'15"	4'40"	4'12"	3'51"	42.7	140
121.9	400	6'40"	5'56"	5'19"	4'51"	4'27"	48.8	160
125.0	410	6'50"	6'04"	5'24"	4'58"	4'35"	50.0	164
137.2	450	7'29"	6'45"	6'00"	5'24"	4'57"	55.0	180
150.0	492	8'11"	7'16"	6'33"	5'57"	5'28"	60.0	197
152.4	500	8'19"	7'23"	6'39"	6'03"	5'33"	61.0	200
167.6	550	9'09"	8'15"	7'20"	6'36"	6'03"	67.0	220
182.9	600	10'	9'00"	8'00"	7'12"	6'36"	77.2	253
198.1	650	11'	9'45"	8'40"	7'48"	7'09"	79.2	260
200.0	656	11'	9'50"	8'44"	7'57"	7'17"	80.0	262
213.3	700	12'	10'	9'20"	8'24"	7'42"	85.3	280
228.6	750	12'	11'	10'	9'00"	8'15"	91.4	300
243.8	800	13'	12'	11'	9'36"	8'48"	97.5	320
250.0	820	14'	12'	11'	9'56"	9'06"	99.9	328
250.1	820	14'	12'	11'	10'	9'09"	100.0	328
259.1	850	14'	13'	11'	10'	9'21"	103.6	340
266.7	875	15'	13'	12'	11'	10'	106.7	350
274.3	900	15'	13'	12'	11'	10'	109.7	360
281.9	925	15'	14'	12'	11'	10'	112.8	370
289.6	950	16'	14'	13'	11'	11'	115.8	380
297.2	975	17'	14'	13'	12'	11'	118.9	390
300.0	984	17'	15'	13'	12'	11'	120.0	394
304.8	1000	17'	15'	13'	12'	11'	121.9	400
350.0	1148	19'	17'	15'	14'	13'	140.0	459
381.1	1250	21'	19'	16'	15'	14'	152.4	500
400.0	1312	22'	19'	17'	16'	15'	160.0	525
450.0	1476	25'	22'	20'	18'	16'	179.9	590
457.2	1500	25'	22'	20'	18'	16'	182.9	600
500.0	1640	27'	24'	22'	20'	18'	199.9	656
500.1	1641	27'	24'	22'	20'	18'	200.0	656
533.4	1750	29'	26'	23'	21'	19'	213.4	700
548.6	1800	30'	27'	24'	22'	20'	219.4	720
579.1	1900	32'	28'	25'	23'	21'	231.6	760
600.0	1969	33'	29'	26'	24'	22'	240.1	788
609.6	2000	33'	30'	27'	24'	22'	243.8	800
625.0	2051	34'	30'	27'	25'	23'	250.0	820
685.8	2250	37'	33'	30'	27'	25'	274.3	900

| 35mm | | Projection speed (frames per second) | | | | | 16mm | |
| | | 16 | 18 | 20 | 22 | 24 | | |
metres	feet			Running time			metres	feet
700.0	2297	38'	34'	31'	28'	26'	280.0	919
750.0	2461	41'	36'	33'	30'	27'	300.0	984
762.2	2500	42'	37'	34'	30'	28'	304.8	1000
800.0	2625	44'	39'	35'	32'	29'	320.0	1050
900.0	2953	49'	44'	39'	36'	33'	360.0	1181
914.4	3000	50'	44'	40'	36'	33'	365.8	1200
990.6	3250	54'	48'	43'	39'	36'	396.2	1300
1000.0	3281	55'	49'	44'	40'	36'	400.0	1312
1066.7	3500	58'	52'	47'	42'	39'	426.7	1400
1142.9	3750	62'	56'	50'	45'	42'	457.2	1500
1219.2	4000	67'	59'	53'	48'	44'	487.7	1600
1250.0	4101	68'	61'	55'	50'	46'	500.0	1640
1295.3	4250	71'	63'	57'	51'	47'	518.1	1700
1371.5	4500	75'	67'	60'	54'	50'	548.6	1800
1447.7	4750	79'	70'	63'	57'	52'	579.1	1900
1500.0	4922	82'	73'	66'	60'	55'	600.0	1969
1524.0	5000	83'	74'	67'	61'	56'	609.6	2000
1600.1	5250	87'	78'	70'	63'	58'	640.0	2100
1676.3	5500	91'	82'	73'	66'	61'	670.5	2200
1752.5	5750	96'	85'	77'	70'	64'	701.0	2300
1828.8	6000	100'	89'	80'	73'	67'	731.5	2400
1904.9	6250	104'	93'	83'	76'	69'	762.0	2500
1981.1	6500	108'	96'	87'	79'	72'	792.4	2600
2000.0	6562	109'	97'	87'	80'	73'	800.0	2625
2057.3	6750	112'	100'	90'	82'	75'	822.9	2700
2133.6	7000	117'	104'	93'	85'	78'	853.4	2800
2209.7	7250	120'	108'	96'	88'	80'	883.9	2900
2285.9	7500	125'	111'	100'	91'	83'	914.4	3000
2362.1	7750	129'	115'	103'	93'	86'	944.8	3100
2438.4	8000	133'	118'	107'	97'	89'	975.4	3200
2500.0	8203	137'	121'	109'	99'	91'	1000.0	3281
2590.7	8500	142'	126'	113'	103'	94'	1036.3	3400
2743.2	9000	150'	133'	120'	109'	100'	1097.3	3600
2895.5	9500	159'	141'	126'	115'	105'	1158.2	3800
3000.0	9843	164'	146'	131'	119'	109'	1200.0	3937
3048.0	10000	167'	148'	133'	121'	111'	1219.2	4000

Note: Running times above ten minutes are rounded to the minute.

Another method for calculating running times involves the use of the following table (valid only for lengths expressed in metres):

Frames per second	35mm	16mm
24	27.36	10.97
22	25.08	10.03
20	22.80	9.12
18	20.52	8.21
16	18.24	7.29

For example, in order to establish the screening time of a 16mm print of 219.4 metres at 24 frames per second, the equation is:

$$219.4 : 10.97 = 20 \text{ minutes.}$$

Appendix 2
Moving Image Archives

The following is a list of the institutions belonging to FIAF, Fédération Internationale des Archives du Film/International Federation of Film Archives (Rue Defacqz 1, B-1000 Bruxelles, Belgium; Fax: (32–2) 534 4774; e-mail: info@fiafnet.org; *Journal of Film Preservation*: JFP@fiafnet.org; website: www.cinema.ucla.edu/FIAF/fiaf.html). The directory, updated on 9 June 2000, lists all affiliates regardless of their status (members or associates). Additional information on the archives and other institutions affiliated to FIAF, their representatives and their telephone numbers is to be found in the FIAF website, or may be obtained in a booklet from the FIAF Secretariat at the address above. A comprehensive list of 577 FIAF and non-FIAF institutions is available in Wolfgang Klaue (ed.), *World Directory of Moving Image and Sound Archives* (Munich: K.G. Saur, 1993).

Albania
ARKIVI SHTETEROR QËNDROR I FILMIT I R. SE SHQIPERISE (ARCHIVE D'ÉTAT DU FILM DE LA RÉPUBLIQUE D'ALBANIE) – Rruga Aleksander Moisiu 76, Tirana, Albania; Fax: (355–42) 649 70

Algeria
CINÉMATHÈQUE ALGÉRIENNE – Centre Algérien de la Cinématographie, 49, rue Larbi Ben-M'hidi, Alger, Algérie; Fax: (213–2) 73 82 46

Angola
CINEMATECA NACIONAL DE ANGOLA – Caixa Postal 3512, Luanda, R.P. de Angola

Argentina
FUNDACIÓN CINEMATECA ARGENTINA – Salta 1915 piso 2°, 1137 Buenos Aires, Argentina; Fax : (54–11) 43 06 05 92; e-mail: info@cinemateca.org.ar; Web: www.cinemateca.org.ar

Australia
NATIONAL FILM AND SOUND ARCHIVE/SCREENSOUND AUSTRALIA – GPO Box 2002, Canberra ACT 2601, Australia; Fax: (61–2) 6248 21 65; Web: www.screensound.gov.au

Austria
FILMARCHIV AUSTRIA – Obere Augartenstrasse 1, A–1020 Wien, Österreich; Fax: (43–1) 216 13 00 100; e-mail: augarten@filmarchiv.at; Web: www.filmarchiv. at/filmarchiv

ÖSTERREICHISCHES FILMMUSEUM – Augustinerstrasse 1, A–1010 Wien, Österreich; Fax: (43–1) 533 70 56 25; e-mail: Peter.Konlechner@serv.univie.ac.at

Azerbaijan
DÖVLÄT FILM FONDU – 69 ave. Matbuat, Baku, Azerbaijan; Fax: (994–12) 939 296

Bangladesh
BANGLADESH FILM ARCHIVE/MINISTRY OF INFORMATION – 12, Gajnavi Road, College Gate, Mohammadpur, Dhaka–1207, P.R. of Bangladesh; Fax: (88–02) 865553 attn Film Archive

Belgium
CINÉMATHÈQUE ROYALE/KONINKLIJK FILMARCHIEF – rue Ravenstein 23, 1000 Bruxelles, Belgium; Fax: (32–2) 513. 12. 72; e-mail: filmarchive@ledoux.be

Bolivia
CINEMATECA BOLIVIANA – Casilla 99 33, La Paz, Bolivia; Fax: (591–2) 32 53 46; e-mail: cinbol@datacom.bo.net

Bosnia-Herzegovina
KINOTEKA BOSNE I HERCEGOVINE – Alipasina 19, 71000 Sarajevo, Bosna y Herzegovina; Fax: (387–71) 66 86 78; e-mail: kinoteka@bih.net.ba

Brazil
CINEMATECA BRASILEIRA – Largo Senador Raul Cardoso 207, São Paulo, Brasil 04021.070; Fax: (55–11) 5084 23 18; e-mail: acervo-atec-cb@sti.com.br

CINEMATECA DO MUSEU DE ARTE MODERNA – Caixa Postal 44, 20001–970 Rio de Janeiro, Brasil; Fax: (55–21) 240 63 51/220 31 13

Bulgaria
BULGARSKA NACIONALNA FILMOTEKA – ul.Gourko 36, 1000 Sofia, Bulgaria; Fax: (359–2) 87 60 04

Burkina Faso
CINÉMATHÈQUE AFRICAINE DE OUAGADOUGOU/FESPACO – 01 BP 2505, Ouagadougou 01, Burkina Faso; Fax: (226) 31 25 09; e-mail: sg@fespaco.bf; Web: www.fespaco.bf

Canada
AUDIO-VISUAL ARCHIVES SECTION – SECTION DES ARCHIVES AUDIO-

VISUELLES/ VISUAL & SOUND ARCHIVES/ARCHIVES VISUELLES ET SONORES, NATIONAL ARCHIVES OF CANADA/ARCHIVES NATIONALES DU CANADA – 395, Wellington Street, Ottawa K1A ON3, Canada; Fax: (1–613) 995 65 75

CINEMATHEQUE ONTARIO – 2 Carlton Street, Suite 1600, Toronto M5B 1J3, Ontario, Canada; Fax: (1–416) 967 94 77

LA CINÉMATHÈQUE QUÉBÉCOISE – 335, Boulevard de Maisonneuve Est, Montréal H2X 1K1, Canada; Fax: (1–514) 842–1816; Web: www.cinematheque.qc.ca

Chile
FUNDACION CHILENA DE LAS IMAGENES EN MOVIMIENTO – Clemente Fabres 814 C, Providencia Santiago de Chile; Fax: (56–2) 225 40 39; e-mail: fuchim@entelchile.net

China
CHINA FILM ARCHIVE – N°3, Wen Hui Yuan Road, Xiao Xi Tian, Haidian District, 100088 Beijing, China; Fax: (86–10) 6225 93 15; e-mail: cfafad@263.net

HONG KONG FILM ARCHIVE – Rm 716, 7/F, UC Fa Yuen Street Complex 123A, Fa Yuen Street, Mongkok, Kowloon, Hong Kong, China; Fax: (852) 2311 5229; e-mail: awstong@email.usd.gov.hk; Web: www.usd.gov.hk/hkfa

China (Taiwan)
CHINESE TAÏPEI FILM ARCHIVE – 4F, N°7 Ching-Tao East Road, Taipei, Taiwan, China; Fax: (886–2) 2392-6359; e-mail: fact@ms12.hinet.net; Web: www.ctfa.org.tw

Colombia
CINEMATECA DISTRITAL – Carrera 7a n°22–79, Bogotá, DC Colombia; Fax: (57–1) 283 77 98

FUNDACION CINEMATECA DEL CARIBE – Apartado Aéreo 50504, Barranquilla, Colombia; Fax : (57–53) 51 25 31; e-mail: cinemate@metrotel.net.co

FUNDACION PATRIMONIO FILMICO COLOMBIANO – Carrera 13 No.13–24 Piso 9° Auditorio, Bogotá, D.E., Colombia; Fax: (57–1) 342 14 85

Croatia
HRVATSKA KINOTEKA/HRVATSKI DRZAVNI ARHIV/CROATIAN CINE-MATHEQUE – Marulicev trg 21, 01 Zagreb, Croatia; Fax: (385–1) 619 06 18

Cuba
CINEMATECA DE CUBA – Calle 23, 1155, entre 10 y 12, Vedado, La Habana 4, Cuba; Fax: (53–7) 33 30 78 attn Cinemateca; e-mail: cinemateca@icaic.inf.cu

Czech Republic
NARODNI FILMOVY ARCHIV – Malesická 12/14, 130 00 Praha 3, Czech Republic; Fax: (420–2) 69 73 057; e-mail: nfapraha@ms.anet.cz

Denmark
THE DANISH FILM INSTITUTE/MUSEUM & CINEMATHEQUE – Vognmager-
gade 10, DK – 1120 København K, Denmark; Fax: (45) 33 74 35 99; e-mail:
museum@dfi.dk & cinematek@dfi.dk; Web: www.dfi.dk

Ecuador
CINEMATECA NACIONAL DEL ECUADOR – Casa de la Cultura Ecuatoriana,
Casilla 17–01–3520 – Quito, Ecuador; Fax: (593–2) 223 391/566 070; e-mail:
c.c.e.@uio.satnet.net

Egypt
AL-ARCHIVE AL-KAWMY LIL-FILM (NATIONAL FILM ARCHIVE) – c/o Egyptian Film Center, City of Arts, Pyramids Avenue, Guiza, Egypt; Fax: (20–2) 585 47 01

Finland
SUOMEN ELOKUVA-ARKISTO – PL 177, 00151 Helsinki , Finland; Street address:
Pursimiehenkatu 29–31A, Helsinki, Finland; Fax: (358-9) 615 40 242; e-mail:
sea@sea.fi; Web: www.sea.fi/

France
ARCHIVES DU FILM ET DU DÉPÔT LÉGAL/CENTRE NATIONAL DE LA
CINÉMATOGRAPHIE – rue A.Turpault, 7bis, 78390 Bois d'Arcy, France; Fax:
(33–1) 34 60 52 25

BIBLIOTHÈQUE DU FILM (BIFI) – 100 rue du Faubourg St Antoine, F-75012
Paris, France; Fax: (33–1) 53 02 22 49; Web: www.bifi.fr

CENTRE GEORGES POMPIDOU – Département du Développement Culturel,
F–75191 Paris Cedex 04, France

CINÉMATHÈQUE DE BRETAGNE – 2 av. Clemenceau, BP 6611, 29266 Brest
Cedex, France; Fax: (33–2) 98 43 38 97

CINÉMATHÈQUE DE TOULOUSE – 69, rue du Taur – BP 824 –, F–31080
Toulouse Cedex 6, France; Fax: (33–5) 62 30 30 12

CINÉMATHÈQUE FRANÇAISE/MUSÉE DU CINEMA – 4, rue de Longchamp,
75116 Paris, France; Fax: (33–1) 53 65 74 97; e-mail: cinematec–fr@magic.fr

CINÉMATHÈQUE UNIVERSITAIRE – Centre Censier, 13, rue Santeuil, F-75005
Paris, France; Fax: (33–1) 45 87 48 94 attn Cinémathèque; e-mail: Cinematheque–Universitaire@univ–paris3.fr

ÉTABLISSEMENT CINÉMATOGRAPHIQUE ET PHOTOGRAPHIQUE DES
ARMÉES – Fort d'Ivry, 94205 Ivry s/Seine Cedex, France; Fax: (33–1) 49 60 52 06;
e-mail: ecpa@calva.net

FORUM DES IMAGES/VIDEOTHÈQUE DE PARIS – Porte Saint-Eustache, F-75001 Paris, France; Fax: (33–1) 40 26 40 96; e-mail: jylepinay@vdp.fr

LA CORSE ET LE CINEMA/CINÉMATHÈQUE RÉGIONALE – B.P. 50, 7, route de Bastia, F–20 537 Porto Vecchio Cedex, Corse; Fax: (33–4) 95 70 59 44

MUSÉE DEPARTEMENTAL ALBERT KAHN – 14, rue du Port, 92100 Boulogne–Billancourt, France; Fax: (33–1) 46 03 86 59

Germany
BUNDESARCHIV–FILMARCHIV – Postfach 310 667, D-10636 Berlin, Bundesrepublik Deutschland; Fax: (49–30) 8681 310; e-mail: barch@barch-fa.b.uunet.de

DEUTSCHES FILMINSTITUT/DIF – Direction, Documentation, Information – Schaumainkai 41, D–60596 Frankfurt/M, Bundesrepublik Deutschland; Fax: (49–69) 62 00 60; e-mail: Deutsches.Filminstitut@em.uni-frankfurt.de; Web: www.filminstitut.de

DEUTSCHES FILMINSTITUT/DIF/FILMARCHIV – Kreuzberger Ring 56, D–65205 Wiesbaden, Bundesrepublik Deutschland; Fax: (49–611) 970 00 15; Web: www. filminstitut.de

DEUTSCHES FILMMUSEUM – Schaumainkai 41, 60596 Frankfurt a.M., Bundesrepublik Deutschland; Fax: (49–69) 212 378 81; e-mail: info@deutsches-filmmuseum.de; Web: www.deutsches-filmmuseum.de

FILM MUSEUM BERLIN – Potsdamer Strasse 2, 10785 Berlin, Bundesrepublik Deutschland; Fax (49–30) 300 903 13; e-mail: info@filmmuseum-berlin.de; Web: www.kinemathek.de

FILMMUSEUM/MÜNCHNER STADTMUSEUM – St Jakobs-Platz 1, 80331 München, Bundesrepublik Deutschland; Fax: (49–89) 233 239 31; e-mail: filmmuseum@compuserve.com

Greece
TAINIOTHIKI TIS ELLADOS – Canari Street 1, 10671 Athinai, Hellas, Greece; Fax: (30–1) 362 84 68

Hungary
MAGYAR FILMINTEZET/FILMARCHIVUM – Budakeszi út 51/b, H–1021 Budapest, Hungary; Fax: (36–1) 200 87 39; e-mail: h12283sur@ella.hu

Iceland
KVIKMYNDASAFN ISLANDS – Vesturgata 11–13, 220 Hafnarfjördur, Iceland; Fax: (354–5) 65 59 94

India
NATIONAL FILM ARCHIVE OF INDIA – Law College Road, Pune 411 004, India;
Fax: (91–212) 567 00 27

Indonesia
SINEMATEK INDONESIA – Pusat Perfilman H.Usmar Ismail; Jl. HR. Rasuna
Said – Kuningan, Jakarta 12940, Indonesia; Fax: (62–21) 526 84 54; e-mail:
snematek@indo.net.id

Iran
NATIONAL FILM ARCHIVE OF IRAN (FILM-KHANE-YE MELLI-E IRAN) –
P.O. Box 5158, Tehran 11365, I.R. of Iran; Fax: (98–21) 38 51 27 10/83 24 85

Ireland
FILM INSTITUTE OF IRELAND/IRISH FILM ARCHIVE – 6, Eustace Street,
Dublin 2, Ireland; Fax: (353–1) 677 87 55; e-mail: archive@ipc.ie

Israel
ISRAEL FILM ARCHIVE/JERUSALEM CINEMATHEQUE – P.O. Box 8561,
Jerusalem 91083, Israël; Street address: Hebron Road, 91083 Jerusalem, Israël;
Fax: (972–2) 673 30 76; e-mail: festival@jer.cine.org.je; Web: www.jer.cine.org.il

STEVEN SPIELBERG JEWISH FILM ARCHIVE – Humanities Building, Hebrew
University, Mt Scopus, Jerusalem, Israel 91905; Fax: (972–2) 581 20 61; e-mail:
msjfa@pluto.mscc.huji.ac.il; Web: sites.huji.ac.il/jfa

Italy
ARCHIVIO AUDIOVISIVO DEL MOVIMENTO OPERAIO E DEMOCRATICO –
Via F. S. Sprovieri, 14, I–00152 Roma, Italia; Fax: (39–06) 583 313 65; e-mail:
aamed@mbox.vol.it; archivio@mbox.vol.it

CINETECA DEL COMUNE DI BOLOGNA – Via Riva di Reno 72, 40122 Bologna,
Italia; Fax: (39–051) 20 48 21; e-mail: Cinetecasegreteria@comune.bologna.it;
Web: www.cinetecadibologna.it

CINETECA DEL FRIULI – Via G. Bini – Palazzo Gurisatti, 33013 Gemona (Udine),
Italia; Fax: (39–0432) 97 05 42 e-mail: cdf@cinetecadelfriuli.org; Web: www.
cinetecadelfriuli.org

CINETECA SARDA/SOCIETÀ UMANITARIA – Viale Trieste 118/126, 09123
Cagliari, Italia; Fax: (39–070) 275 271

FONDAZIONE CINETECA ITALIANA – Villa Comunale, via Palestro 16, 20121
Milano, Italia; Fax: (39–02) 79 82 89; e-mail: cinetecaitaliana@digibank.it

FONDAZIONE SCUOLA NAZIONALE DI CINEMA/CINETECA NAZIONALE –
Via Tuscolana 1524, 00173 Roma, Italia; Fax: (39–06) 721 16 19; e-mail:
snccn@tin.it; Web: www.snc.it

MUSEO NAZIONALE DEL CINEMA/FONDAZIONE MARIA ADRIANA PROLO; Via Montebello 15, I – 10124 Torino, Italia; Fax: (39–011) 812 25 03; e-mail: museo-cinema@to2000.net

Japan

NATIONAL FILM CENTER/THE NATIONAL MUSEUM OF MODERN ART, TOKYO – 3-7-6, Kyobashi, Chuo-ku, Tokyo, 104–0031 Japan; Fax: (81–3) 3561–0830; e-mail: okajima@momat.go.jp; Web: www.momat.go.jp/

Korea (DPR of)

CHOSON MINJUJUI INMINGONGHWAGUK KUGGA YONGHWA MUNHONGO (NATIONAL FILM ARCHIVE OF D.P.R.K.) – 15 Sochangdong, Central District, Pyongyang, D.P.R. of Korea; Fax: (850–2) 381 44 10/381 21 00

Korea (Republic of)

KOREAN FILM ARCHIVE – 700, Seocho-dong, Seocho-gu, Seoul 137–718, Republic of Korea; Fax: (82–2) 582 62 13; e-mail: kfa@cinematheque.or.kr; Web: www.cinematheque.or.kr/

Latvia

INTERNATIONAL CENTRE OF CINEMA (ICC); 14 Marstaju str., P.O. Box 626, LV–1047 Riga, Latvia; Fax: (371) 782 04 45; e-mail: arsenals@latnet.lv

Luxembourg

CENTRE NATIONAL DE L'AUDIOVISUEL – BP 105, L–3402 Dudelange, Grand Duché de Luxembourg; Fax: (352) 520 655

CINÉMATHÈQUE MUNICIPALE DE LUXEMBOURG – 10, rue Eugène Ruppert, L – 2453 Luxembourg, G.D. de Luxembourg; Fax: (352) 407 519

Macedonia

KINOTEKA NA MAKEDONIJA – P.O. Box 161, 91000 Skopje, Makedonija; Fax: (389–91) 22 00 62; e-mail: kinoteka@ukim.edu.mk

Mexico

CINETECA NACIONAL – Av. México-Coyoacán 389, Col.Xoco, C.P. 03330, México, D.F., México; Fax: (52–5) 688 42 11/688 12 08; e-mail: acervo@cineteca. spin.com.mx; Web: www.cnca.gob.mx/cnca/cineteca/bienv.htm

FILMOTECA DE LA UNAM – San Ildefonso 43, Centro, 06020 México, D.F., México; Fax: (52–5) 702 45 03 e-mail: trujillo@servidor.unam.mx; Web: www. unam.mx/filmoteca

FUNDACION CARMEN TOSCANO I.A.P./ARCHIVO HISTORICO CINE-MATOGRAFICO ING. SALVADOR TOSCANO – Av. de las Palmas 2030, Col. Lomas de Chapultepec, 11000 México, D.F., México; Fax: (52–5) 251 07 09

Morocco
CINÉMATHÈQUE MAROCAINE – B.P. 421, Quartier Industriel, Av Al Majd, Rabat, Maroc; Fax: (212–7) 79 48 79

Netherlands
FILMMUSEUM – Postbus 74782, 1070 BT Amsterdam, Nederland; Street address: Vondelpark 3, 1071 AA Amsterdam, Nederland; Fax: (31–20) 683 34 01; Web: http://www.filmmuseum.nl; e-mail: filmmuseum@nfm.nl

NETHERLANDS AUDIOVISUAL ARCHIVE – P.O. Box 1799, NL – 2280 DT Rijswijk; Street Address: Visseringlaan 3, Rijswijk, Holland; Fax: (31–70) 307 04 28

New Zealand/Aotearoa
THE NEW ZEALAND FILM ARCHIVE / NGĀ KAITIAKI O NGĀ TAONGA WHITIĀHUA – P.O. Box 11449, Wellington, New Zealand; Fax: (64–4) 382 95 95; e-mail: nzfa@actrix.gen.nz; Web: www.nzfa.org.nz

Nicaragua
CINEMATECA NACIONAL DE NICARAGUA; Apartado Postal 4642, Managua, Nicaragua; Fax: (505–2) 28 29 53

Norway
THE NATIONAL LIBRARY OF NORWAY, RANA DIVISION/SOUND AND IMAGE ARCHIVE – P.O. Box 278, 8601 Mo i Rana, Norway; Fax: (47) 75 15 54 60; Web: www.nbr.no

NORSK FILMINSTITUTT – Postboks 482 Sentrum, N–0152 Oslo 1, Norge; Fax: (47) 22 47 45 99; e-mail: museum@nfi.no; Web: www.nfi.no

Peru
FILMOTECA DE LIMA/MUSEO DE ARTE – Paseo Colón 125, Lima 1, Perú; Fax: (51–1) 425 11 01; e-mail: filmolima@blockbuster.com.pe; Web: www.filmotecadelima.com

Poland
FILMOTEKA NARODOWA – ul. Pulawska 61, 00975 Warszawa, Polska; Fax: (48–22) 845 50 74

Portugal
CINEMATECA PORTUGUESA/MUSEU DO CINEMA – Rua Barata Salgueiro, 39, 1250 Lisboa, Portugal; Fax: (351) 21 969 3571

Rumania
ARHIVA NATIONALA DE FILME – CINEMATECA ROMANA – 4–6, rue Dem I. Dobrescu, sector 1, Bucuresti, România; Fax: (40–1) 313 04 83/314 69 84

Russia

GOSFILMOFOND OF RUSSIA – 142050, Belye Stolby, Moskovskaia Oblast, Russia; Fax: (7-096) 794 23 90/(7–095) 546 05 42/(7–095) 229 42 77/(7–095) 546 05 12

Slovakia

NATIONAL CENTRE FOR AUDIOVISUAL ART – Grösslingova 32, SK–811 09 Bratislava, Slovakia; Fax: (421–7) 363 461

Slovenia

ARHIV REPUBLIKE SLOVENIJE/SLOVENSKI FILMSKI ARHIV – Zvezdarska 1, p.p. 21, 1127 Ljubljana, Slovenija; Fax: (386–61) 216 551; e-mail: ars@ars.sigov.mail.si; Web: www.sigov.si/ars

SLOVENSKA KINOTEKA – Miklosiceva 28, 1000 Ljubljana, Slovenija; Fax: (386–61) 133 02 79; Web: www.kinoteka.si

South Africa

NATIONAL FILM, VIDEO AND SOUND ARCHIVES – Private Bag X236, Pretoria 0001, South Africa; Fax: (27–12) 344 51 43; e-mail: arg02@acts2.pwv.gov.za

Spain

CENTRO GALEGO DE ARTES DA IMAXE – Durán Loriga, 10 baixo, E–15003 A Coruña, España; Fax: (34–981) 20 40 54; Web: www.cgai.org; e-mail: dir@cgai.org

EUSKADIKO FILMATEGIA/FILMOTECA VASCA – B.P. 1017, 20080 San Sebastián, España; Fax: (34–943) 46 99 98; e-mail: filmoteca@facilnet.es

FILMOTECA DE LA GENERALITAT DE CATALUNYA – Portal de Santa Madrona 6–8, 08001 Barcelona, España; Fax: (34–93) 316 27 81; e-mail: arxiufilmo@correu.gencat.es

FILMOTECA DE LA GENERALITAT VALENCIANA – Plaça de l'Ajuntament 17, Edificio Rialto, 46002 Valencia, España; Fax: (34–96) 352 50 79; e-mail: filmoteca.gv@cultura.m400.gva.es

FILMOTECA ESPAÑOLA – Carretera de la Dehesa de la Villa s/n, 28040 Madrid, España; Fax: (34) 91 549 7348 Web: www.mcu.es

Sweden

CINEMATEKET/SVENSKA FILMINSTITUTET – PB 27126, S-102 52 Stockholm, Sweden; Street address: Filmhuset, Borgvägen 1–5, Stockholm; Fax: (46–8) 661 18 20; Web: www.sfi.se

Switzerland

CINÉMATHÈQUE SUISSE – Case postale 2512, CH–1002 Lausanne, Suisse; Fax: (41–21) 320 48 88; e-mail: lausanne@cinematheque.ch

Thailand
THE NATIONAL FILM ARCHIVE – Tavasugree, Samsen, Bangkok 10300, Thaïland; Fax: (66–2) 280 11 95; e-mail: thaifilm@infonew.co.th

Turkey
SINEMA-TV ENSTITÜSÜ – 80700 Kişlaönü – Beşiktaş, Istanbul, Türkiye; Fax: (90–212) 211 65 99; e-mail: sinematv@msu.edu.tr

United Kingdom
BFI COLLECTIONS DEPARTMENT/NATIONAL FILM AND TELEVISION ARCHIVE – 21, Stephen Street, London W1P 2LN, UK; Fax: (44–207) 580 75 03; Web: www.bfi.org.uk

FILM AND VIDEO ARCHIVE/IMPERIAL WAR MUSEUM – Lambeth Road, London SE1 6HZ, UK; Fax: (44–207) 416 5379; e-mail: film@iwm.org.uk; Web: www.iwm.org.uk/archive.htm

NORTH WEST FILM ARCHIVE – Minshull House, 47–9 Chorlton Street, Manchester, M1 3EU, UK; Fax: (44–161) 247 30 98; Web: www.nwfa.mmu.ac.uk

SCOTTISH FILM AND TELEVISION ARCHIVE; 1 Bowmont Gardens, Glasgow; G12 9LR, Scotland, UK; Fax: (44–141) 337 74 13; Web: www.scottish screen.demon.co.uk

WALES FILM AND TELEVISION ARCHIVE/ARCHIF FFILM A THELEDU CYMRU – Unit 1, Science Park, Aberystwyth, Ceredigion, SY23 3AH, UK; Fax: (44–1970) 626 008

United States
ACADEMY FILM ARCHIVE – Center for Motion Picture Study, 333 S. La Cienega Blvd, Beverly Hills, CA 90211, USA; Fax: (1–310) 657 54 31; e-mail: mfriend@oscars.org

ANTHOLOGY FILM ARCHIVES – 32 Second Avenue at Second Street, New York, NY 10003, USA; Fax: (1–212) 477 27 14

ARCHIVO DE IMAGENES EN MOVIMIENTO/ARCHIVO GENERAL DE PUERTO RICO – Apartado Postal 9024184 San Juan, Puerto Rico 00902–4184; Fax: (1–787) 722 90 97

DEPARTMENT OF FILM AND VIDEO/THE MUSEUM OF MODERN ART – 11 West 53rd Street, New York, NY 10019, USA; Fax: (1–212) 333 11 45

GEORGE EASTMAN HOUSE/MOTION PICTURE DEPARTMENT – 900 East Avenue, Rochester, NY 14607, USA; Fax: (1–716) 271 3970; e-mail: film@geh.org; Web: www.eastman.org

HUMAN STUDIES FILM ARCHIVES – National Museum of Natural History,

Room E307, Stop 123, Smithsonian Institution, Washington, DC 20560, USA; Fax: (1–202) 357 22 08; e-mail: hsfa@nmnh.si.edu; Web: nmnhwww.si.edu/gopher-menus/HumanStudiesFilmArchives.html

MOTION PICTURE, BROADCASTING AND RECORDED SOUND DIVISION/ LIBRARY OF CONGRESS (MP/B/RS) – 101 Independence Ave SE, Washington, DC 20540–4690, USA; Fax: (1-202) 707 23 71; e-mail: mbrs@mail@loc.gov; Web: Library of Congress: lcweb.loc.gov/; Motion Picture & Television Reading Room: lcweb.loc.gov/rr/mopic/; National Film Preservation Board: lcweb.loc.gov/film/; National Film Registry: lcweb.loc.gov/film/titles/; National Digital Library: lcweb2.loc.gov/ammem/

NATIONAL CENTER FOR FILM AND VIDEO PRESERVATION/AMERICAN FILM INSTITUTE – John F. Kennedy Center for the Performing Arts, Washington, DC 20566, USA; Fax: (1–202) 252 31 26; Web: www.afionline.org

PACIFIC FILM ARCHIVE – University of California, Berkeley Art Museum, 2625 Durant Avenue, Berkeley, CA 94720–2250, USA; Fax: (1-510) 642 48 89; Web: www.bampfa.berkeley.edu

SPECIAL MEDIA ARCHIVES SERVICES DIVISION/NATIONAL ARCHIVES & RECORDS ADMINISTRATION – 8601 Adelphi Road, College Park, MD 20740–6001; Fax: (1–301) 713 69 04; Web: www.nara.gov

UCLA FILM AND TELEVISION ARCHIVE – 302 East Melnitz, 405 Hilgard Ave, Los Angeles, CA 90095–1323, USA; Fax: (1–310) 206 31 29; Web: www.cinema.ucla.edu

WISCONSIN CENTER FOR FILM AND THEATER RESEARCH – 412 Historical Society, 816 State Street, Madison, WI 53706, USA; Fax: (1–608) 264 64 72

Uruguay
ARCHIVO NACIONAL DE LA IMAGEN – SODRE – Casilla de Correo 1412, 11.000 Montevideo, Uruguay; Fax: (598–2) 96 32 40

CINEMATECA URUGUAYA – Casilla 1170, Montevideo, Uruguay; Fax: (598–2) 409 45 72; e-mail: cinemuy@chasque.apc.org; Web: www.cinemateca.org.uy

Vatican
FILMOTECA VATICANA – Palazzo San Carlo, 00120 Città del Vaticano, Vaticano; Fax: (39–06) 69 88 53 73; e-mail: fv@pccs.va

Venezuela
ARCHIVO AUDIOVISUAL DE VENEZUELA/BIBLIOTECA NACIONAL – Apartado Postal 6525, Caracas 1080, Venezuela; Fax: (58–2) 941 86 22; e-mail: daudiov@bnv.bib.ve; Web: www.bnv.ve

FUNDACION CINEMATECA NACIONAL – Final Av. Este 2, Edif. José Vargas, Piso 14, Quebrada Honda, Caracas 1015–A, Venezuela; Fax: (58–2) 576 29 12/576 15 48; e-mail: cinema@cinemateca.org.ve; Web: www.cinemateca.org.ve

Vietnam
VIETNAM FILM INSTITUTE – 523 Kim Ma Street, Ba Dinh District, Hanoi, Vietnam; Fax: (84–4) 834 91 93; e-mail: vfa@fpt.vn

Yugoslavia
JUGOSLOVENSKA KINOTEKA – Knez Mihailova 19/I, 11000 Beograd, Jugoslavia; Fax: (381–11) 62 25 55

Appendix 3
Identification of Méliès Films by the Star Film Trademarks, 1896–1913

Throughout his career, French filmmaker Georges Méliès included the logo of his production company (Star Film) in the films made by himself or his brother Gaston between 1896 and 1912, with the aim of discouraging illegal duplication and plagiarism. The logo is often visible in the image itself (sometimes as part of an object in the set decoration), as a title card before the beginning of the film, and on the leader of each print (in the form of an embossed inscription: see Plate 18). The logo does not appear systematically in all titles, nor in all scenes; however, its presence is frequent enough to help identify a film as a Méliès production and to determine its approximate date of shooting. The chart was compiled by Jacques Malthête for the French journal *1895*, no. 24, June 1998, and is reproduced here by kind permission of the author.

1896 – 1897
(1898: no trademark)

1899 – 1900

1901 (Dec.) – 1902 (Dec.)

1902 (Dec.) – 1903 (Jan.)

TRADE MARK
★
STAR
Registered

1903 (Feb.–Dec.)

COPYRIGHT 1903
BY
Geo. MÉLIÈS

1903 (Dec.)

COPYRIGHTED
BY Geo. MÉLIÈS 1904
Trade Mark ★ Star

1904

COPYRIGHTED
BY Geo. MÉLIÈS 1904
PARIS NEW-YORK
Trade Mark ★ Star

1904 – 1905

COPYRIGHTED
BY Geo. MÉLIÈS 1906
PARIS NEW-YORK
Trade Mark ★ *Star*

1906 – 1908

(1909: no trademark
1910: no film
1911-1913: no trademark)

Appendix 4
Identification of Eastman Kodak Film Stock by its Edge Codes, 1913–28

Beginning in 1916, the Eastman Kodak company manufactured most of the film stock used for production and distribution. (Its only significant rivals were Agfa, Brifco, Gevaert and, for a few years, Pathé.) Eastman Kodak marked its film stock with date codes along the edges (see Plate 22): their presence is of invaluable help in establishing the approximate date of films made during the silent era and in the following decades. The edge code symbols can be found between the perforations and the edge of the film, immediately after the word 'Kodak', which is repeated along the length of the print. The same procedure was implemented from 1917 for the prints manufactured in the United Kingdom, and from 1925 for those made in Canada. Edge codes were used after 1928, with the same sequences of symbols recurring every twenty years.

In 1927 Kodak bought the laboratories which produced Pathé film stock in France. From that year, Pathé film still bears the name of the original company along the edges of the print, but sometimes the Kodak date codes for the United Kingdom can also be found on the copy.

In the early years of their adoption, when date codes were used on prints manufactured in the first months of the year, the symbols were reproduced immediately after the word 'Kodak'; prints made during the second half of the year had the codes printed about 10mm after the company's corporate name.

Please note that the codes indicate the year when the film stock was manufactured. The date does not necessarily correspond to the year when the film was exposed or processed; this means that a date code may be earlier than the year in which the film was shot.

Codes are printed on the film by means of a photographic process, and appear as black characters on a clear background in the stock on which they were originally inserted. Obviously, these codes can be duplicated on a print of later generation, where they will appear as clear characters on a black background. In the next print generation the codes become again black marks on a clear background, as in the original (only slightly faded), and so on after each generation. This should be kept in mind in order to avoid confusion when codes from a certain year appear on a film made at a much later date, or when several different codes are found on the same print.

The above rules do not necessarily apply to 'reversal' film stock (see p. 6). In this case, clear characters often appear on black edges; occasionally, the codes are in black on a clear background.

Kodak film stock manufactured before the introduction of date codes can sometimes be dated as well: between 1913 and 1916, the stock is marked with the word 'Eastman'. The letters are stencilled in large capital letters from 1913 to the first half of 1914 (see Plate 47). From the second half of 1914 and throughout 1915, the letters become smaller and are preceded by a small rectangle placed two or three frames away. From the beginning of 1916 until the introduction of the edge code in the same year, the rectangle is replaced by two black dots.

Year	United States (Rochester)			United Kingdom (Harrow)		Canada	
1913–Summer 1914	ʁ ᴀ S ʇ ᴎ ᴀ ⅄ (stencilled "EASTMAN")						
Summer 1914–End 1915	▬ E A S T M A N						
Early 1916	•• E A S T M A N						
1916	●						
1917	■			▼			
1918	▲			L			
1919	●	●		▬			
1920	■	■		▼	▼		
1921	▲	▲		L	L		
1922	●	■		▬	▬		
1923	●	▲		▼	L		
1924	▲	■		▬	L		
1925	■	●		▼	▬	●	L
1926	▲	●		▬	▼	●	▬
1927	■	▲		L	▬	●	▼
1928	● ● ●			L	▼	L	●

Source: Harold Brown

Appendix 5
Identification of Pathé Films by their Edge Marks

From April 1905, the French production company Pathé distributed films identified by an inscription on both edges of the prints, between the perforations (see Plates 49, 51 and 52). From 1905 to the end of 1912, these were in large stencilled block letters; by the end of 1912, the characters become smaller and thinner. In the following chart, boxes divided by a dotted line indicate that each edge of the film stock has a different text. In positive prints made between 1921 and 1927 the inscription is followed by four digits: the first two correspond to the year.

1899–April 1905	[no writing along the edges]
April–December 1905	PATHE FRERES PARIS 1905
1906–April 1907	PATHE FRERES PARIS
May–December 1907	PATHE FRERES -------- 14 RUE FAVART PARIS
1908	PATHE FRERES 14 RUE FAVART PARIS -------- EXHIBITION INTERDITE EN FRANCE ET EN SUISSE
1909–1911	PATHE FRERES 14 RUE FAVART PARIS -------- EXHIBITION INTERDITE EN FRANCE EN SUISSE EN BELGIQUE [or ET EN BELGIQUE]
End 1911–1912	PATHE FRERES 14 RUE FAVART PARIS -------- EXHIBITION INTERDITE EN FRANCE EN SUISSE EN BELGIQUE ET EN ITALIE
End 1912–13	[same text, smaller type, italics]
1913	[same text, smaller type, print]
End 1913–14	[same text, taller and narrower print]

1914	PATHE FRERES PARIS [in taller, narrower print] or [no wording along the edges]
1921	PATHE CINEMA FRANCE 16 .. or 17 .. or PATHE CINEMA PARIS 16 .. or 17 ..
1922	[the same] 18 .. or 19 .., 20 .., 21 ..
1923	[the same] 22 .. or 23 .., 24 .., 25 ..
1924	[the same] 26 .. or 27 ..
1925	[the same] 28 .. or 29
1926	[the same] 30 .. or 31
1927	[the same] 32 .. or 33 .., 34 .., 35 .., 36 ..

Sources: Gerhard Lamprecht, (unpublished MS); Harold Brown, *Physical Characteristics of Early Films as Aids to Identification.*

Appendix 6
Film Mutilation and How to Prevent It (1924)

Inspection of Machines Proving Success in Ending Damage to Prints

The effort to eliminate much of the damage to motion picture prints caused by defective projection machines by having inspectors examine the equipment of theatres in territories of the various Film Boards of Trade which have adopted the method, is proving highly successful. The move, which followed a widespread agitation for solving the problem of bad prints in which *Motion Picture News* actively participated through its editorial columns, has been in operation for some time in Philadelphia, and a recent report from the Board in that city states that seventy-five percent of the 300 machines examined by its inspector were found to be defective.

It was estimated that more than $50,000 worth of film was destroyed annually in the Philadelphia territory as a result of defective projectors. Much of the trouble has already been eliminated through the system of inspection now in practice there.

The Albany Film Board of Trade is one of the latest to appoint a booth inspector. This action followed complaints made by nearly all exchange managers in that territory of film being returned in bad condition. Several machines in deplorable condition have already been found. The owners have been notified to place their machines in proper shape, while a list of all machines in poor condition has been furnished each exchange. Exhibitors who do not make the necessary repairs will be refused film. It is expected, as a result of this move on the part of the Board of Trade, that exhibitors will soon receive film in far better condition than in the past.

(From *Motion Picture News*, July 19, 1924)

Film Mutilation and How to Prevent It

Every year the loss through needless film mutilation runs into staggering sums and of course someone has to pay the bill. There are several contributing causes to this waste, as will be pointed out in the pages that follow, and it is with the frank purpose of giving exchange managers, exhibitors, and projectionists helpful facts with which they may not be familiar that this book is published.

Needless film mutilation may be caused by defective manufacture, faulty laboratory methods, poor inspection in the exchanges, careless handling in the projection room and worn or imperfectly adjusted projection machines, and, while it is difficult in many cases to fix the exact responsibility, each possible source of damage will be fully discussed.

The Film

The film can be blamed only when the manufacture is defective. The base or support of motion picture film, which is of standardized thickness, is made from cotton and with reasonable care will fulfill the requirements of commercial use but due to the nature of its origin consideration should always be given to the fact that it has physical limitations. The Eastman Kodak Company with its years of experience in the manufacture of motion picture film (it was Eastman film that first made motion pictures possible) quite naturally observes every possible precaution to assure itself that the quality of its product is kept uniform. Samples from all coatings are thoroughly tested for their photographic and physical properties and must pass careful scrutiny of inspectors whose sole duty is to find flaws or imperfections.

The matter of accurate perforating is of the utmost importance and is only accomplished by constant vigilance on the part of experts to keep the machines at the highest degree of precision.

Recent changes in the perforation dimension of Eastman positive film was adopted only after exhaustive practical tests had proved its greater endurance and wearing properties.

As a final check against photographic quality and physical characteristics, test lengths are run through regular commercial projectors, under exactly the same conditions as would be encountered in the theaters.

The Laboratory

Improvements in equipment and methods of manipulation in all the important laboratories have reduced the possibility of affecting the physical properties of the film during the printing, developing and finishing operations to an extent as to be almost negligible.

The Exchange

Investigation of the general procedure in the inspection and repair of prints indicates that a considerable proportion of the burden of print mutilation begins in the film exchanges. It is not so much that the exchange starts the damage as that it fails to stop it. Inspections are invariably too rapid to be thorough. Splicing is carelessly done with the result that the films are frequently sent to the theatres in such poor condition as to be unable to withstand ordinary projection, to say nothing of the super requirements, particularly with respect to high speed of projection and rapid rewinding, which are all too frequently the case. In rewinding, care should be taken to see that the 'rewind' is properly lined up so that the film will feed from the one reel to the other without striking the edges of the reels. The use of defective reels causes untold damage in the rewinding operation. Cinching occurs when the person rewinding attempts to tighten the roll. This causes scratches on both sides of the film.

Cupping the film to detect damaged edges, perforations, or loose splices is very apt to crack or split the film, more especially on subjects which have had repeated projection on projectors using high amperage. Careful inspection and repairs in the exchanges will result in better service to the exhibitor, eliminate breaks which are the frequent cause of film damage, reduce the amount of replacements due to break-down, and make the subjects available for constant service. Longer commercial life means increased earning capacity.

The Exhibitor

Good projection adds patronage and increased revenue to the theatre.

Good projection is entirely dependent on the skill of the projectionist and the condition of the film and the projection machine. Through constant use projection machine parts become worn and out of adjustment. Projectors should never be permitted to get in this condition. Replacement parts are readily available and for the most part inexpensive, and any expenditure in this connection will improve projection and materially help in the reduction of unnecessary film loss.

Careful study of the following pages will be helpful to all concerned with motion picture film.

Splices

Splicing, whether done in the film laboratories, film exchanges or projection rooms, has such direct bearing on the welfare of the film as to call for special and constant attention.

Much film is ruined by poor splicing. Splices that are wide, stiff, buckled and out of line cause the film to jump the sprockets resulting in torn perforations or breaks. Perforations in the vicinity of a splice of this kind will always be found to be strained or broken out. Stiff and buckled splices are caused by excessive scraping of the film, or a too liberal application of cement or both. The use of a poor quality cement results in splices pulling apart especially in the film gate or trap. This constitutes a hazard; therefore, all weak or otherwise bad splices should be remade before protection. Figure 1 shows the well known full-hole splice which is the most widely

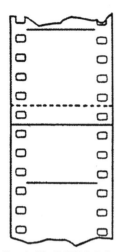

FIG. 1. The Full Hole Splice
Generally Recommended.

used and if properly made gives the best all-around results.

Pamphlets on splicing instructions may be had without charge on application to the Eastman Kodak Company, Rochester, N.Y.

Whenever film is damaged on a projector, it is generally customary to lay the cause of the trouble to one or more of three different things; namely, sprockets, idlers, and tension exerted on the film by the springs in the gate or film trap.

While it is true that in most cases the trouble can be traced to one or more of these points, it must be admitted that the direct cause of a great amount of film damage is never definitely settled between the film Exchanges and the Projectionists, especially when the projectors in question have been gone over quite carefully and everything has been found to be in apparently good condition.

In cases of this kind, it is only natural to assume that the film stock is at fault. There are, however, various projector parts, generally considered more or less unimportant which, as a rule receive little or no attention on the part of the Projectionist. The result is that film trouble is apt to start at any one of them.

The following résumé covers the more important points which must be given careful attention by the Projectionists, if the maximum wearing qualities are to be obtained from the film.

Tension on Springs in Gate or Trap

One of the principal sources of trouble is the use of excessive tension exerted on the film by the springs in the gate or trap. A great variation will be found in tension on various projection machines being used in the trade. Moreover, there are some Projectionists who are not familiar with the amount of tension which should be used, and as far as we know, there is no set standard which is generally accepted as being correct.

It is common practice to set the springs just tight enough to hold the film stationary at the speed which is used in a given theatre. For proper screen reproduction the speed of a projector should be determined by the action of the picture. This is very seldom done, the average program being run at one set speed regardless of the action. This cannot be considered the fault of the Projectionist as he is under a certain time limit to project a given number of reels.

Excessive tension as high as 34 ounces has been found to exist on certain projection machines and causes badly nicked and pulled out perforations. Heavy tension on one side can be caused by a poorly adjusted, weak or broken spring and results in an uneven pull-down strain on the film.

On projectors using the gate a stop or catch is provided which holds the gate in the same position each time it is closed.

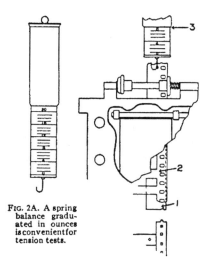

FIG. 2A. A spring balance gradu-ated in ounces is convenient for tension tests.

FIG. 2B. Tension tests are made on each side. 1 is the film, 2 the pressure plate and 3 is the spring balance at 8 ounces.

Projectors using a trap door or pressure plate are not provided with a stop of any kind, thereby allowing varying amounts of tension to be applied to the film. The trap door or plate should never be let back against the film with great force as this results in exceptionally heavy tension, which must be withstood by the film until the door or plate has worked back to its proper position. The proper tension exerted by the springs should be 8 ounces for each spring or 16 ounces combined tension. Below Figure 2 is given the proper method of making a tension test.

Referring to illustration B: first the tension on one side and then on the other is taken by using one half of a strip of film about 8″ long. This strip is prepared by slitting a piece of film down through the center. Care should be taken to observe that the perforations on this strip of film are free of the teeth on the intermittent sprocket and are held properly in place by the tension shoe before proceeding further. After fastening the end of the strip of film to the balance a straight even upward pull is made until the 8 ounce mark is reached. At this point the film will start to pull from the gate if the spring is set properly.

The combined tension of both sides is then checked as shown in Figure 3, using a full width piece of film placed in the gate so that

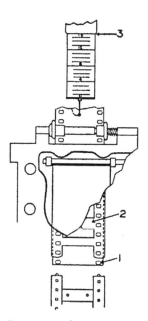

FIG. 3. A tension test is then made on both sides. 1 is the film; 2 the pressure plate and 3 the balance at 16 ounces.

both sides of the shoe hold it firmly against the aperture plate. After making sure that the perforations on this strip of film are not engaged by the sprocket teeth proceed as before with a straight upward pull until the 16 ounce mark is reached. At this point if both springs are adjusted correctly the film can be pulled from the gate. To make this test correctly, the projector should be cold, using film of the average thickness.

The tension springs on some projectors can be regulated by means of small set screws while on others no adjusting device has been provided and springs must be bent by hand, but in doing this great care must be taken to get the proper adjustment.

Sprockets

Through carelessness and neglect sprockets are frequently left on projectors until the teeth develop bad hooks and knife-like edges. Film damage caused by under-cut teeth is unmistakable in appearance and in many cases film is practically ruined after one or two showings if run on a projector equipped with such sprockets. (Figure 4)

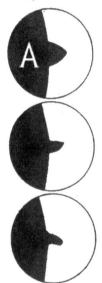

The changing of an intermittent sprocket must be done with great care as the shaft can be bent very easily. Equipped with the proper tools any competent Projectionist can make the change but in many cases it may be advisable to have the work done at the factory to insure the best results.

Before placing new sprockets on projection machines, a careful examination should be made of the teeth to be sure that none of them have been damaged by coming in contact with one another or some other hard surface. If a sprocket is accidentally dropped on the floor the teeth are likely to be burred or bent and if used on a projection machine, will cause untold damage to film. This will be true even if only one tooth has been damaged.

FIG. 4. Sprockets taken from projectors actually in daily use. Sprocket A is a new sprocket.

Adhesion of Emulsion to Shoe or Film Tracks

All new film should be waxed to insure against adhesion or sticking in the gate or trap of the projector. When unwaxed film is run, it is necessary to clean the shoes frequently, otherwise the accumulation of hardened emulsion on the shoes acts as a hold-back causing a greatly increased pull-down strain which always results in mutilated perforations. Needless to say, a new print can be completely ruined in this manner at one showing.

In removing the hardened emulsion deposits from the film tracks and tension shoes use no steel or iron implement such as a screw driver, safety razor blade or file. Instead use a dampened cloth and if necessary a coin as this will not scratch the highly polished surface.

Guide Rollers

The guide rollers located above the gate or film-trap are there for the purpose of properly guiding the film down past the aperture to the intermittent sprocket. If these rollers are out of line with the sprocket, the teeth will naturally strike the film perforations off-center.

On some projectors these rollers are adjustable by means of a collar and set-screw, while on others there is no regulating device. Certain manufacturers using the latter type, rely on the proper centering- to be made at the factory, nevertheless there are times when an adjustment is found to be necessary and it is very important that great care should be used in lining up the guide rollers with the intermittent sprocket, otherwise damaged perforations will result. See Figures 5 and 6.

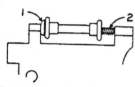

FIG. 5. This guide roller is not adjustable. Spring 2 is supposed to hold it snugly against the washer 1. If it is not properly aligned return the head to the manufacturer.

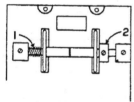

FIG. 6. This guide roller may be adjusted by loosening the set screw in collar 2 and then after centering tightening the screw. Great care should be taken not to "spring" the shaft.

If these rollers bind, the face of the rollers will develop ridges which will roughen the edge of the film as shown in Figure 7. It is also well to examine new rollers closely as in some cases they are received from the factory in a semi-finished condition, and have rough faces against which the edge of the film comes in contact.

Friction Take-up

The take-up adjustment should be checked up closely from time to time. An excessive pull can always be detected by the film making a 'singing' sound at the take-up sprocket. The sprocket, of course, acts as a hold back or brake and puts a strain on the film, when starting on a small hubbed reel. This is sometimes enough to cause very severe damage to the upper side of the perforation. Figure 8 shows the sprocket damage resulting from a tight take-up.

Proper setting of the spring is a simple matter and care should always be taken to keep the friction disc, whether

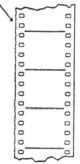

FIG. 7. The arrow shows where the film edge has been chewed away by bent reels or imperfect alignment of the upper magazine.

FIG. 8. The teeth of this sprocket have been under-cut because the take-up was too tight.

leather, cork or fiber, absolutely free from oil. Contrary to some opinions oil will not cause smoother operation in a case of this kind, but will really create a certain amount of suction which in turn results in an uneven, excessive pull.

Tension on Upper Magazine Shaft or Spindle

Some widely used makes of projectors have an adjustable spring tension on the upper magazine shaft or spindle. Proper adjustment of this spring is important. If set too loosely the film will come from the feed roll with a jerky motion. This is especially noticeable if used with a bent reel, which is bad for any film, particularly film which is in a dried-out condition or badly worn.

If the tension is too tight the effect would not be noticeable on a full reel of film, but the tension on the last 50 or 75 feet would be sufficient to cause serious perforation damage when a small hubbed reel is used. It is not uncommon for the film to break under this strain.

Sprocket Idlers

All sprocket idlers must be properly adjusted. If set too far from the sprockets, the film is liable to jump out of place and ride over the teeth, whereas, if they are set too close they will ride the film, causing creasing, especially on the lower sprocket which acts as a brake on the friction take-up.

The small lock nuts on all idler adjusting screws should always be kept tight. Failure to observe this rule will allow the idlers to drop, not only causing creasing but otherwise weakening and permanently marking the film.

It has been found that the safest distance to set an idler from a sprocket is the thickness of two pieces of film. Some manufacturers recommend the thickness of one piece of film but this is insufficient as the distance between the sprocket and idler is too small to allow the average splice free passage.

When the idlers are properly adjusted, it should be possible to move any idler from side to side without danger of touching the sprocket teeth. Badly worn idlers mark the film and should be replaced immediately.

Intermittent Film Guide

The intermittent film guide, is for the purpose of holding the film snugly against the intermittent sprocket but otherwise has nothing to do with the steadiness of the picture. Filing the openings in the film guide holders is sometimes necessary to insure the proper amount of side clearance for the sprocket teeth. Moving the film guide from side to side while the projector is running will determine whether or not

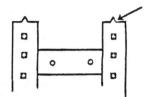

FIG. 9. The arrow shows where the teeth have been grooved to a knife-like sharpness by coming in contact with the wall of the film guide. This will ruin film.

the teeth have sufficient clearance. Figure 9 shows the results of the wearing of the teeth against the wall of the guide, thereby developing sharp edges which cut into the film.

There is a right and a wrong way to install this film guide in the holder. Figure 10 shows proper installation – pointed end down. If in the reverse position as in Figure 11 the pointed end will present a shoulder to the film against which all splices must strike. This strain is so great as to cause torn perforations or even a break in the film especially if the splices are stiff, thick or buckled.

Many Projectionists have found it advisable to substitute a slightly lighter film guide holder spring for the stiff one now furnished by the manufacturers. By this small change, less strain is put on the film at this point, with absolutely no change in screen results, wide and stiff splices, especially, going through with greatly decreased resistance thereby lessening the chance of film breakage due to the yielding of the film guide.

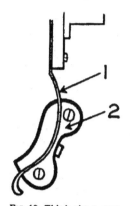

FIG. 10. This is the correct position for the film guide. Arrow 1 shows the guide holder and 2 is the film guide.

One of the main reasons for picture unsteadiness is an excessive amount of play between the moving parts of the intermittent movement, due to wear. Readjustment is made by means of an eccentric bearing but care must be taken to see that it is not set too tightly, otherwise the parts will bind.

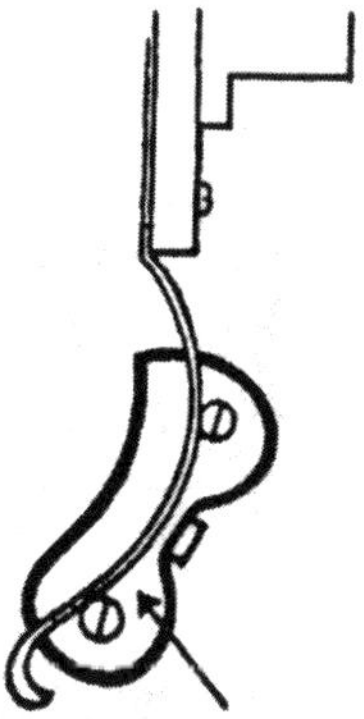

Projector models using an eccentric bearing at each end of the intermittent shaft should be checked carefully after an adjustment has been made, to see that both bearings are lined up correctly, otherwise the intermittent sprocket will run out of true, resulting in the breaking out of the perforation on one side of the film.

Some projectors provide for a side adjustment of the intermittent shaft by means of a collar and set-screw. Proper alignment is necessary to ensure against the intermittent sprocket striking the film perforations off-center.

Excessive wear of the pin-cross type of intermittent movement results in flat sides on the pins, thereby causing a slightly quickened pull-down which gives an added strain on the film perfora-

FIG. 11. Here the film guide is upside down allowing the film to strike the sharp end of the guide. Stiff splices won't last under these conditions.

tions. On newer models these pins are equipped with rollers insuring smoother operation.

Proper Alignment of Upper Magazine

One widely used projection machine has an adjustment on the top magazine which allows for its proper alignment. Unless great care is taken to see that the magazine is in line, the film coming from the valve rollers will not feed squarely under the idle roller. This generally causes fractured film to crack from the perforations to the edge of the film.

This improper alignment also causes film breaks resulting from film with nicked edges and from loose splices coming in direct contact with the side of the valve.

Size of Idler Rollers

The idler roller on the same machine mentioned above is ½″ diameter and causes the film to make a sharp turn on itself. On a roller of this size film which has been dried out and thus has become brittle may break especially if there is an improper amount of tension on the feed roll.

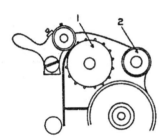

FIG. 12. Shows 1 the feed sprocket and the small roller 2.

If trouble of this nature is encountered the substitution of a larger roller, preferably the diameter of a sprocket namely, ¹⁵⁄₁₆″ is practical remedy. This means but a small amount of work, as only a simple extension is necessary to allow the proper amount of clearance and it will be found to be well worth while. Figures 12 and 13 illustrate the ½″ roller and how the large idler roller can be installed in its place.

Reels

Bent reels and reels with loose and sharp edged flanges should be discarded immediately. Fig. 7, on page 199, plainly shows what happens to the film when such reels are used.

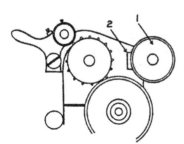

FIG. 13. Here a 15/16″ idler replaced the smaller one shown in Fig. 12. The bar, 2. is the only other alteration necessary. The larger idler makes the film last longer.

Framing

In framing a picture, it is common practice to move the framing lever very quickly. Figure 14 shows what happens to the film when the framing lever is given a sharp, downward blow on a projector where the complete intermittent carriage moves as one unit. Figure 15 shows the same damaging result on a model on which the intermittent sprocket *only* moves in synchronism with the framing lever.

Film Loops
Excessively large upper or lower loops either cause a rattle in the film guard above or allow the film to drag in any oil which may be present below. The film also has a tendency to jump the sprockets, which can take place if the idlers are set too far from the sprockets.

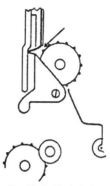

FIG. 14. Suddenly jerking the framing lever on this machine puts a kink in the film shown by the arrow. Frame carefully and slowly.

The practice of resetting loops while the projector is running should be discouraged as in many cases the sprocket teeth strike outside of the perforations, or otherwise damage the film.

Film Tracks or Trap Shoes
Many scratches are caused by worn film tracks, or trap-shoes as they are known on one of the projectors, allowing the face of the film to scrape against the recessed aperture plate.

Such tracks or trap-shoes together with all tension shoes or door pads that show a 'wavy' or badly worn-down surface, should be replaced by new ones.

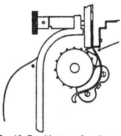

FIG. 15 On this type of projector, also in common use, buckling of the film will occur if framing is done too rapidly.

Fire or Valve Rollers
The valve rollers of both magazines should always be kept clean. Care should be taken to see that they revolve freely as a sticking roller can cause bad emulsion scratches especially if it is worn, thereby allowing the center of the roller to come in direct contact with the face of the film. This is especially true of the upper magazine rollers around which dirt and small pieces of film very often accumulate.

Adjustment of Film Trap Door
On one make of projection machine the film trap door is designed so that it can be easily removed by merely lifting it from its holder. In replacing this film trap door care should be taken to see that it is seated properly, as unless this is done one is liable to ruin the intermittent sprocket, bend the shaft as well as ruin the film which happens to be running through the projector at the time.

Strippers on Upper and Lower Sprockets

On some projectors, so called strippers or stripping plates are provided to prevent, by any chance, the film from winding around or 'following' the sprockets as well as to remove any accumulation of dirt that may tend to form at either side of the sprocket teeth. In resetting these strippers after the replacement of sprockets, extreme care must be taken to see that they do not come in contact with the teeth as this will cause the teeth to wear to a sharp edge which will damage any film coming in contact with it.

Unnecessary Oiling

Flooding the mechanism with oil is unnecessary and causes oil to get on the film. Dust then adheres to the film making good clear projection impossible. This practice also is a fire hazard as oily film will catch fire a great deal easier than that which is clean. Aside from the intermittent case, one drop of good oil in each oil hole will be sufficient for the average day's run.

One Method of Tracing Film Damage

Film damage can sometimes be more easily traced if it will be remembered that certain projectors run the film emulsion or dull side against all three sprockets, while on others the support or shiny side, only touches the sprockets. For example; if film is received showing tooth marks on the emulsion side, it is fairly simple to determine on what make or makes of projectors this film has been run, especially if the investigator has familiarised himself with the different types of sprocket teeth.

Why Film Should Be Waxed

In conclusion, special attention is drawn to the desirability of waxing new prints along the perforations to prevent unsteadiness and premature breakdown.

In making the light sensitive emulsion of motion picture film one of the chief ingredients is gelatin – a substance which readily absorbs and gives off moisture. In freshly developed film the gelatin contains a considerably higher percentage of moisture than is found in seasoned film, and when in this condition it is easily affected by heat, tending to make it soft and tacky particularly in a moist atmosphere. The first point at which new film comes in contact with unusual temperature is at the aperture plate of the projector where the light is concentrated, producing heat to a degree which softens the gelatin and causes it to collect on the tension springs or shoes where it rapidly dries and forms a flint-like deposit. As the new film is projected, the hardened deposit of gelatin continues to accumulate and offers further resistance, causing scratches along the perforations. As the resistance increases there is the added danger of the teeth of the intermittent sprocket tearing and damaging the perforations, sometimes to an extent where injury to the print is irreparable.

Careful waxing produces, under the action of heat, a smooth and polished surface on the gelatin along the perforations; provides against undue straining during the first projections of new prints; materially benefits successive runs, and greatly prolongs the commercial life of the prints.

Cold wax should never be used as it is impossible to apply it evenly. There is also the danger with the cold method of over-waxing with the result that, in contact with the heated pressure springs, the wax melts and spreads over the picture. A very slight application is all that is necessary and is best accomplished by a waxing machine which deposits a thin layer of hot wax along the perforations. New prints treated in this manner require no further waxing.

Source: Promotional booklet for projectionists distributed by the Eastman Kodak Company, 1924.

Appendix 7
The Film Prayer

I am celluloid, not steel; O God of the machine, have mercy. I front four great dangers whenever I travel the whirling wheels of the mechanism.

Over the sprocket wheels, held tight by the idlers, I am forced by the motor's might. If a careless hand misthreads me, I have no alternative but to go to my death. If the springs at the aperture gate are too strong, all my splices pull apart. If the pull on the take-up reel is too violent, I am torn to shreds. If dirt collects in the aperture, my film of beauty is streaked and marred, and I must face my beholders – a thing ashamed and bespoiled. Please, if I break, fasten me with clips; never with pins. Don't rewind me – my owner wants that privilege, so that he may examine me, heal my wounds, and send me rejuvenated upon a fresh mission.

I travel many miles. I am tossed on heavy trucks, sideways and upside down. Please see that my own band is wrapped snugly around me on the reel, so that my first few coils do not slip loose in my shipping case, to be bruised and wounded beyond the power to heal. Put me in my own shipping case. Scrape off all old labels so I will not go astray.

Speed me on my way. Others are waiting to see me. The 'next day' is the last day I should be held. Have a heart for the other fellow who is waiting, and for my owner who will get the blame. Don't humiliate me by sending me back without paying my passage.

I am a delicate ribbon of celluloid – misuse me and I disappoint thousands; cherish me and I delight and instruct the world.

Source: Advertising sheet [not dated, ca. 1920] by A. P. Hollis, Edited Pictures System, Inc., 330 West 42nd Street, New York, NY.

Index